# The Peach Blossom Fan

(T'ao-hua-shan)

# The Peach Blossom Fan

## (T'ao-hua-shan)

By K'ung Shang-jen

(1648-1718)

Translated by Chen Shih-hsiang and Harold Acton

With the collaboration of Cyril Birch

UNIVERSITY OF CALIFORNIA PRESS

Berkeley • Los Angeles • London

Note on Illustrations

The illustrations are from a Chinese edition
of the play published in 1917,
but stylistically they are modelled on woodcuts
made for a fine late-Ming edition (early
seventeenth century) of T'ang Hsien-tsu's famous play
*The Peony Pavilion.*

University of California Press
Berkeley and Los Angeles, California
University of California Press, Ltd.
London, England
Copyright © 1976, by
The Regents of the University of California
ISBN 0-520-02928-3
Library of Congress Catalog Card Number: 74-27294
Printed in the United States of America

# Contents

# Preface

The late Chen Shih-hsiang and I first collaborated in translating some modern Chinese poems while we were together in Peking in the nineteen-thirties. We undertook the present translation one summer over twenty years ago. It was a pleasant distraction from more arduous labours — a holiday task and, for me, a spiritual return to China when I had no chance of returning there in the flesh. Shih-hsiang was occupied at the time with teaching duties at Berkeley and with his researches into early Chinese poetry and criticism. At my suggestion, we devoted delightful hours to *The Peach Blossom Fan* — for its own sake rather than for publication, though we hoped it might be published eventually. We completed a draft of all but the last seven scenes, and in this unfinished state the manuscript lay until Chen's untimely death in May 1971. Now Cyril Birch, Shih-hsiang's colleague at Berkeley for eleven years, has very kindly undertaken to complete the work by adding his own translation of these late scenes and by revising our draft throughout. The complete English version of this fine play is offered here as a tribute to the memory of a dear friend.

Many popular Chinese plays fail to qualify as literature, being no more than plain scripts for brilliant actors to display their virtuosity. *T'ao-hua-shan — The Peach Blossom Fan* appears to be a luminous exception, for it is a highly poetic chronicle play composed by a distinguished scholar, K'ung Shang-jen, who was born soon after the events he portrayed. As a vivid evocation of the downfall of the Ming dynasty, it deserves to be better known to students of Chinese literature and history.

The great Ming dynasty endured close on three hundred years, from 1368 to 1644. It purchased stability at the price of atrophy in certain aspects of the national life, most notably in the art of government; yet there was continuing advance during those centuries in philosophy and the arts, in trade and the growth of cities.

Though the idea would have been inconceivable to men of the time, 1644 was the last year, forever, in which a Chinese ruler

vii

would occupy the Imperial throne. By the early years of the seventeenth century, dynastic decline was rapidly accelerating. The historical background has been described in *Annals and Memoirs of the Court of Peking* by E. Backhouse and J. O. P. Bland (Boston: Houghton Mifflin, 1914), and biographies of the principal characters are given in the two invaluable volumes of *Eminent Chinese of the Ch'ing Period* (1644-1911), edited by Arthur W. Hummel (Washington: Library of Congress, 1943).

The failing grasp of the last Ming emperors was further loosened by a succession of disastrous famines which drove thousands to brigandage under the leadership of men like Li Tzu-ch'eng. From the province of Shensi, rebellion spread to Shansi, out and down across Honan, southwest into Szechuan. Capturing city after city, Li Tzu-ch'eng assumed the title of Emperor and marched into Peking in April 1644, where the unfortunate Ming Emperor Ch'ung-chen ended his troubles by committing suicide. A month later, Li's two hundred thousand troops were defeated by the Chinese general Wu San-kuei, whose family Li had exterminated. Into the power vacuum, at the invitation of Wu San-kuei, marched the newly consolidated nation of the Manchus. Swiftly they became masters of North China and established a dynasty of their own, the Ch'ing, which was to yield only to the republican forms of the twentieth century.

Following the suicide of the Emperor Ch'ung-chen, remnants of the Ming court fled south to Nanking. Here for a few short months of 1644-45 the attempt was made to restore Ming rule by proclaiming Prince Fu as Emperor Hung-kuang. It was a vain hope, and the faction-riven armies of the Ming court at Nanking soon melted before the Manchu advance.

Fairbank and Reischauer, *In East Asia: The Great Tradition* (Boston: Houghton Mifflin, 1958), identify "many classic features" of the Ming decline: "effete and feckless rulers, corrupt favorites misusing their power, factional jealousies among the officials, fiscal bankruptcy, the impact of natural disasters, the rise of rebellion and, finally, foreign invasion." All items of this melancholy catalogue are visible in *The Peach Blossom Fan* — although, as we should perhaps expect of a moralist, K'ung Shang-jen tends to stress the first three elements of waning political integrity and personal relations.

The egregious example of the corrupt favourite was a vicious dictator, the eunuch Wei Chung-hsien. It was a prime folly of the late Ming rulers to deliver power into the hands of such men as he, untrained and ignorant controllers of the Imperial harem, who rose from underling to dominant status by their accumulation of private wealth and by the elimination of rival influences on the Emperor. Wei Chung-hsien was disgraced and hanged himself in 1627, but his bane invests the play through his creatures Ma Shih-ying and Juan Ta-ch'eng.

The latter was as villainous in real life as in the play. After the disgrace of his powerful eunuch patron, Juan went into retirement for about fifteen years. During this time he composed elegant poems and dramas, some of which were still performed at the beginning of the present century. After ignominious and vain attempts to curry favour with more reputable scholar-officials, he was reinstated in office by his crony Ma Shih-ying, who had become Grand Tutor of the Emperor and dominated the court through bribery, extortion, and the sale of degrees and offices. Juan easily won the favour of the last Ming claimant to the throne by pandering to his passion for theatricals. Our play corroborates the anecdote in *Annals and Memoirs* that while the Manchu troops were investing Yangchow, the newly installed Ming Emperor Hung-kuang was asked by eunuchs the cause of his despondency. His reply: "What distresses me is that in all my court there is not an actor worthy of the name." The picture of the refugee court at Nanking leaving its hard-pressed armies unfed while it rehearsed Juan Ta-ch'eng's play *The Swallow Letter*, or searched the highways and byways for attractive singing-girls, destroys one's sympathy for the fading Ming regime, but it leaves the impression of truth.

With equal authenticity, our playwright K'ung Shang-jen establishes the members of the Revival Club as the forces of light. The Club was an offshoot of the Tung-lin or Eastern Forest Party, a loosely organized group of literati who in the late Ming years had called for a return to fundamental Confucian ideals; they attacked governmental corruption, and in consequence were virtually wiped out by Wei Chung-hsien's purges of the 1620s. It was a stroke of genius on K'ung Shang-jen's part to select Hou Fang-yü, brilliant young spokesman for the Revival Club, as the romantic hero. The love relationship at the center of the drama is based on solid fact, the liaison of Hou Fang-yü with the beautiful singing-girl Li Hsiang-chün, "Fragrant Princess." At the age of sixteen, this girl in actual life showed surprising strength of character. Her unwavering devotion to her lover, her delicacy of sentiment, were in accordance with venerable Chinese ideals. We find many chaste and

virtuous concubines in Chinese history. Hou Fang-yü himself, like
the scholarly young heroes of most Chinese plays, strikes the
Westerner as rather effete in comparison with such women. Had
not Fragrant Princess firmly put her foot down, Hou might have
been misled into abetting the designs of the villainous Juan Ta-
ch'eng.

Yang Wen-ts'ung, who introduced Fragrant Princess to Hou
Fang-yü and then undertook — without success — to deliver her to
another man when Hou was out of the way, played such an
ambiguous role because he had friends in both camps. In spite of
his connection with the Revival Club, he was a brother-in-law of
the unscrupulous Ma Shih-ying and on intimate terms with Juan
Ta-ch'eng. Though a talented painter, poet, and official who died
for the Ming cause, Yang could be guilty of shoddy behaviour. He
seems to have been more irresponsible than wicked, a convivial
type fond of social and literary gatherings, and an instinctive
matchmaker. Early in life he had studied painting under Tung
Ch'i-ch'ang, the most admired painter and critic of the Ming
dynasty. According to Osvald Sirén, in *Chinese Paintings* (London:
Lund Humphries, 1956), Yang Wen-ts'ung's best paintings were
"exceedingly free expressions of his own poetic spirit, album
leaves, fans or small pictures of bamboo branches or epiden-
drums." It was therefore appropriate that he should have converted the bloodstains on Fragrant Princess' fan into the peach
blossoms which give the play its title.

Chinese theatre audiences have always shown a strong partiality
for scenes of martial action. The story of *The Peach Blossom Fan*
revolves around events in the south, the abortive restoration of
Ming rule in Nanking. The decisive northern campaigns provide
only a distant backdrop to the play: neither the destruction of
Peking by the bandit Li Tzu-ch'eng, nor the admission of the
Manchu forces by the renegade general Wu San-kuei, assumes any
direct significance in the action. The central military role is
assigned to Shih K'o-fa, President of the Board of War at the
restoration court in Nanking, who stands out as a true hero. His
frank and eloquent memorials to the Throne were suppressed by
Ma Shih-ying; the provisions and munitions he appealed for never
arrived. After his gallant defence of Yangchow, which lasted seven
days, the Manchu conquerors made attempts to win him over with
the most cogent arguments, but he was a stalwart Confucian for
whom loyalty was one of the chief virtues. Failing in his attempt
at suicide, he was beheaded, and there followed a ten-day massacre

of the inhabitants of Yangchow. Our playwright, however, in a rare instance of poetic licence, honours the legend that Shih K'o-fa escaped the city and drowned himself.

General Tso Liang-yü was another Ming patriot associated with the Eastern Forest Party. In April 1645 he published a denunciation of Ma Shih-ying and moved against the corrupt government at Nanking, which he saw as inimical to the aspirations for a Ming revival. But the confusion created by his advance helped to weaken Nanking's defence against the Manchus. Against orders, his troops pillaged and fired the city of Kiukiang, and Tso died the same night.

Of the "Four Guardian Generals" Huang Te-kung, Kao Chieh, Liu Tse-ch'ing, and Liu Liang-tso, Huang remained loyal to the Ming and committed suicide; Kao Chieh, a former bandit and associate of the rebel leader Li Tzu-ch'eng, was in permanent conflict with the other generals, and it is hard to understand why Shih K'o-fa tolerated him and deplored his loss as a blow to the Ming cause. As in the play, Kao Chieh accepted an invitation to Hsu Ting-kuo's residence, where he was murdered after a banquet, like so many other generals before and after him. The remaining two "Guardian Generals" both became traitors.

As Backhouse and Bland point out, had there been a single strong man among the last Ming claimants to the throne, their dynasty might have been restored and China spared three centuries of rule by the alien Manchus. The wonder is that loyalty to an ideal in the actual state of China should have inspired so many brave and distinguished martyrs. When *The Peach Blossom Fan* was first performed, older members of the audience, like the old Master of Ceremonies in the prologue, wept as they remembered the leading characters and the episodes with which they were connected.

The author of *The Peach Blossom Fan*, K'ung Shang-jen (1648-1718), was a descendant of Confucius who spent many years completing his family genealogy and re-editing the history of Confucius' birthplace. A great authority on ancient rites and music, and a discriminating collector of antiques in his native Shantung, he was invited to lecture before the Manchu Emperor K'ang-hsi when the latter visited Ch'ü-fu. Consequently he became a Doctor of the Imperial Academy and held other official posts oddly at variance with the usual career of a dramatist. *The Peach Blossom Fan* was completed in 1699 after three revisions. It won immediate popularity; but we may well assume that it was the reading in the Manchu Imperial palace of this threnody for the Ming which led to K'ung Shang-jen's dismissal from office in the spring of the following year.

HAROLD ACTON, K.B.E.

Florence,
1973

# Introduction:

# *The Peach Blossom Fan* as Southern Drama

The centers of governmental power have clustered in the north, on the dusty Yellow River plains, through most of Chinese history as at the present time. To past residents of this region, "the south" did not mean the tropical southern coast where Canton lies, but the Yangtze Valley with its silk and tea and porcelain, its rich trade towns like Soochow and Yangchow, its landscapes lovingly recorded by the painters, and its preeminence in all the arts. Much of the action of *The Peach Blossom Fan* centers on Nanking, which holds a special place even among the glamorous cities of the south: for this reason it is especially appropriate that the play, as we shall show, should be in the "southern" style. Nanking in the fifth and sixth centuries of our era served as capital for native dynastic houses which, however decadent, ill-fated, and short-lived, at least kept alight the lamp of Chinese culture when the north was in the hands of overlords from beyond the frontiers. In the seventeenth century, when K'ung Shang-jen was writing his play, the mere mention of the Nanking pleasure-quarter on the banks of the Ch'in-huai River was still enough to bring wistful sighs from anyone who had dallied there only in his youth, or never at all. *The Peach Blossom Fan* draws constantly on the fading glories of yore to weave a backdrop of nostalgia for its tale of sad decline.

As terms in the history of Chinese drama, *northern* and *southern* define two generic types of play which at different times dominated the national stage. Readers of English have begun to know northern-style plays in translations such as S. I. Hsiung's *Lady Precious Stream* and *Romance of the Western Chamber,* but they have barely even heard of southern plays. By northern we mean, essentially, Yuan drama, which under the rule of the Yuan

or Mongol dynasty (1280-1368) furnished the first Golden Age of
the Chinese theatre. This Yuan or northern-style play (the Chinese
term is *tsa-chü*) is governed by the strictest conventions. It is quite
short: four acts with the option of a "wedge," a short prefatory or
interpolated segment. Each act of a northern play consists essentially of a song-set, a sequence of a dozen or so arias surrounded
by dialogue. The arias are composed in a single musical mode and
are allocated to a single character, obviously the lead character in
the play. There is a freshness and naturalness about the poetry of
these songs which perfectly matches the forceful action and the
vigour of the dialogue: crude and creaky mechanisms somehow
don't detract from the vital energy of the best of these plays.
There is much self-introduction and soliloquy, much narration of
offstage action, too much recapitulation of earlier scenes, but
overall a remarkably tight organization of events into the four
nucleic acts. The third act is usually climactic; the fourth will
usually show the finest poetry, as the singer builds up images to
explore the significance of what has been presented.

Although the southern style of drama has actually a longer
history than the northern, dating back at least to the Sung dynasty, which preceded the Yuan, it did not come to dominance
until the sixteenth and seventeenth centuries, during which time
the Ming dynasty (1368-1644) yielded place to the Ch'ing or
Manchu (1644-1911). Hundreds of southern-style plays (*nan-hsi*
or *ch'uan-ch'i*) were written during these years. *The Peach Blossom Fan*, completed in 1699, was one of the last of the great ones.

The southern-style play contrasts strongly with its Yuan coun-
terpart. In place of the tight four-act structure, with its concentra-
tion of dramatic situation around the songs of a single lead player,
we are shown a sort of undulating cavalcade. There are many
scenes: *The Peach Blossom Fan*, with forty plus, is not unduly
long, for *Peony Pavilion* (*Mu-tan t'ing*) has fifty-five. The scenes
vary in length and kind from short transitional, when narrative
business is conducted without a great deal of singing, to lengthy
"grand scenes" with many of the cast assembled for some crucial
confrontation. Often there will be contrasting groupings of characters in a play (as for example, in *The Peach Blossom Fan*, the
young hero Hou Fang-yü and his friends over against the Ma
Shih-ying-Juan Ta-ch'eng clique). The "cavalcade" effect is created
by the alternation of such groupings through successive scenes.

The traditional Chinese stage used no sets, and so there is
complete freedom of movement and much scenic description

(vicarious stage-setting) in dialogue and songs: Scene 8, "A River-side Occasion," is a conspicuous example. The well-peopled "grand scene" will usually offer spectacular costuming and a feast of song with particularly fine arias for solo, duet, or choral rendering — for in the southern drama all characters may sing. This is the most striking departure from the Yuan convention of the single singing role. Certain other types of scene are also prescribed for the southern play: it must, by convention, contain at least a minimum number of love scenes, martial scenes, and comic scenes. As a matter of course, we find all these in *The Peach Blossom Fan,* for K'ung Shang-jen matched the story he had to tell quite precisely with the requirements of the genre.

The extraordinary length of the southern play (even further exaggerated by the use of very slow tempi for many of the songs) meant that one could hardly take in a complete performance at one sitting. The fifteen-day New Year's holiday, or the protracted birthday celebration of a high official or a member of the Imperial family, were favoured occasions for a performance which might spread over four or five evenings. The audience, knowing the play as every Chinese audience always seems to, would attend at its discretion: the connoisseurs for the great musical treats, the servants for the comic interludes, the children for the battle scenes. But because of the strenuous demands imposed by such a performance, the troupes themselves developed the practice of offering only selected scenes. They would construct a program for a single evening of scenes from three or four different plays, chosen to suit the particular resources of the company. These "selected scenes" were the ancestors of the Peking Opera plays of today.

Anyone who has seen Peking Opera, the classical theatre of China in its present incarnation, will be aware of the importance of role-types. The juvenile lead, the ingenue, and so on, are perhaps not so different from what we know in the West, but distinction of type is carried to a far higher degree. On an actor's role-type (or an actress' — only in certain historical periods were women barred from stage performance) depended the pitch of his voice, the pattern of his makeup, the manner of his gait and gesture, the way he sat down or held a fan.

Among the numerous *dramatis personae* of a play like *The Peach Blossom Fan* there would inevitably be several characters belonging to the same role-type. Thus the general Liu Liang-tso, the villainous grand secretary Ma Shih-ying, the singing-teacher Su K'un-sheng, and the minstrel Chang Yen-chu are all assigned to the *ching* or "painted-face" role: each would have special facial make-up, deep voice, tall stature (platform shoes), and exaggerated stride. The stage direction in the text of the play reads not just "enter Liu Liang-tso," but "enter the painted-face, costumed in armour as General Liu Liang-tso." By having a single *ching* actor play more than one of these parts, the size of the acting company could of course be held down below the level of a huge cast. The *ch'ou* or comic role-type in *The Peach Blossom Fan* plays the parts of the storyteller Liu Ching-t'ing, the bookseller Ts'ai Yi-so, a variety of servants and attendants, and an important female part, the singing-girl Cheng T'o-niang. We can imagine her as conspicuously ugly with her tart's makeup, lewd gestures, and regular caterwaul of a singing voice, since one of her major functions is to offset the demure elegance of the ingenue (*tan*) role, Fragrant Princess.

The poetic diction of the songs of the plays is a kind of loosened-up derivative of classical Chinese verse. Each song is composed to a specific, set metrical pattern. This is true of northern drama also, but the repertoire of available patterns is much larger for the southern style. It runs into hundreds, and one of the most jealously cherished aspects of the playwright's skill was his selection of the perfect metrical pattern for the effect he desired. Since each metrical pattern would imply a particular basic melody, he was also something of a composer, or at least arranger, of music. The accompaniment of the songs involved much use of gongs and drums for the martial sequences, but the most characteristic feature of southern drama was the use of the flute (as against the harsher stringed instruments of the northern style) to accompany much of the solo singing. The effect was of refinement almost to the point of languor, as the tremulous slow line of the flute, the modulations of high soprano or falsetto, and the delicate sway of sleeve and fan united to explore the last subtle suggestion of the lyrical text.

Buried among the hundreds of southern-style plays, hardly ever performed and seldom even read today, are scenes of great verbal beauty, lively passion, or effective comedy. There are only a handful of plays, though, which taken as a whole can match *The Peach Blossom Fan* for quality. Only one is available in a relatively complete (though prosaic and flat) English version: *The Palace of Eternal Youth* (*Ch'ang-sheng tien*) by Hung Shen (Peking: Foreign Languages Press, 1955). A musical comedy which enjoyed modest success on the Broadway stage in 1946, *Lute Song* by Will Irwin and Sidney Howard, was based on the early-Ming southern-style masterpiece of that title, but Irwin and Howard presumably relied on the French translation made by A. P. L. Bazin as early as 1841, for there is still no complete English version of *Lute Song* (*P'i-p'a chi*). In another year or so, I hope to complete an English translation of *Peony Pavilion* (*Mu-tan t'ing*), which the master-dramatist T'ang Hsien-tsu was finishing just about the time Shakespeare wrote *Romeo and Juliet*.

In some ways, *The Peach Blossom Fan* is the most interesting of all these plays. It tells the story of the intrigues and treachery that led to the downfall of the Ming dynasty in 1644, fifty years before the play was written: the protagonists, as Sir Harold Acton makes clear in his preface, are all historical characters. The love affair (central to every southern play) is brilliantly integrated with the more weighty matter of the plot, for it is between a young scholar (Hou Fang-yü), who as a loyalist opposes corrupt officials selling out to the Manchu conquerors, and a courtesan of great strength of character, Fragrant Princess, who resists court bullies to follow her love. The martial scenes (also obligatory) perfectly reflect the unhappy progress of the Ming cause and depict in vivid terms the gallant but ultimately futile loyalty of generals like Huang Te-kung and Shih K'o-fa.

There can be no happy ending, given the historical authenticity of the action: the play ends with a Taoist ceremony of mourning for the fallen dynasty, and the resolve of the remaining loyalists to enter seclusion in the hills rather than serve an alien regime. The world of *The Peach Blossom Fan* is that late-Ming world of gross corruption, of callousness and cowardice and the breakdown of a long-cherished order. Yet the quality of life revealed in the play is of extraordinary cultivation and sensibility. There is a great poignancy in this contrast, and we are led to a deep respect for Hou Fang-yü, Liu Ching-t'ing, and Shih K'o-fa, as in their different ways they follow their doomed ideals.

The textual history of K'ung Shang-jen's play is fairly straightforward: it was printed within the author's lifetime, and subsequent editions have introduced few variations in the text. In revising the Chen-Acton translation, I have followed the excellent edition put out by the People's Literature Press in Peking in 1959, deriving much help from the copious annotations by Wang Chi-ssu and Su Huan-chung. The translation is complete except for a very few places — for example, in Scene 32 where the directions for the ceremonial of eulogy have been abridged to omit long strings of instructions of the "Kneel! Rise! Kneel!" kind from the Master of Ceremonies' speech. These commands, in performance, would punctuate an elaborate posturing dance, but they make for boring reading.

Chen and Acton have exploited the resources of English to reproduce with great success the high poetry of many songs, the contrasting low punning and bawdy badinage, the formal greetings and compliments between scholars, and the sometimes rather stiff and artificial soliloquies and speeches of self-introduction. No other genre in Chinese literature draws so widely on the resources of the language. One feature of these Ming-Ch'ing plays presents a perennial problem to the translator: this is the passion for allusion. In the present translation, many allusions have been footnoted; many more have been sacrificed to the interests of readability. In my own rendering of the final scenes, I followed Chen and Acton's lead by paraphrasing when the closest translation would have impossibly retarded the movement of the verse. To illustrate this, let me quote from Liu Ching-t'ing's ballad in the final scene. He is lamenting the fall of the Nanking court. Throughout his song, he moves back and forth between the recent disastrous collapse of the Ming regime and the comparable events of a thousand years earlier "when the house of Sui destroyed the Ch'en." So, when he comes to the despicable career of the traitor Juan Ta-ch'eng, he sings:

> Past faults [admitted by Juan Ta-ch'eng in his own play]
>     *Spring Lantern* [*Riddles*] he should recognize over again;
> But cliques and groupings he rejoins so that no seam shows;
> Borrowing a sword to kill his foe, [like the treacherous]
>     Elder of Endless Joy [Feng Tao, a tenth-century Chief
>     Minister],
> Rubbing shoulders, flattering the eminent in the Halfway-to-
>     Leisure Hall [the villa by the West Lake built by the
>     notorious traitor, the Southern Sung minister Chia Ssu-
>     tao].

In line with the decisions made at similar knotty junctures by Chen and Acton, I decided to paraphrase rather than translate, to read:

> Careless of past faults, Juan Ta-ch'eng
> Fawned on the might of Ma Shih-ying,
> Tricked and betrayed all who opposed him,
> Slaughtered his foes with borrowed blade.

This kind of rendering obviously obscures much of the erudition, and with this some of the depth and richness of the original. But it seems regrettably unavoidable if the play is to be enjoyed at all in English; and it is worth insisting that the true glory of *The Peach Blossom Fan* lies not in these precious displays of pedantry, but in those songs, the great majority, whose language and imagery are clear, direct, and deeply moving.

Cyril Birch

# Principal Characters

### (in order of appearance)

The **Master of Ceremonies** of the Imperial Temple in Nanking
**Hou Fang-yü**, a young scholar of distinction
**Ch'en Chen-hui** ⎫
**Wu Ying-chi** ⎬ fellow members of the Revival Club
**Liu Ching-t'ing**, a veteran minstrel of renown
**Li Chen-li**, proprietress of an elegant house of pleasure and foster mother of the heroine
**Yang Wen-ts'ung**, painter, poet, and official
**Fragrant Princess** [Li Hsiang-chün], the heroine
**Su K'un-sheng**, her singing-teacher
**Juan Ta-ch'eng**, corrupt politician, dramatist and poet
**Ting Chi-chih** ⎫
**Shen Kung-hsien** ⎬ poet-musicians
**Chang Yen-chu** ⎭
**Pien Yü-ching** ⎫
**K'ou Pai-men** ⎬ professional singing-girls
**Cheng T'o-niang** ⎭
General **Tso Liang-yü**, commander of the Wu-ch'ang garrison
General **Shih K'o-fa**, President of the Board of War at Nanking
**Ma Shih-ying**, Governor of Feng-yang and Grand Secretary
General **Yuan Chi-hsien**
General **Huang Te-kung**
**Emperor Hung-kuang**
General **Liu Tse-ch'ing**
General **Kao Chieh**
General **Liu Liang-tso**
**Lan Ying**, a famous painter
**Ts'ai Yi-so**, a Nanking bookseller
**Chang Wei** (Chang the Taoist), former commander of the Imperial Guard in Peking
**Huang Shu**, Inspector General
**T'ien Hsiung**, adjutant to General Huang Te-kung
**Hsu Ch'ing-chün**, a magistrate's runner

# Prologue
## 1684

[*Enter an old man with a long white beard. He is the former **Master of Ceremonies** of the Imperial Temple. He now wears a felt cap and a broad-sleeved Taoist robe.*]

**Master of Ceremonies** [*sings*] :
Where in the world is a quainter curio
In jade or bronze than I, my face patined with age?
Though superannuated, lone and lost,
Why should I shrink when striplings mock at me?
I extirpate old sorrows from my breast,
And where there's wine and song I'm apt to linger.
When filial duty and loyalty reign, the universe will thrive
And the fruit of longevity grow superfluous.

[*Speaks*] : The sun beams brightly on a world well governed. The flowers bloom in the first year of the cycle; the mountains are free from bandits; the whole earth belongs to the blessed. Formerly an official of the Board of Rites, I used to announce the ceremonies in the Imperial Temple of Nanking. Since my post was humble, I need not reveal my name. Happily I have been spared most calamities. During ninety-seven years of life I have seen the rise and fall of many generations. Now another cycle has dawned. Our ruler is supremely wise and virtuous, and his ministers are loyal and efficient. The people are quiet and contented after an uninterrupted succession of good harvests. During this twenty-third year of K'ang-hsi's reign,[1] twelve kinds of auspicious omens have appeared.

---

1. K'ang-hsi was the reign-title of the Emperor Sheng-tsu who reigned 1662-1723; hence the date would be 1684. In earlier dynasties an emperor would occasionally change his reign-title in midrule, but the custom from the fifteenth century onwards was for the reign-title to be coterminous with the reign itself. It is thus possible (though strictly speaking, incorrect) to refer to an emperor (e.g., the Emperor Sheng-tsu) by his reign-title (as the Emperor K'ang-hsi or the K'ang-hsi Emperor). In this play, Ch'ung-

**Voice from Backstage:** What were the omens?

**Master of Ceremonies** [*counting on his fingers*]: The Chart of
Revelation emerged from the Yellow River, and the Holy
Scripture from the River Lo.[2] We have seen both the Fortunate Star and the Felicitous Cloud; the sweet dew and the
fruitful rain have fallen; the phoenix pair have returned and
the unicorn roams at large. The bean-pods burst and the
orchid flourishes; the sea is calm and the Yellow River clear.
All the omens are complete. Is this not a matter for congratulation? My old body is glad to survive in so wondrous a
world, and I have been enjoying innumerable excursions. Last
night, in the Garden of Great Serenity, I saw a new play
entitled *The Peach Blossom Fan.* The events it portrays took
place in Nanking not long ago, during the last years of the
Ming dynasty. The rise and fall of an empire are evoked in a
story of meeting and separation. Both plot and protagonists
were drawn from life. Not only did I hear tell of the originals;
I saw them with my own eyes. How amusing it was to
recognise my decrepit self in a minor role! I was stirred so
deeply that I laughed and wept, raged and cursed by turns.
Needless to say, the audience had no idea that I was included
in the drama.

**Voice from backstage:** Who was the author of this remarkable
play?

**Master of Ceremonies:** Perhaps you gentlemen do not realize that
famous playwrights never divulge their names. Suffice it that
in distributing praise and blame he follows the tradition of
his ancestor, the author of the *Spring and Autumn Annals;*
by melodic means he revives the lofty style of the classic
Odes, and demonstrates the quality of his upbringing.[3]

**Voice from backstage:** It must be the Mountain Hermit of the
Cloud Pavilion.

---

chen is the reign-title used for the Emperor Chuang-lieh-ti (the last Ming emperor, who
ruled from 1628 to 1644), and Hung-kuang is the reign-title assumed by Prince Fu in his
attempt, 1644-45, to restore the dynasty.

2. These magical events were actually legendary happenings of high antiquity.

3. The author of the *Spring and Autumn Annals* was Confucius [K'ung Tzu], who
also compiled the "classic Odes" or *Book of Songs.* K'ung Shang-jen, our playwright,
counted himself a descendant of Confucius in the sixty-fourth generation. "Mountain
Hermit of the Cloud Pavilion" was one of K'ung Shang-jen's sobriquets.

**Master of Ceremonies:** You are not mistaken.

**Voice from backstage:** The play will be performed at today's assembly. Since you are one of the characters and a veteran familiar with the latest tunes, please favour us with a synopsis. We shall listen with rapt attention.

**Master of Ceremonies:** It is summarized in a song by the Taoist priest Chang Wei. [*Sings*]:

The young scholar Hou, residing in Mo-ling,
Lost his heart to a southern beauty there.
But love was wounded; evil slandering
Soon forced asunder this too happy pair.
Chaos was loosened; warriors ran wild;
A worthless debauchee the Throne defiled;
Murderous traitors sprang from civil strife.
Forever ended was the blissful life
Of our fond lovers; he in fetters lay,
While she true heroism did display.
Aided by Su and Liu, with all their might,
The Emperor and his Premier fled by night.
Over the misty waves I gaze and falter:
Who is to chant the patriot's lament?
The painted fan of peach blossoms was rent,
And true love's token shattered at an altar.
How matters went astray, we shall disclose.

**Voice from backstage:** Bravo, bravo! But your masterly trills sometimes made it difficult for us to follow the meaning. Please oblige us with a short outline of the plot.

**Master of Ceremonies** [*sings*]:
Within and without the court, traitors Ma and Juan[4] hide
    their blades;
Liu and Su astutely plot to foil their machinations;
Master Hou's life of rapture falls into ruin;
Chang the Taoist tells the fates of dynasties in a song.

[*Speaks*]: Before I have finished speaking, Master Hou steps onto the stage. Your attention please!

---

4. A note on pronunciation: it is unfortunate that the romanization of the surname Juan suggests a Spanish pronunciation. Actually the initial "j" should be something like a weak French "j."

# PART I

## SCENE 1
# The Storyteller

1643, SECOND MONTH

[*Enter Hou Fang-yü in the robes of a scholar.*]

**Hou** [*sings*] :

On Grieve-Not Lake beside the Poet's Tower,[1]
The weeping willows burgeon once again.
The sun is setting: hill and river blend
In perfect beauty, and the traveller is tempted
To drink, recalling beauties long ago,
Painted and powdered in the southern courts.
Sad thoughts come with twilight, while the swallows
Frolic regardless of the fall of kings.

[*Recites*] :

Hushed is the courtyard, cold the kitchen stove;
And I have risen late from heavy slumber.
Though flowers bloom, fatigue invades the limbs,
And while it rains at every dawn of day,
And trees around the royal tombs decay,
The river swollen with the melted snows
Washes away the palace's foundations.
I write new poems grieving for the past;
An exile's sorrow, dreaming dreams of home.
Where will the swallows choose to nest this year,
In my village home far west of the misty waters?

[*Speaks*] : My name is Hou Fang-yü, and I am a native of

---

1. Grieve-not Lake and the Poet's Tower (built for the fourth-century poet Sun Ch'u) were located just to the west of the city wall of Nanking.

[5]

Kuei-te in the heart of the empire. I am descended from a long line of scholars and officials; my father and grandfather were Ministers of State, and both set up their standards in the Eastern Forest.[2] Trained in poetry and the classics, I have won distinction in the world of letters and allied myself with the Revival Society. My early writings were influenced by those master-spirits Pan Ku and Sung Yü; in maturity I am drawing nearer to Han Yü and Su Tung-p'o.[3] I have written in praise of wine in the Yueh-hua Palace, despite my reluctance to plant more flowers in the garden at Loyang.[4] Since finishing my examinations last year, I have been staying on the shore of Grieve-Not Lake. But the clouds of war continue to cover us, and news from home is scarce. It is mid-spring and the green grass stretches to the dim horizon, but where shall I find a companion for my homeward journey? The yellow dust rises from the earth, but here I sit in solitary exile. Oh! Grieve Not, Grieve Not! How can I fail to grieve? Fortunately, my literary friends Ch'en Chen-hui and Wu Ying-chi are staying over Ts'ai Yi-so's bookshop. We often meet and cheer each other's solitude. Today we shall gather at the Fair City Monastery and enjoy the splendour of the plum blossoms. I must start immediately or I shall be late. [*He proceeds to sing*] :

New warmth invades the breeze,
Mist 'whelms the river glade.
We stroll through flowery leas
With wine in jars of jade.
Thrilled by a sudden flute

---

2. The Tung-lin or Eastern Forest Party was a school of intellectuals who organized opposition to the corrupt dictatorship of the eunuch Wei Chung-hsien and his secret police. The Fu-she Society for the revival of ancient learning was an offshoot of the Eastern Forest Party whose aim was to "make friends by means of literature" and help its members prepare for the civil service examinations. Wu Ying-chi, who appears in this play, in historical fact recorded over two thousand members of this influential society, here translated as the "Revival Club."

3. Pan Ku, died A.D. 92, eminent historian; Sung Yü, third century B.C. statesman and poet whose works form part of the *Elegies of Ch'u* [*Ch'u-tz'u*]; Han Yü, 768-824, poet and essayist, leader of the influential "plain style movement" of the T'ang dynasty; Su Tung-p'o or Su Shih, 1036-1101, leading poet and essayist of the Sung dynasty.

4. Hou Fang-yü uses these allusions to compare himself with the poet Tsou Yang (c. 206-129 B.C.), guest in the Yueh-hua Palace built by Prince Hsiao of Liang, and with the poet Shih Ch'ung (died A.D. 300), owner of a famous garden outside Loyang.

The pilgrim's heart is mute.
Don't pass by Swallow Lane:
New owners are repainting
The lintels of your friends
Who will not come again.          [*Exit.*]

[*Enter Ch'en Chen-hui and Wu Ying-chi.*]

**Ch'en** [*sings*] :
The royal power is fading from Nanking.
The war-flags wave, the drums of battle beat.
One dreads to cross the river, though it flows
So placidly through willow groves and orchards.

[*Each announces his name.*]

**Ch'en**:  What is the latest news of the roving bandits?

**Wu**:  Yesterday I saw an official report. After defeating the national-
al armies, the bandits are drawing near the capital. Tso
Liang-yü, the Earl of Ning-nan, has retreated to Hsiang-yang,
and central China is totally unprotected. The fate of the
dynasty is sealed. We might as well enjoy the spring while it
lasts.

**Ch'en** and **Wu** together [*singing*] :
Spring floods the air, but wind and rain
Have scattered petals of the pear,
And so dawn seems dishevelled and in pain.

**Hou** [*re-entering*] :  Greetings! So the two of you came betimes.

**Wu**:  Of course. We could not bear to keep you waiting.

**Ch'en**:  I sent my servant ahead to sweep the monastery courtyard
and serve refreshments.

**Servant** [*entering in haste*] :  When it is cold, the wine's not warm
enough; when flowers bloom, the trippers are too many. . . .
We arrived too late, Your Honour. Let us all go home.

**Ch'en**:  What do you mean, too late?

**Servant**:  Master Hsu from the Wei Palace is giving a party in
honour of the blossoms. The whole monastery is crammed
with his guests.

**Hou**:  Let us go up the river then, and visit the beauties of the
Water Pavilion.

**Wu:** Why trouble to go so far? Do you know that brilliant minstrel Liu Ching-t'ing of T'ai-chou? He is highly esteemed by such connoisseurs as the Ministers Fan Ching-wen and Ho Ju-ch'ung, and I hear that he lives nearby. On this languid spring day, would it not be pleasant to listen to him?

**Ch'en:** That is also a good suggestion.

**Hou** [*angrily*]: Pock-marked Liu was a toady of Juan Ta-ch'eng, Bearded Juan, the eunuch's adopted son. I would rather avoid such a creature.

**Wu:** Apparently you do not know the facts. Since the despicable Juan persisted in patronising singers and dancers and flattering the powerful at court instead of resigning, I wrote an impeachment exposing his crimes and demanding his punishment. When at last his troupe of artists discovered that he was a member of the treacherous Ts'ui and Wei cliques, they all walked out on him in the middle of a performance, and pock-marked Liu was among them. In my opinion Liu deserves our respect.

**Hou:** I should never have expected to find such high principles in a man of that sort. Let us pay him a visit. [*They proceed together.*]

**Hou, Wu,** and **Chen** together [*singing*]:
Random pipe-notes in the Courts of the Transcendents
Where the secluded Alchemist
Watches "the vast sea turn into mulberry groves."[5]

**Servant:** Here we are. I'll knock at the door. [*Shouts*]: Is pock-marked Liu at home?

**Ch'en:** Fie, fie! He is a celebrity: you should address him as *Master* Liu.

**Servant:** Master Liu, open the door!

[*Enters Liu – a "ch'ou" or comedian type with a white beard, a skull cap, and a blue gown.*]

**Liu** [*sings*]:
Green moss and weeds grow rank and high
Beside my long-locked door.

---

5. The sea's giving place to mulberry groves is a common Taoist (i.e., "Alchemist") metaphor for the mutability of all phenomena.

Woodsmen and fishingfolk amble nigh
To praise the times of yore.

[*Seeing the visitors, he exclaims*]: Oh, Masters Ch'en and Wu! Forgive my ignorance of your arrival. Who is the gentleman you have brought along with you?

**Ch'en:** This is our friend Hou Fang-yü of Honan, whose fame is in the ascendant. He has long admired your art and hopes to hear you.

**Liu:** I am overwhelmed. Pray be seated and drink some tea. [*They sit, and **Liu** continues*]: You gentlemen are such fine scholars, so familiar with the *Records of the Historian,* the *Comprehensive Mirror,* 6 or whatever; what pleasure or instruction could you hope to gain from my vulgar discourse? [*He points at his courtyard and sings*]:

In the forsaken garden, a withered pine leans over a
broken wall;
On the fragrant grass of the palace ruins, the silky
showers fall.
The Six Great Dynasties' decay7 brings thoughts too
sad to render;
In telling tales I often weep, because my heart's too
tender.

**Hou:** You are excessively modest. Please favour us with a sample of your skill.

**Liu:** Since you honour me with your company, I dare not disappoint you. But I fear that my crude versions of history and blind man's tales are unworthy of your ears, so I shall comment on a chapter of Confucius's *Analects* instead.

**Hou:** How strange! One would hardly expect you to choose such a theme.

**Liu** [*laughing*]: You scholars discuss the *Analects,* why shouldn't

---

6. The *Records of the Historian* [*Shih-chi*] is by Ssu-ma Ch'ien, 145 to c. 90 B.C., who after his reformation of the calendar took up and completed the monumental work begun by his father, the history of China from the earliest ages to his own time. The *Comprehensive Mirror* [*Tzu-chih t'ung-chien*] was the history of China by Ssu-ma Kuang, 1019-1086.

7. The Six Dynasties were those which from the third through the sixth centuries maintained their capital at Chien-k'ang, modern Nanking.

I? Today you will judge my slender claim to learning. [*Recites*]:

"I dwell among green hills: you ask me why.
My soul at ease, I smile without reply.
The peach petals are swept along the stream
To other lands outside this mortal dream."[8]

[*He claps his "wakener-board" and continues, speaking*]: I
shall tell how the crime of three powerful clans who con-
spired against their ruler was exposed. I shall also tell how
wonderously Confucius succeeded in the reform of music.
The great doctrine of the Way was on the wane. Avarice and
covetousness were deeply embedded in the heart of man. On
returning to Lu from the state of Wei, our great Sage began
to restore the true principles of music. So profoundly were
performers affected by the result that they were ashamed to
realize they had been serving the wrong masters, and abandoned those tribes of malefactors. The theatres of the
mighty, which had been full of glowing colour and vibrant
melody, were deserted in a twinkling. Truly fearsome, truly
marvelous was the influence of the Sage! [*He sings to drum
or ta-ku accompaniment, keeping rhythmic time*]:

The great Sage of antiquity was most versatile in magic;
He could sway the wind and rain,
And turn handfuls of peas into armies of warriors.
When he saw that the turbulent nobles
Had lost all sense of propriety in their dancing and music,
He played a subtle trick on them.
Hence the lowest of slaves
Began to behave like the highest of heroes.

[*Liu claps his board and continues, speaking*]: The first
player to leave for the state of Ch'i was good Master Chih.
And why did he leave for Ch'i? I'll tell you. [*He drums and
sings*]:

Alas, he exclaimed,
Why should I ring the bell for these three clans?
I must have been blind to wallow in such mire.
I shall leave at once,

---

8. A poem by the great T'ang master Li Po, 699-762.

1. The storyteller Liu Ching-t'ing to the three scholars
   Hou Fang-yü, Ch'en Chen-hui and Wu Ying-chi:
      "I fear that my crude versions of history and
   blind man's tales are unworthy of your ears. . . ."

Setting forth with long swift strides towards the
   northeast;
There I shall join my old comrades and win fresh laurels.
I shall play for the delight of Master K'ung himself,
Who forgot the flavour of meat
For three months after hearing my performance.
And the virtuous Duke Ching
Will also be moved to tears by my art.
Even if the usurpers have swallowed
The heart of a leopard and the gall of a bear,
I doubt if they would pursue me to Ch'i,
The land of Chiang T'ai-kung's descendants![9]

[*Liu claps his board and continues speaking*]: The second
master's name was Kan. He left for the state of Ch'u. The
third master, Liao, retired to the state of Ts'ai. The fourth
one was Ch'üeh, who went to the state of Ch'in. Why did
these three leave? I'll tell you. [*He drums and sings*]:

All these musicians, who played at every banquet,
Had lost their leader now;
One by one they embarked on a new career.
The second master said: "See the usurper
Grasp his rice-bowl in the hall!
Why should we blow trumpets
And beat drums for his entertainment?
Our leader has left for the state of Ch'i;
Nobody can make him return.
As for me, I propose to play for Hsiung Yi, the King
   of Ch'u,
Committing myself to his powerful protection."
The third master said: "Though the state of Ts'ai,
South of the river, is not extensive,
It is near the capital
And in the heart of the central plain."
The fourth master gazed towards the south and said:
"I can see a new imperial spirit
Rising from the state of Ch'in,
Which has strong armies and fortifications;

---

9. Chiang T'ai-kung, twelfth century B.C., legendary octogenarian who consolidated
the Chou dynasty. He was said to exercise authority over the spirits of the unseen
universe, and hence was often depicted over doors to frighten away evil spirits.

Thither I shall take my lute."
All three of them pointed at the usurpers and said:
"We have endured your tyranny too long;
Henceforth we shall make you wince at the sound of
    our names."

[*Liu claps his board and continues speaking*]: One drummer
named Fang Shu went to the Yellow River region, and
another named Wu to the Han River region. The junior
leader's name was Yang and the gong-beater's name was
Hsiang, and these repaired to the seacoast. The manner of
their leaving was different. I'll tell you. [*He drums and
sings*]:

Altogether there were four drummers and gong-beaters.
"Our theatre remains in confusion," said they,
"And we have no desire to stay.
Disgusted with our fiendish patrons,
We shall seek employment elsewhere,
Even though it is unlikely that we shall fare better.
Let us sail a light boat to the Peach Blossom Spring;[10]
At least we may win renown
As fishermen of the lakes and rivers."

[*Liu claps his board and continues speaking*]: These four
made the wisest decision. Hearken to their speech! [*He
drums and sings*]:

"The trees of coral soar a hundred feet, vermilion in
    the sunlight;

---

10. Under the Tsin dynasty, 265-420, the poet T'ao Ch'ien wrote of a fisherman of
Wu-ling who, following a stream without noticing its length, suddenly came to a grove of
flowering peach trees. Fascinated by the beauty of the trees and the abundance of
scented plants, he wandered on until he reached a spring below a hill. He left his boat
and entered a narrow passage which widened as he advanced towards a country of
well-tilled fields, ponds of clear water, bamboos and mulberries, and pleasant cottages.
The inhabitants were highly civilised and law-abiding. He asked where they had come
from, and was told that their ancestors had fled from the tyranny of the Ch'in dynasty
in the third century B.C. and had found refuge in this country cut off from the rest of
the world. After leaving them, the fisherman reported his adventure to the governor of
his district, who sent out men to investigate this unknown region; but they lost their
way. Hence the expression *t'ao-yuan,* Peach Blossom Spring, became a metaphor for a
place of retirement where the sage could live happily, far from the noise and turmoil of
the world. The allusion is of course anachronistic here, from the lips of a contemporary
of Confucius (sixth century B.C.).

The crystal palace of the sea-god is built on a terrace
   of pearls.
The Dragon King will invite us to a banquet
Where golden boys and jade girls excel earthly mortals.
Phoenix flutes and ivory pipes
Will be tuned to the dragon's most exquisite melodies;
For this time, *others* will play while *we* shall listen.
Though the usurpers may try to pursue us down the rivers,
There will be thousands of leagues between us
In which they will lose their way.
We need not fear to be friendless
Among the mountains and distant waters,
For all men within the four seas
And beyond the horizon are our comrades.
We should tear the paper windowpane
And look at the real world.
We have saved ourselves from the abyss by divine
   inspiration.
Even if sea becomes land, and land sea,
The vision of our Sage endures in the Six Canons.[11]

[*Standing up, **Liu** speaks*]: Thank you for listening! I have
shown what trifling talents I possess.

**Ch'en:** Superb! None of our modern pundits could express himself so well. You are indeed a consummate artist.

**Wu:** Since leaving Juan, Liu has not cared to seek another patron.
This last recital was autobiographical.

**Hou:** I perceive he has a noble character, untainted by worldli-
ness. He is truly one of us. Story-telling is merely one of his
minor accomplishments.

**Ch'en, Wu,** and **Hou** together [*singing*]:

The deep red dust is suddenly clear,
And all shines bright as snow.
The warm spring light is suddenly chill;
The Sage solves all below.

---

11. The oldest enumeration of Chinese classics gave only five *ching* or canons: *I
ching* [*Book of Changes*]; *Shu ching* [*Book of Historical Documents*]; *Shih ching* [*Book
of Songs*]; *Li chi* [*Record of Rites*]; *Ch'un ch'iu* [*Spring and Autumn Annals*]. The
*Yueh chi* [*Record of Music*] was later added as the sixth canon, but it is usually classed
as one of the books of the *Li chi*.

[*They laugh, and continue*] :

Your mocking satire, our delight,
Each phrase at once caress and bite,
The triple beat of Yü-yang drum
To judgment come![12]

**Liu** [*sings*] :

Please come another day;
And if to Peach Blossom source
You fail to find the way,
To this old fisherman have recourse.

**Wu:**  Which of your other colleagues left the house of Juan?

**Liu:**  We are all dispersed. Only the master-singer Su K'un-sheng remains in this neighborhood.

**Hou:**  I should like to meet him too, and hope you will both pay me a visit.

**Liu:**  Of course we should be most honoured.

[*Each sings a line of the following quatrain*] :

**Liu:**

After my song is sung, the sun is setting.

**Ch'en:**

The fragrance of fallen petals fills the courtyard.

**Wu:**

Terraces and towers seem myriad blades of grass.

**Hou:**

Spiritual discourse and imperial strategy melt into the void.

---

12. The "triple beat of Yü-yang drum" alludes to the drumming to whose accompaniment Mi Heng cursed the tyrant Ts'ao Ts'ao in the time of the Three Kingdoms (third century A.D.).

# The Singing-Master

[*Li Chen-li, the heroine's foster mother, enters. She is the hostess of an elegant house of pleasure.*]

Li [*sings*] :
   With delicate firm strokes I paint my eyebrows.
   The doors of these red chambers are seldom closed;
   The drooping willows by the wooden bridge
   Cause riders to dismount.
   I shall embroider the bag of my reed-organ and tighten
      the strings of my lute.

[*Recites a quatrain*] :

The pear blossoms are like snow, the grass like mist;
Spring settles on the banks of the Ch'in-huai River.
A row of pleasure-chambers fronts on the water,
Reflecting from each window a lovely face.

[*Speaks*] : My name is Li Chen-li. I have won fame in the world of "mists and flowers," and high rank in the circles of "wind and moon."[1] I was educated in the old tradition of my calling. Though I have escorted countless guests along the bridge to the pleasure-quarters, the rose of my complexion has not faded and my charms are as fresh as ever. I have adopted a daughter of exquisite grace, who has recently begun to appear at social functions. She is very shy and utterly enchanting; so far she has had no experience behind the hibiscus-embroidered bed-curtains. I happen to know a former magistrate named Yang Wen-ts'ung who is the brother-in-law of Ma Shih-ying, Governor of Feng-yang, and a sworn brother of Juan Ta-ch'eng. Whenever he visits us, he lavishes praise on my adopted daughter and promises to introduce an influential patron to "comb her hair."[2] On such a fine spring day, I expect he will pay me a visit. [*Calls*] : Draw the curtains, maid, and sweep the floor. See that everything is ready for our guests.

**Voice from backstage:** Aye, aye, ma'am.

---

1. Metaphors for romantic love.
2. I.e., to deflower her. In the case of a young courtesan-to-be of exceptional beauty and talent — like Fragrant Princess — this was an honour for which young gallants would

[*Yang Wen-ts'ung enters.*]

**Yang**: This magnificent view of the three mounts is like a masterpiece of painting. The romance of the Six Dynasties is a
perennial theme of poetry. I am Yang Wen-ts'ung, a retired
magistrate. Since I am on the best of terms with Mistresss Li,
the famous hostess of the Ch'in-huai River, I'll take advantage of the fine weather to call on her. Here is her house. [*He
enters it.*] Where is Mistress Li? [*On seeing her*]: The plum
petals have fallen and the willow floss turned yellow. The
courtyard is filled with soft harmonies of spring. How can we
extract the utmost enjoyment from it?

**Li**: Let us climb to the upper chamber. Up there we can burn
sweet incense, sip tea, and enjoy some poetry.

**Yang**: That sounds delightful. [*Both climb the stairs. He recites*]:

The bamboo screen suggests bars of a cage
For the bird on his perch;
Flower shadows seem like a cover
For the fish in the bowl.

[*Looking round, he says*]: This must be the sitting-room of
your charming daughter. Where is she now?

**Li**: She has not finished dressing.

**Yang**: Please ask her to join us.

**Li** [*calls*]: Come out, my dear. His Honour Yang has arrived.

**Yang** [*examining the poems hanging on the walls*]: These are all
gifts from famous masters of calligraphy. What a choice
collection! [*He reads them out loud to himself.*]

[*The heroine, a **Girl** of about 16, enters in an
exquisite dress.*]

**Girl** [*sings*]:
Returning from the scented land of dreams,
I leave the red quilt embroidered with mandarin ducks,[3]
To redden my lips and dress my hair.

---

eagerly vie. If the process led to a more enduring attachment, there was always the
possibility that the young man might purchase the girl's freedom from her "adoptive
mother — i.e., the madam of the house — and install her as his wife, or at least secondary
wife. This is what indeed happens, in the play, between Hou Fang-yü and Fragrant
Princess: the vows of fidelity and plans to marry are not to be taken as mere lovers'
rhetoric but as perfectly serious intentions. Their union, however, was not regarded by
others as totally binding: see Scene 6, n. 4.

3. The mandarin duck and drake were emblems of conjugal fidelity.

I shall con some recent poems
To dispel the languor of spring.

[*Says to Yang*] : Your Honour, a thousand blessings!

**Yang:** I have not seen you for several days, and you have grown
much lovelier in the meantime. What profound truth the
poems on this wall express! I see that some were written by
my dearest friends. Since they have paid you such a compliment, I must join them. [**Mistress Li** *promptly brings him a
brush and ink-slab.* **Yang** *holds the brush in silence before
saying*] : I doubt if I could ever compete with these masters.
To conceal my failings, I shall contribute a sketch of orchids.

**Li:** I can assure you it will be appreciated.

**Yang:** Here is a fist-shaped rock by Lan T'ien-shu.[4] I'll paint some
orchids beside it. [*Sings*] :

The white wall gleams like silk for me to paint on:
Fresh leaves, sweet buds, an aura of mist and rain.
Here a fist-rock bursts with ink-splashed energy,
There specks of moss are elegantly scattered.

[*Standing back to survey his finished painting, he says*] : I
believe it will do. [*Sings*] :

No match for the splendid vigor of the Yuan masters,
But at least our ladies will have orchids to set them off.

**Li:** This is a genuine work of art. It vastly improves the room.

**Yang:** Don't mock me! [*To the* **Girl**] : Please tell me your name
so that I can inscribe it here.

**Girl:** I am too young to have a name.[5]

---

4. Lan T'ien-shu or Lan Ying (1578 to after 1660), who appears later in the play. He
was one of the most accomplished painters of his time, a last representative of the Che
school.

5. The Chinese had a number of personal names. At birth a male received a "milk
name" which was used by relatives and neighbours. On entering school he was given a
"book name" to be used by schoolmasters, schoolfellows, officials, and in literary
connections. At marriage he was given a "great name," *tzu,* or style, *hao,* for use by
acquaintances. Every writer or scholar took one or more "studio names," *pieh-hao.* If he
won a literary degree, entered official life, or had official rank, he took an official name,
*kuan-ming.* After death he might be given a posthumous name. Names usually had some
appropriate significance. A girl received a milk name, a marriage name, and perhaps a
nickname. "Fragrant Princess" corresponds to the last.

**Li:** We should be obliged if Your Honour would choose one for her.

**Yang:** According to the *Tso chuan*,[6] "the fragrance of the orchid pervades a whole nation, it captivates all mankind." Why not call her *Fragrant Princess*?

**Li:** That is perfect. Fragrant Princess, come and thank His Honour.

**Fragrant Princess** [*curtseying*]: I thank Your Honour kindly.

**Yang** [*laughing*]: It provides us with a name for the house also. [*As he writes the inscription, he reads it aloud*]: In the springtime of the Year of the Horse during the reign of Ch'ung-chen,[7] I painted these orchids in the Abode of Entrancing Perfumes, in order to win a smile from Fragrant Princess. Signed, Yang Wen-ts'ung of Kweiyang.

**Li:** Both the calligraphy and brushwork are supreme. I can never thank you enough. [*All sit down.*]

**Yang:** Surely Fragrant Princess is the greatest beauty in the land. What training in the arts has she received?

**Li:** I brought her up so tenderly that she has only just begun to study in earnest. The day before yesterday I found a teacher to instruct her in the art of lyric.

**Yang:** Who is he?

**Li:** A certain Su K'un-sheng.

**Yang:** I know him well. He used to go by the name of Chou Ju-sung, and lived in Wusi. He deserves the highest praise. What tunes has he taught her so far?

**Li:** "The Four Dreams of the Jade Tea-House."[8]

**Yang:** How much has she learned?

**Li:** Only half "The Peony Pavilion." Dear daughter, as His Honour Yang is an old friend of ours, do bring your music book and sing a few tunes for him.

---

6. *Tso chuan*, the important commentary on the *Spring and Autumn Annals*, was attributed to Tso Ch'iu-ming, a supposed disciple of Confucius. The work was actually written later than the time of Confucius; it dates from about the first century of our era.

7. On Ch'ung-chen, see Prologue, n. 1. The "Year of the Horse" was 1643.

8. I.e., the plays of T'ang Hsien-tsu, 1550-1617, the outstanding dramatist of the Ming period. "Jade Tea-house" was his "studio name."

**Fragrant Princess:** I dare not.

**Li:** Don't be silly. In our profession, sleeves and skirts are in constant motion. Why not sing when you have the chance? [*Sings*] :

Born amid powdered faces and painted eyebrows,
Nurtured as one of the orioles and flowers,
A tuneful voice is your only source of wealth.
Be not too prodigal with your emotions, but learn to sing
Songs of the morning breeze and broken moon.
Beat gentle time with your ivory castanets,
Bear off the singer's prize,
And princes will tether horses at your gate.

[*Su K'un-sheng enters, in everyday garb.*]

**Su:** On my way to the songbird in the emerald chamber, I stop to gaze at the peonies by the porch. Since leaving the house of Juan, I have been teaching music to the loveliest courtesans. Isn't this better than waiting on the whims of an eunuch's foster son? [*He steps in.*] Ah! Your Honour Yang, it is an age since we have met!

**Yang:** I congratulate you on your entrancing pupil.

**Li:** Master Su has arrived. Run and welcome him, dear daughter.

[*Fragrant Princess curtseys.*]

**Su:** Let us avoid formalities. Have you memorized the song we practised yesterday?

**Fragrant Princess:** I have, sir.

**Su:** Since His Honour Yang is present, let us hear it. We should take advantage of his criticism.

**Yang:** I shall be content merely to listen.

**Su** and **Fragrant Princess** [*sitting opposite each other, sing*] :
Clusters of purple, witching hues of red,
Now blossom from below and overhead,
Even from dried-up wells and broken walls.
How shall we spend so glorious a day?

**Su** [*stopping*] : Your rhythm is weak. The accent should fall on

"spend" and "glorious"; don't run them together. Again!
[*The last line is repeated. Then they continue*]:

**Su** and **Fragrant Princess** [*singing*]:
    Where at this hour can perfect bliss be found?
    Now twilight gathers, and the day has fled.
    The many-coloured clouds are drifting round
    The green-tiled roofs, and gusty showers fall. . . .

**Su** [*interrupting*]: The word "showers" should be stressed, and
    sung from deep in the throat. [*The last line is repeated. Then
    they continue*]:

**Su** and **Fragrant Princess** [*singing*]:
    Over the misty waves doth float
    A fragile painted boat.
    Yet by the cloistered maid these things are seen
    Only as visions on a painted screen.

**Su**: Well done, well done! You have sung it without a mistake.
    Let us continue.

**Su** and **Fragrant Princess** [*singing*]:
    The cuckoo's tears have stained the verdant hills,
    The willow branches droop as drunk with wine;
    New peonies reign; but when the spring is gone,
    What will survive of their bright sovereignty?

**Su** [*interrupting*]: This line is new to you, try it again. [*They
    repeat the last line and then continue*]:

**Su** and **Fragrant Princess** [*singing*]:
    Now feast your gaze in sheer serenity:
    Behold the twittering swallows, how they fare,
    Flashing their tails like scissors through the air,
    While orioles drop their notes like rounded pearls.

**Su**: Better and better! Now we have mastered another melody.

**Yang** [*to Li*]: I'm delighted to discover that your daughter has
    such talent. She is certain to reach the peak of her profession.
    [*To Su*]: Yesterday I met Hou Fang-yü, the son of Minister
    Hou. He has brilliant prospects as well as literary genius, and
    he is looking for a beautiful mate. Have you heard of him,
    old friend?

**Su**: He is a fellow countryman of mine, a youth of exceptional
    promise.

2. Su K'un-sheng (to Fragrant Princess, who has just sung
for Yang Wen-ts'ung and Madam Li Chen-li): "Well done,
well done! You have sung it without a mistake."

**Yang**: A match between such a couple should be very successful. [*Sings*] :

> The sixteen-year-old maid, as fair as emerald jade,
> Is ripe for nuptial bliss — how ravishing her song!
> Her suitor rides with silken gifts and trinkets for
>     her hair.
> Hand in hand they will drain the cups of wine,
> While friends chant verses in congratulation;
> The halls are freshly garnished for the wedding.
> A couple perfectly matched,
> Year after year they will abide together,
> In a peach tree grove beside the sweet spring waters.

**Li**: I hope you will persuade this young gentleman to pay us a visit. It would be wonderful if such a match could be arranged.

**Yang**: I promise to keep it in mind.

**Li** [*sings*] :

> My daughter is more precious to me than rarest pearls,
> Her voice is purer than the new-born oriole's;
> But her virgin youth is barred by many doors,
> Unnoticed by the passing wanderer.

> [*Speaks to all*] : This day should be celebrated. Let us drink some wine below.

**Yang**: With the greatest pleasure.

>    [*Exeunt, each one singing*] :

**Yang**:
> Outside the curtain, flowers fill the courtyard.

**Li**:
> The oriole feels drunk, the swallow drowsy.

**Fragrant Princess**:
> My crimson kerchief holds a heap of cherries.

**Su**:
> Waiting to fling them at P'an's chariot![9]

---

9. P'an Yueh was a third-century poet renowned for his exceptional handsomeness. Women would pelt his carriage with flowers and fruits when he rode in the capital.

# The Disrupted Ceremonies

1643, THIRD MONTH

[*Enter two* **Temple Servants**, *both clowns.*]

**First Servant**: For generations, the sacrificial peas[1] have been symbols of this rite.

**Second Servant**: Ever since the days of my old grandad's might.

**First Servant**: The sacrificial vessels at each altar are catalogued in the books.

**Second Servant**: Count them like stooks.

**First Servant**: In the beginning and middle of each month, we light the candles and open the door.

**Second Servant**: Sweep the floor.

**First Servant**: Kneel down and greet the Master of Ceremonies as soon as he is sighted.

**Second Servant**: Make sure that everything is righted. But you have bungled all the words.

**First Servant**: If you can do better, go ahead.

**Second Servant**: Grain tribute is brought to the treasury all the year round.

**First Servant**: Bragging of wealth by the pound.

**Second Servant**: The whole family lives under a green-tiled roof with scarlet walls.

**First Servant**: Leading a wife to the stalls.

**Second Servant**: Dry timber is felled as soon as an axe you seize.

**First Servant**: Plundering neighbours' trees.

**Second Servant**: Year in, year out, no vegetable need you eat.

**First Servant**: Nothing but salted meat.

**Second Servant**: Shame on you, you have made a hash of it with your cheap rhymes. [*Both laugh.*]

---

1. In early youth, Confucius was reputed to have used peas to imitate the arrangement of a ritual altar, thereby indicating his precocious interest in the rites.

**First** and **Second Servant** together: We prepare the rites of the Imperial Academy in Nanking. After six months of idleness, we are back in the middle of spring, the season for sacrifice. All the ritual vessels and provisions have arrived from the Minister's office. Let us set them in proper order.

[*They set out the altar.*]

**First Servant**: Chestnuts, dates, fresh water-roots.

**Second Servant**: Ox, sheep, pig, rabbit, and deer.

**First Servant**: Fish, spinach, celery, bamboo shoots, and garlic.

**Second Servant**: Salt, wine, incense, silk, and candles.

**First Servant**: The list is complete. Keep an eye on everything, for we shall be blamed if the stewards pilfer.

**Master of Ceremonies** [*entering*]: Fie on you! If you don't pilfer, well and good. Why cast aspersions on others?

**First Servant**: [*bows with folded hands*]: I beg your pardon. I was referring to those who shall be nameless since they are shameless. Of course a respectable person like you would be blameless.

**Master of Ceremonies**: Let us not waste words. It is already daybreak. You should light the candles and incense.

**Second Servant**: Aye, aye, sir. [*Exeunt.*]

[*Libationer appears in his official robes.*]

**Libationer** [*sings*]:
The smoke of incense clouds the pillared hall
Where scarlet candles flame beside the altar.
And now the orchestra strikes up a prelude;
The vessels, food and wine are all prepared.

[*His Assistant appears in his official robes.*]

**Assistant** [*sings*]:
The ranks are drawn up
For the observance of ceremonies in the Southern Academy.

**Libationer**: I am the Libationer in the Imperial Academy of Nanking.

**Assistant**: I am the Assistant Libationer. Today is the day of sacrifice at the Temple of Confucius, and we are about to begin the ceremony.

[*They stand on either side of the stage.* **Wu Ying-chi** *enters.*]

**Wu** [*sings*] :
    The drum is booming; soon it will be dawn.
    The scholars file before the Almond Altar.

[*Enter* **Four Scholars** *of the Imperial Academy.*]

**Four Scholars**, together [*singing*] :
    Of yore this music and these rites inspired three
        thousand disciples.
    Today we shall again behold our Sage.

[**Juan Ta-ch'eng** *enters in formal attire, his face covered with a heavy beard.*]

**Juan** [*sings*] : I have brazened myself to join this solemn gathering.

**Wu**: I, Wu Ying-chi, together with my comrades Yang Wei-tou, Liu Po-tsung, Shen K'un-t'ung, and Shen Mei-sheng, am ready to attend the sacrifice.

**Four Scholars**: Let us take our appointed places.

**Juan** [*hiding his face behind his sleeve*]: Having nothing else to do in Nanking, I came to see the ceremony. [*He takes up a position in the front rank.*]

**Master of Ceremonies** [*enters and calls*] : Go to your places. Stand in even ranks. Bow; kneel; prostrate yourselves; arise! [*Thrice repeated.*]

**All** together [*singing*] :
    A hundred feet above the clouds, the golden tablet gleams;
    Behold our Sage enthroned in majesty,
    His four supreme disciples sit beside him,
    While strains of music bid his spirit welcome.
    Let us prostrate ourselves below the steps,
    We who have studied poetry and the classics
    That we may come into his heritage.
    Now tremble in his presence, struck with awe.

[*After burning paper offerings, all salute each other.*]

**Libationer** and **Assistant** [*singing*]:
    Facing the north, we celebrate together
    Our Sage's glory with the spring's return;
    Observing all the hallowed regulations,
    The time and order of each sacrifice.

**Wu** [*leading the Scholars' chorus*]:
    Let us unite in worship of the Sage,
    Like his disciples in a nobler age.

**Juan** [*sings*]:
    What joy to stroll the capital,
    A man of pleasure,
    Without official duties
    To rob me of my leisure.

[*Exeunt **Libationer** and **Assistant**. **Juan** bows to all.*]

**Wu** [*startled*]: Are you not whiskered Juan? What are you doing at the sacrifice? This is an insult to the Sage. You are a disgrace to the world of letters. [*Shouting*]: Away with you!

**Juan** [*angrily*]: I am a distinguished Doctor of Literature, descended from a famous family. Why should I not be allowed to attend the sacrifice? What sin have I committed?

**Wu**: At court and outside it, your guilt is notorious. You have covered your face with a mask and lost your conscience. How dare you set foot in this temple? Did not my public impeachment say enough about your crimes?

**Juan**: That was precisely why I attended these ceremonies, to confess what is in my heart.

**Wu**: Let me tell you plainly who and what you are. [*Sings*]:

    Godson of Wei, godson of K'o,[2]
    To any family you will go.
    With Ts'ui Ch'eng-hsiu, and T'ien Erh-ching,[3]

---

2. Wei is Wei Chung-hsien, 1568-1637, one of the most powerful eunuchs in Chinese history, whose persecution of able generals and ministers weakened the Chinese defences against the threatening Manchus. K'o-shih was the Emperor Hsi-tsung's wet-nurse and supposedly Wei's plaything. On the Emperor's death, Wei hanged himself to escape trial, and K'o-shih was executed.

3. Leading associates of Wei Chung-hsien's clique.

Consorting in stealth,
You guzzle iniquities and gobble filth.
Shooting secret arrows into the Eastern Forest,[4]
Weaving your plots in the Western Shed,[5]
Beware, beware — men will not be misled.

**Scholars** [*singing in unison*]:
Ha! behold the melting glacier,
The baseless, toppling iron pillar!

**Juan**: Brothers, you revile me without trying to understand my
motives. You do not realize that I am a disciple of the great
Chao Chung-i. When the Grand Eunuch Wei rose to power, I
had retired to the country to mourn the death of my parents.
How could I have harmed anyone? On what grounds do you
accuse me? [*Sings*]:

To such injustice Heaven once responded
By sending frost in midsummer.
Hide me under no black bowl
To suffer slander
No more substantial than a shadow.[6]
Why did I cultivate Wei Chung-hsien?
To try to save the upright censors,
Wei Ta-chung, Chou Ch'ao-jui!
For their sake, my good name
Gladly I sacrificed.

[*Speaks*]: Have you forgotten Master K'ang Hai of yore,
who curried favour with the eunuch Liu Chin in order to save
the life of an upright man?[7] If I associated with Wei Chung-
hsien, it was to protect my noble friends of the Eastern
Forest Party. How can I be blamed for this? [*Sings*]:

Every problem demands a fair solution,
But I have been ten times wronged,
Yet no one rises to defend me;

---

4. See Scene 1, n. 2.

5. The notorious torture-chamber of the court secret police.

6. The frost in midsummer was sent down by Heaven, in an ancient legend, to
convince the king of the loyalty of an unjustly slandered minister. The black bowl is an
image for an impenetrable cloud of unwarranted suspicion.

7. Liu Chin, a eunuch who became virtual head of the government under the Ming
Emperor Wu-tsung. A cabal formed against him, and he was executed in 1510.

I am vilified by all.
These giddy striplings break wind in my face. . . .

**Wu**: How dare you use such language here!

**All**: It is insufferable that a traitor like you should speak so foully in the temple of Confucius.

**Master of Ceremonies**: It is absolutely monstrous. Old as I am, I long to thrash the traitor! [*Beats* **Juan**.]

**Wu**: Pummel his face and pull out all his hair!

　　　　[*Everybody attacks Juan.*]

**All** [*singing*] :
　　Damned spawn of a eunuch!
　　You should not even be allowed
　　To worship the Sage;
　　A disgrace to the world of letters!
　　We shall wage war against you and your like
　　And drive you to the farthest wilderness,
　　To feed wolves and tigers with your swinish carcass.

**Juan**: Have you done with assaulting me? [*To* **Master of Ceremonies**] : Even an old gaffer like you has the nerve to strike me!

**Master of Ceremonies**: I can thrash you as vigorously as any man.

**Juan** [*gazing ruefully at his beard*] : I have lost half my beard. How shall I ever appear in public again? [*He runs off the stage, singing*] :

　　This volley of fists has laid me low,
　　I am in agony;
　　My arms feel broken, my back as well.
　　I flee from this place of torment.

**Wu** and **All** [*singing*] :
　　Between the virtuous and the vile
　　There is always a clear distinction,
　　And this man's crimes are heavy and solid as lead.
　　Not long ago his power could reach to Heaven —
　　Today how ignominious was his flight!
　　His scholar's hat was beaten flat;
　　It is time for him to burn his ink and brushes.

**Wu:** This incident has avenged the Eastern Forest Party and brought honour to the Academy of Nanking. We should presevere in this resolute course, and prevent all such villains from showing themselves again in public.

**Chorus:** Hear, Hear! We have done a righteous deed before the Sage's gate.

**Wu:** Between light and darkness we should champion light.

**Chorus:**
Alas, 'tis never easy to decide
Which be the winning, which the losing side.

**Wu:**

Heaven may loosen Chaos; 'tis for Man
To conjure Order wheresoe'er he can.

---

SCENE 4

# The Play Observed

## 1643, THIRD MONTH

[*Juan Ta-ch'eng enters, in obvious distress.*]

**Juan** [*sings*]:
The old game is played out,
My former colleagues scattered.
The hair grows white upon my temples,
No spirit is left in my song.
Insulted by these upstarts without cease,
How shall I ever sleep and eat in peace?

[*Speaks*]: Until recently I enjoyed a triumphant career. Power, fame, and rank were within my grasp. Unfortunately, I was tempted by vanity and greed to join the eunuch Wei's party. For a time I became one of his foster sons. While his influence was spreading like fire, I was like a wolf within sight of its prey. Now that it has dwindled to cold ashes, I am more like a wretched owl in a withered forest. Everybody curses me and spits in my face; I am assaulted from every side. Alas, I am a scholar who has absorbed a whole library of

books. Why did I attach myself to that evil eunuch? I was
neither demented nor delirious, yet how could I have made
such a blunder as to become his henchman? [*Stamps his
foot.*] When I think of the past, I am filled with mortifica-
tion. Luckily, this huge city affords a shelter for all sorts. I
have a spacious mansion in Breeches' Bottom, which I have
embellished with gardens and pavilions, and here I have
trained a private troupe of singers and dancers. Should any
high official deign to associate with me, I would go to any
expense to gratify him. Perhaps I may still win some good
man's sympathy, and the chance to amend past errors. . . .
[*Whispers*]: But if Heaven allowed dead ashes to flare up
again, I would waste no further thought on my reputation. I
would commit every crime again to my heart's content!
Yesterday I was grossly insulted by the young urchins of the
Revival Club in the temple of Confucius. Though they were
to blame, I was rash to expose myself. But I am anxious to
find a way to propitiate them. [*He scratches his head in
thought and sings*]:

Coxcombs combined, a feather-pated crew,
To cheat and slander my distinguished name.
Like whirling winds they tore away the beard
About my lips — these very lips, the same
That uttered purest poetry; broke this wrist
Whose calligraphic skill once brought me fame.
Nor can I find revenge, but only hide
Indoors in all my shame.

First Servant [*entering with a letter*]: Few notabilities come this
way; all the fine birds are flown, alackaday! [*To Juan*]: Your
Honour, here is a note requesting the loan of your troupe of
players.

Juan [*reading it aloud*]: "Your friend Ch'en Chen-hui salutes
you." Aha, this comes from a great celebrity. Why would
such a great man as this stoop to borrowing my troupe of
players? What did his messenger have to say?

Servant: He says there are two other gentlemen named Fang
Mi-chih and Mao P'i-chiang who are drinking with him at the
Crowing Cock Inn. They are all agog to enjoy your new play,
*The Swallow Letter.*

**Juan:** Run upstairs, choose the best costumes, and summon the leading players. See that they brush themselves up and hasten to oblige the scholars. You go with them, take my greetings, and keep a careful eye on everything.

>          [*Exit* **First Servant**. *Several players cross the stage, followed by another* **Servant** *carrying costumes.* **Juan** *beckons to him.*]

**Juan** [*whispers*]: When you get there, listen carefully to their remarks while they watch the play.

**Servant:** As you command, sir. [*Exit.*]

**Juan** [*chuckling to himself*]: Ha-ha, I never expected them to apply to me. This is an encouraging sign. I'll sit in my study and wait for the servant's report. [*Exit.*]

>          [**Yang Wen-ts'ung** *enters.*]

**Yang:** In the hope of hearing the latest tunes, I have come to call on my old crony. He excels in composing lyrics and plays as I do in painting and calligraphy. Today I have a chance of hearing his latest song for *The Swallow Letter*. Here is the Stone Nest Garden. How exquisitely all the rocks and flowers are arranged. It must have been designed by the famous Chang Nan-yüan.[1] [*Pointing at the rocks and flowers, he sings*]:

Flowering groves carefully spaced,
Rocks mantled with moss,
Create the effect of a landscape
By Ni Tsan or Huang Kung-wang.[2]

[*Looking up, he reads from a tablet*]: "The Hall of Lyrics. Calligraphy by Wang To."[3] What vigorous characters! Red carpets strew the ground; this is where he rehearses his plays. [*Sings*]:

---

1. Chang Nan-yüan or Chang Lien was a landscape architect of the late Ming and early Ch'ing period who designed many famous gardens in Chekiang and Kiangsu.

2. Ni Tsan, 1301-1374, and Huang Kung-wang, 1269-1354, were two of the most celebrated figures of the Yuan dynasty, which was a golden age of Chinese painting.

3. Wang To, 1592-1652, was an eminent poet, painter, and calligrapher who attained the exalted post of President of the Board of Rites, first under the Ming and then again under the Manchus.

A thatched pavilion completes the picture.
There in his high black cap he directs the players
With silver lute and crimson clappers.

[*Speaks*]: Maybe I shall find him in the flower garden.
[*Sings*]:

But why closed gates, a scene forlorn?
Is he writing new poems or revising old ones?

[*Standing still, he listens and says*]: Somebody seems to be chanting; it must be old Juan reading aloud. Brother Juan, come and relax awhile. Don't give up all your time to literature!

**Juan** [*enters, laughing*]: I was wondering who had come to see me. So it is you! Sit down, sit down.

**Yang:** Why shut yourself indoors on a fine spring day?

**Juan:** My four plays are being printed, so I have to scrutinize the proofs for mistakes.

**Yang:** So that explains it. I heard you had finished rehearsing *The Swallow Letter,* and I long to see it.

**Juan:** Unfortunately my actors are away.

**Yang:** Where have they gone?

**Juan:** They have gone to entertain some friends of mine.

**Yang:** Would you let me see a copy of the script? I should enjoy nothing better than to read it with some wine beside me.

**Juan** [*to servants*]: Bring the wine. His Honour Yang and I will quench our thirst.

**Voices from backstage:** Aye, aye, sir.

[*Wine and refreshments are brought in. Yang and Juan drink while reading the play.*]

**Yang** [*sings*]:
Column by column, new poems flow onto paper,
Each line as gold freshly sifted from sand.
A beautiful woman speaks her reverie,
As mist drifts over the sea and far clouds form.

[*Speaks*]: While reading this passage, I feel I have fallen in love! [*Sings*]:

Though willow buds whiten, and hair be sprinkled with snow,
The swallow retains a fragment of spring in its beak.

**Juan:** My doggerel and commonplace tunes must strike you as absurd. Pray drink some more wine.

**First Servant** [*entering hastily*]: I bring my random words to allay my master's concern. Your Honour, I have been watching the performance at the Crowing Cock Inn. They have finished three scenes, so I hurried back to report.

**Juan:** What were the comments of the audience?

**Servant:** All expressed the highest admiration. [*Sings*]:

They nodded their heads and beat time in approval.
They forgot their wine cups to lap every line of the play.

**Juan:** Their approbation seems to have been genuine. What else did they say?

**Servant** [*sings*]:
They exclaimed:
"A true genius with a remarkable pen!"

**Juan:** Oho! I am surprised that they were so complimentary. What else?

**Servant** [*sings*]:
They said: "His style is that of an immortal,
Expressing himself in human speech.
In modern letters his art stands supreme."

**Juan** [*feigning embarrassment*]: This is too much; they are exaggerating. But I shall look forward to hearing their comments when they have seen more of it. Be quick and find out, then run back and tell me. [*Servant obeys. Juan laughs aloud*] I never guessed those young men were so discerning! [*To Yang*]: No heel-taps! [*Sings*]:

Ah, I have seen
All the landscapes of the southern school,
Read all the old romances.
I have toiled till dusk in my tower or rain pavilion,
Toiled on from nightfall under a lamp;
I have drained my heart's blood in solitary composing.
At last I have found discriminating hearers!

**Yang:** Who are these gentlemen?

**Juan:** Ch'en Ting-sheng, Fang Mi-chih, and Mao P'i-chiang — all men of the deepest culture. They have proved their esteem for me.

**Yang:** These persons are seldom addicted to praise, but your *Swallow Letter* is so fine in versification and melody that their admiration is natural.

**First Servant** [*returning*]: I ran out like a rabbit; I fly back like a raven. Your Honour, now that they have seen half the play, I have returned with another report.

**Juan:** How did the audience respond?

**Servant** [*sings*]:
> They called Your Honour "Pride of the south,
> Chief ornament of the Eastern Forest,
> Worthy of the Han-lin Academy itself."

**Juan:** Every sentence is so laudatory that I feel embarrassed. What else?

**Servant** [*sings*]:
> They added: "But why did you join the traitors Ts'ui and Wei,
> And turn against your old friends?

**Juan** [*frowning angrily*]: That was only a passing misjudgment; there was no need to bring it up again. What else?

**Servant:** They said more in the same strain, but being your humble servant I dare not repeat it.

**Juan:** Never mind, proceed.

**Servant** [*sings*]:
> They said: "Your Honour called a stranger his father,
> And became his foster son;
> Utterly shameless and heartless,
> Fawning on your protector like a cur."

**Juan** [*furiously*]: So they starting reviling me again! I cannot endure it. [*Sings*]:

> What have politics to do with art?
> I lent them my latest music and poetry
> To increase their enjoyment of wine and flowers.
> Alas, it was in vain.
> They never tried to fathom my motives,

But only heaped on me the vilest abuse.
I am overwhelmed by so many insults.

**Yang:** Why did they attack you?

**Juan:** I cannot imagine. Recently I went to worship at the temple of Confucius, where I was set upon and beaten by five young graduates. Now I have lent them my play and private actors to propitiate them, only to reap further calumnies. I must find a remedy, or I shall never dare step out-of-doors.

**Yang:** Don't worry, elder brother, I have been pondering a solution.

**Juan:** You give me a ray of hope. I shall be grateful for your advice.

**Yang:** The leaders of the graduates is Wu Tzu-wei, and the leader of the nobles is Ch'en Ting-sheng. If these stop attacking you, your peace will be restored.

**Juan:** Of course; but who would venture to defend me?

**Yang:** I think Hou Fang-yü might be approached. He is their boon companion in the literary club as well as at the wine table. Both are influenced by his opinions. Only yesterday I heard that he was feeling lonely for lack of employment. He longs for a girl companion, and I have found him one ideal in every respect. Her name is Fragrant Princess. She excels in beauty as in the gentle arts; I am sure he will be captivated by her. Now if you provide a dowry, he would be obliged to show some gratitude. I could then ask him to speak in your favour, which would lead to a general appeasement.

**Juan** [*clapping his hands and laughing*]: Excellent! What a splendid idea. Hou's father was my classmate, so he is almost a nephew to me. I feel I should do whatever I can for him. But what will it cost me?

**Yang:** About two hundred silver *taels*[4] should suffice for the wardrobe and banquet.

**Juan:** I can easily afford it. I'll send three hundred over to your house. Spend the money as you think fit.

**Yang:** That is too large a sum. [*Sings*]:

---

4. *Tael* was the former monetary unit; it was worth close to one ounce avoirdupois of silver, varying in different localities.

A young willow leans over the gate
For the lover to climb in late.

**Juan** [*sings*]:
My poems and music proved inadequate;
Only this beauteous girl may serve as bait.

**Yang** [*sings*]:
Upon your bounty will depend their fate.

---

SCENE 5

# A Visit to the Beauty

1643, THIRD MONTH

[*Hou Fang-yü, elegantly gowned, enters singing.*]

**Hou** [*sings*]:
The golden glory has not quite departed,
The fragrance of the southern courts still lingers;
These misty meadows melt into my soul,
While breezes coax the budding flowers to open,
But wind and rain will pass, and likewise spring.

[*Speaks*]: Too long I have been roving with only my books
and sword for company, and no prospect of seeing my home.
During this third month I have been steeped in nostalgia for
the bygone Six Dynasties. As a wanderer I suffer from
homesickness, nor can I help being stirred by the spring
scenery. Yesterday I met Yang Wen-ts'ung, who sang the
praises of Fragrant Princess Li, of her youthful grace and
exceptional beauty. He also told me that Su K'un-sheng was
giving her singing lessons, and proposed that I should buy her
trousseau. Alas, my purse is almost empty; I cannot afford
what I ardently desire. Today is the Festival of Pure Brightness.[1] I feel so lonely that I shall take a stroll through the

---

1. The Ch'ing-ming Festival, corresponding to the Christian Easter, was usually in
early April. On this day offerings were made to the dead, while their graves were put in
good order; it was also a time for picnics and excursions into the country, when houses
were decorated with foliage.

meadows. Perhaps I may have a chance to visit the beauty's house.

[*Sings*] :

I gaze towards the Forbidden City, where all the beauties
    dwell,
Their gates concealed behind the drooping willows.
Young cavaliers are riding down the highway,
Flourishing elegant reins of purple silk,
But where are the tender couples of young swallows?

**Liu Ching-t'ing** [*entering*] :
An oriole awoke me from my dreams;
My white hair kindles memory's fading gleams.

[*To Hou*] : Where are you going, Master Hou?

**Hou**: Oh, it is Ching-t'ing! What a pleasant surprise! I set out for a walk hoping to meet a companion like yourself.

**Liu**: I shall be glad to keep you company. [*As they stroll, Liu points and says*] : There is the Water Pavilion, beyond the Ch'in Huai River.

**Hou** [*sings*] :
Over the waves a green mist creeps,
Brushing the windows; against the sky,
Bright blossom of the almond peeps
Above the house-wall high.

**Liu** [*pointing*] : Here is Long Bridge. Let us loiter on the way.

**Hou** [*sings*] :
Passing the wine and tea shops
And the noisy vendors of flowers . . .

**Liu**: Ha! This is the old quarter now.

**Hou** [*sings*] :
We saunter across the wooden bridge
To reach a labyrinth of lanes.

**Liu**: In yonder lane the most famous beauties dwell.

**Hou**: It has an air of voluptuous refinement. [*Sings*] :

Over these twin black lacquered gates,
A tender willow droops as if with dew.

**Liu**: That is the house of Mistress Li Chen-li.

**Hou**: And where does Fragrant Princess live?

**Liu**: She is Mistress Li's daughter.

**Hou**: How lucky! I have been longing to meet her, and here we are!

**Liu**: I'll knock at her door. [*Knocks.*]

**Voice from backstage**: Who's there?

**Liu**: It is old Liu, a regular visitor. I have brought a distinguished guest.

**Voice from backstage**: Mistress Li and Fragrant Princess are not at home.

**Liu**: Where are they?

**Voice**: They went to a hamper party at Mistress Pien's.

**Liu**: Oh, of course! I had quite forgotten about it.

**Hou**: Why did they have to go out today of all days?

**Liu**: My legs are tired. Let's sit on these stone steps and rest while I explain. [*Both sit down.*] Just as men become sworn brothers by burning incense together, courtesans become sworn sisters by exchanging kerchiefs. In due course, they hold parties in celebration at times of festival. [*Sings*]:

These beauties become sisters
By knotting silken kerchiefs together.
On days of festival,
They meet in friendly rivalry.

**Hou**: I see; but why do they call it a hamper party?

**Liu**: Each must bring a hamper filled with delicacies. [*Sings*]:

Dainty dishes from the sea,
Succulent rarities from the rivers,
And the choicest of wines.

**Hou**: What do they do on these occasions?

**Liu**: Usually they hold musical contests. [*Sings*]:

They play the lute,
The reed-organ, and the bamboo flute.

**Hou:** How fascinating! Are men allowed to join them?

**Liu:** No, at such times they shun male society. They bolt their doors and climb to an upper storey. Men are only allowed to admire them from below.

**Hou:** Supposing one glimpsed his heart's desire, how could a meeting be arranged?

**Liu:** In that case, a personal trinket might be thrown up into the tower, and the recipient might throw down fruit. [*Sings*] :

If the girl is gratified,
She will descend to offer wine
And make an assignation.

**Hou:** I am tempted to go and see for myself.

**Liu:** There's no harm in trying.

**Hou:** But I don't know where Mistress Pien lives.

**Liu:** Her place is called the Halcyon Lodge; it isn't far from here. I'll show the way. [*As they proceed, each recites one line of a quatrain*] :

**Hou:**

Before the worship at the tombs, each family hangs out
   a willow branch,

**Liu:**

Everywhere the bamboo flute celebrates this festival.

**Hou:**

Three miles of streets are adorned with birds and flowers.

**Liu:**

We cross two bridges over the misty river.

[*Points*] :  Here is the house. Let's go in.

> [*Yang Wen-ts'ung and Su K'un-sheng enter and meet Hou and Liu.*]

**Yang:** In my leisure I search for orioles and flowers.

**Su:** We have come to see powdered faces and painted eyebrows. [*They greet each other.*]

**Yang:** How astonishing to find you in such a resort!

**Hou:** All the more so since I heard you had gone to visit bearded Juan.

**Su:** We happened to come here expressly on your account.

**Liu:** Let us all sit down.

**Hou** [*looking up*]: What a charming lodge! [*Sings*]:

> The windows glowing on the spacious courtyard
> Transport one to a gentle land of dreams.

[*Speaks*]: But where is Fragrant Princess?

**Yang:** She is upstairs.

**Su:** Can you hear the music? [*A flute and a reed-organ are played offstage.*]

**Hou** [*listens and sings*]:
> The fairy organs and phoenix pipes echo among the clouds.

[*Lute and zither play.*]

> What subtle rhythm!
> What a harmony of strings!

[*A yün-lo or small gong is heard.*]

> What jade-like tinkling!
> Each note plucks at my heart.

[*Pan-pipes play.*]

> The phoenix pair soar fluttering through the air . . .

[*Speaks*]: These pipes have seized my soul and borne it away. I can restrain myself no longer. I shall throw my pledge aloft. [*He removes the pendant from his fan and throws it into the upper room, singing*]:

> This treasure from the southern seas
> Is wafted high upon the breeze
> Into the lodge, my beauty's heart to tease.

[*A kerchief full of cherries is thrown down to him.*]

**Liu:** How curious! A shower of fruit.

**Su** [*opening the kerchief*] :  Strange that there should be cherries at this season!

**Hou**:  I wonder who threw them. If it was Fragrant Princess, I shall be overjoyed.

**Yang**:  This kerchief is woven of the finest silk. I'll wager nine to one that it is hers.

> [*Enter Li Chen-li with a teapot in her hand, followed by Fragrant Princess with a vase of flowers.*]

**Liu**:  The light grass trembles under the butterfly's wings, the beauty now descends the Phoenix Terrace.

**Su**:  Look! They advance like goddesses.

**Liu** [*with palms together as in prayer*] :  Amida Buddha!

**Yang** [*whispering to Hou*] :  Observe them carefully. [*All rise.*] That is Mistress Li, and that is Fragrant Princess.

**Hou** [*greeting Mistress Li*] :  I am Hou Fang-yü of Honan. After hearing so much about you I am delighted to have this opportunity. [*To Fragrant Princess*] :  You are indeed a perfect beauty in the flush of youth. My friend Yang's keen eyes have proved him a connoisseur.

**Li**:  May I offer you gentlemen some fresh tea from Tiger Hill? [*She pours tea.*]

**Fragrant Princess** [*showing her vase*] :  These green willows and pink almond blossoms enhance the season's beauty.

**All** [*in chorus of admiration*] :  Delicious, to sip the rarest tea and gaze upon such flowers!

**Yang**:  On this occasion we should be drinking wine.

**Li**:  I have already ordered it. Aunt Pien is occupied with guests in the lodge, so I shall act as hostess in her stead. [*Wine is brought by a maid.*] Would it not be amusing to play some drinking games?

**Liu**:  We await your orders.

**Mistress Li**:  It is not for me to give orders.

**Su**:  However, it is customary.

> [*Mistress Li produces dice and a jar to throw them in.*]

**Li:** Fragrant Princess, you pour the wine when I ask you to, depending on the dice. The rule of the game is that each must give a sample of his talent after every cup of wine. Number one stands for cherry, two for tea, three for willow, four for almond blossom, five for the pendant, and six for the silk handkerchief. Your Honour Hou comes first. [*Fragrant Princess pours Hou a cup; Mistress Li throws the dice and says*]: It's the pendant. Drain your cup, Master Hou, and let us hear your contribution.

**Hou** [*drinks and says*]: I'll improvise a verse. [*Chants*]:

This came from the south for my beauty to wear;
It should hang from her fan like a moon in midair,
To sway and swing at her every turn,
Catching the breeze from her fragrant hair.

**Yang:** How clever!

**Liu:** The pendant is a fine one. I'm only afraid it would sway once too often and get broken!

**Li:** Now it is His Honour Yang's turn to drink. [*Fragrant Princess pours and Yang drinks. Mistress Li throws the dice and says*]: It's the silk handkerchief.

**Yang:** I'll compose a verse about the handkerchief.

**Li:** Please change the metre for variety.

**Yang:** Then I'll make it an examination essay: "The silk that dabs off perspiration evokes the lustrous skin of its possessor. The sweat that moistens the kerchief is spring's hot breath on a lovely face. And whose face is worthy of so fine a fabric? The rosy cheek and white silk blend, enhancing each other's perfection."

**Hou:** That's excellent.

**Liu:** What subtle talent! For this you should pass both provincial and metropolitan examinations at once!

**Fragrant Princess** [*serving wine to Liu*]: Your turn, please, Master Liu.

**Li** [*throwing dice*]: Number two; that stands for tea.

**Liu** [*drinks, but jokes*]: You mean I only get tea to drink, while you drink wine?

**Li**: No, your *forfeit* must be about tea.

**Liu**: Shall I tell the tale of Chang San-lang, drinking tea with his paramour Yen P'o-hsi in *The Men of the Marshes*?

**Li**: That's too long-winded. Just tell us a joke.

**Liu**: All right. Su Tung-p'o and Huang T'ing-chien went to visit the Buddhist monk Fo Yin.[2] Su brought a pot of fine Ting-yao porcelain, and Huang a pound of excellent Yang-hsien tea. All three sat under a spreading pine to savour the brew. The monk said: "Master Huang has a notorious passion for tea, but I don't know about bearded Su's tea-drinking capacities. Why not have a competition now?" Su asked: "How shall we arrange it?" The monk replied, "You ask him a riddle. If he cannot answer at once, I'll put it on record that the Beard [i.e., Su] has beaten the Graduate. He will then ask you a riddle, and if you fail to give a prompt reply, I'll put down that the Graduate has beaten the Beard. In the end we shall make a count. Each must drink a cup of tea on being defeated." "Very well," said Su, and asked: "How can you run a thread through a pin without a hole?" "Scratch away the pinpoint," Huang replied.[3] "Well answered," said Fo Yin. Huang asked: "How can you hold a gourd without a handle?" "By throwing it into the water," said Su. "Another good answer," said Fo Yin. Su asked: "If there is a louse in your breeches, will you see it or won't you?" Before Huang could reply, Su seized a stick to beat him. At that moment Huang was holding the teapot, and it slipped and was shattered on the ground. Su shouted: "Remember this, you monk, the Beard has beaten the Graduate." Fo Yin laughed and said: "But I only heard a crash. The Graduate broke the pot [*hu-tzu*]; the Beard [also *hu-tzu*] did not break the Graduate." [*General laughter.*] This is no laughing matter. Graduates can be dangerous fellows. [*Fingering the teapot*]: They can break a hardware pot, not to mention a soft one! [*Juan hu-tzu,* a pun on Bearded Juan.]

---

2. Su Tung-p'o; see Scene 1, n. 3. Huang T'ing-chien, 1045-1105, was a poet and disciple of Su. Fo Yin was a rollicking Buddhist monk and convivial associate.

3. There are many anecdotes about Su Tung-p'o and his friend the monk Fo Yin. If these particular riddles do not seem to have much point (like the pin), it is probably because they are intended to be pointless, deliberate non-sequiturs to confound the logical processes and thereby liberate true understanding, in approved Zen fashion.

**Hou:** He deserves another drink for his rollicking wit and humour.

**Li:** Fragrant Princess, pour your teacher some wine.

> [*Liu drinks. Mistress Li throws dice and gets number four, almond blossom.*]

**Su** [*sings*]:
The almond blossoms droop within the tower,
And clothes grow thin at this cool evening hour.

**Fragrant Princess** [*pouring wine for Mistress Li*]: It is your turn now, Mama.

> [*Mistress Li drinks and throws dice, getting number one, the cherry.*]

**Su:** Let me sing for you.

"Those cherry lips the pearly teeth betray,
Before a single syllable they say."

**Liu:** Master Su should be fined. The cherries he sings of are not the edible kind.

**Su:** I accept the fine. [*He pours and drinks.*]

**Li:** Fragrant Princess, you will have to pour your own wine.

**Hou:** No, allow me. [*He pours and she drinks.*]

**Li** [*throwing dice*]: Number three. Fragrant Princess must sing about the willow. [*But Fragrant Princess coyly declines.*] My daughter is too shy. Would somebody else perform in her stead? Perhaps Master Liu would oblige us?

**Su:** We are really making him work today!

**Liu:** My name means willow, and I have been afraid of that word all my life. On this Festival of Pure Brightness, there are willow garlands everywhere. Might as well put one on me as a "dog-collar."[4] [*All roar with laughter.*]

**Su:** Oh, that's enough of your jokes!

**Hou:** Having finished the wine, we ought to be taking our leave.

**Liu:** It is seldom that a handsome young genius is brought

---

4. It was a local custom on this festival for children to wear willow garlands which they called "dog-collars."

together with such a radiant girl. [*He pulls **Hou** and **Fragrant Princess** together.*] Why don't you exchange vows over a cup of wine?

[*Fragrant Princess hides her face behind her sleeve and runs out covered with confusion.*]

**Su**: The girl is sensitive. You shouldn't have talked like that in front of her. What is to be done about her trousseau? Has His Excellency Hou any suggestions to offer?

**Hou** [*laughing*]: Would a Graduate object to becoming a Prize Candidate? My case is similar.

**Li**: Since you are so favourably disposed, let us choose an auspicious day.

**Yang**: The fifteenth of the third month is the best time for flowers and the full moon; it is also the best time for mating.

**Hou**: The only drawback is that, being a traveller, I'm short of ready cash. I'm afraid I couldn't make a suitable offer.

**Yang**: Never mind, you can leave that to me.

**Hou**: How could I put you to so much trouble?

**Yang**: I shall be only too pleased to assist you.

**Hou**: I am overwhelmed. [*Sings*]:

Now fate has led me towards the magic peak.
My passions rise like clouds, and in their tumult
My eyes cannot discern the radiant goddess.
This night of spring, these flowers, and the moon
Lighting the silent land, are they illusions?
Nay, for the joyful moment hurries near;
Now for this blessed union I'll prepare.

[*Hou bows farewell.*]

**Li**: I dare not detain you. Let us decide on the fifteenth provisionally. I shall send out the invitations and ask several fair sisters to join us. The finest music should be played for this occasion. [*Exit.*]

**Liu**: Alas, I had forgotten a previous engagement.

**Yang**: Couldn't you postpone it?

**Su**: Admiral Huang's warship is anchored west of the city, and on the fifteenth he is holding a flag ceremony. We shall have to attend it.

**Hou:** What a pity! We shall miss you.

**Yang:** There are plenty of others to make up a merry party. I suggest Ting Chi-chih, Shen Kung-hsien, and Chang Yen-chu.

[*Exeunt, singing*]:

**Su:**
Powdered cheeks are fragrant before the boudoir bright,

**Yang:**
The grace of bygone ages returns to our delight,

**Liu:**
Our outing of today found only hints of spring;

**Hou:**
We think of the fair blossom tomorrow's warmth will bring.

---

SCENE 6

# The Fragrant Couch

1643, THIRD MONTH

[*Enter Mistress Li in gorgeous attire.*]

**Li** [*sings*]:
In short spring jacket, sleeves folded back,
She tunes the zither in the fairy park.
Today in expectation her curtains are raised;
Let not the willow fronds
Hide from view the groom's magnolia-wood boat.

[*Speaks*]: Since Fragrant Princess turned sixteen, I have been worrying night and day about her future. Luckily, Master Yang introduced us to Master Hou, who came to drink wine with us the other day — a distinguished young man of good family. Today is the auspicious day of their union banquet. Soon the guests will arrive, and I am expecting all our fair sisters. To entertain so large a party is quite a responsibility. Where is the maid?

**Maid** [*a clown, enters waving a fan*] :  How I love cracking jokes at a banquet, and eavesdropping under a blanket! But mum, the mistress is calling me! [*To **Mistress Li***] :  What are your orders now, ma'am? More pillows and quilts to be brought for some itching couple?

**Li**:  Fie! The guests are due to arrive, and there you dawdle in a stupid daze. Make haste and draw the curtains, sweep the floor and arrange the chairs.

**Maid**:  Always at your service, ma'am. [***Mistress Li** directs her.*]

**Yang Wen-ts'ung** [*entering in festive garb, singing*] :
　　Like red embroidery, the peach blossoms
　　Make patterns on the lady's banquet board;
　　The screens are spread like golden peacocks' tails;
　　Scent floats from the heraldic incense-burner.
　　The crimson lady seated by the stove[1]
　　Is the ideal mate for him to cherish.

[*Speaks*] :  I have come on behalf of Juan Ta-ch'eng to deliver the wedding gifts. Where is Mistress Li?

**Li** [*coming to greet him*] :  A thousand thanks for helping to arrange this match. The feast is ready, but where is His Honour Hou?

**Yang**:  I imagine he will soon be with us. I have brought a selection of dresses for Fragrant Princess's wardrobe. [*To **Maid**, who brings in chests containing hair ornaments and gowns.*] :  Take them into the bridal chamber and set them out neatly. [***Maid** exits.*]

**Li**:  Such an expense — how kind of you!

**Yang** [*drawing silver bars from his sleeve*] :  Here are thirty taels of silver, to provide the best wines and dishes for the banquet.

**Li**:  You are far too generous! [*She calls **Fragrant Princess**, who enters magnificently dressed.*]  His Honour Yang has showered so many presents on you that you ought to thank him. [***Fragrant Princess** curtseys.*]

---

1. An allusion to Ssu-ma Hsiang-ju, died 117 B.C., a Han dynasty poet whose singing so captivated the young widow Cho Wen-chün that she eloped with him. They set up a small wine shop, where she served the customers and he washed the cups. Shamed by such hippie conduct, her wealthy father took them back into his favour. Ssu-ma's fame as a poet reached the Emperor Wu-ti, who appointed him to high office.

**Yang:** These are mere trifles, no need for such ceremony. Please retire to your boudoir. [*Exit **Fragrant Princess**.*]

**Maid** [*entering breathlessly*]: The bridegroom has arrived.

**Hou** [*entering in his best clothes, followed by several servants*]: Though I did not win the highest degree in the examinations, I now belong to the realm of the Moon Goddess.[2]

**Yang:** Congratulations, brother! You have won the paragon of feminine beauty. In token of my regard for you, I could only bring these paltry offerings as a contribution to your household expenses. I only hope they will add to the evening's enjoyment.

**Hou:** I am struck speechless by your munificence.

**Li:** Pray sit down and have some tea. [*All sit down. The **Maid** waits on them.*]

**Yang:** Is everything ready for the feast?

**Li:** Thanks to Your Honour, the arrangements are complete.

**Yang** [*to **Hou***]: I won't intrude on your private rejoicings. Tomorrow I shall return to congratulate you again.

**Hou:** Why don't you join the party?

**Yang:** In my position that would not be proper.[3] [*He takes his leave.*]

**Maid:** May I remind the bridegroom that it is time for him to change?

[*Hou, onstage, is assisted in removing his gown and donning a new one.*]

**Li:** I must go and help the bride to dress for the banquet. [*Exit.*]

[*Three male guests appear: **Ting Chi-chih**, **Shen Kung-hsien**, and **Chang Yen-chu**.*]

**Three guests** [*recite*]:
Poet-singers are we
Like Chang Hsien and Li Erh of old.

---

2. Successful examination candidates were eulogized as having plucked the blossoms of the mythical cassia tree tended by the goddess in the moon.
3. Yang had been the principal matchmaker.

[*Each announces his name. Then, together, they say*]:

We have come to attend the auspicious banquet for His Honour Hou, and we are punctual to the minute.

**Chang**: I wonder which of the girls I shall sit next to?

**Shen**: I hear that there will be several queens of their profession.

**Chang**: Then we should have no difficulty in winning their favours.

**Ting**: But are you rich enough to afford such luxuries?

**Chang**: Everybody can get some outside help. Look at His Honour Hou. Has he had to spend a penny of his own on this?

**Shen**: Stop gossiping. He is changing his clothes upstairs. Let us go and greet him. [*Together bowing to* **Hou**, *who is still on stage*]:

**Three Guests**: Congratulations!

**Hou**: I thank you all for coming.

[*Enter three singing-girls:* **Pien Yü-ching, K'ou Pai-men,** *and* **Cheng T'o-niang.**]

**Three Girls**: Our passions run riot like grass, ever in a pleasant state of titillation. And though we are as delicate as willow catkins, we are kept busy night and day. [*They greet the guests.*]

**Chang**: From which pavilion of delight have you ladies sprung? Please announce your names.

**First Girl**: Are you the director of the conservatoire to ask us such a question?

**Hou** [*laughing, to* **First Girl**]: I should be happy to learn your honourable name.

**First Girl**: Your humble servant's name is Pien Yü-ching, "Jade Capital."

**Hou**: "Fairy from the Jade Capital" would be more suitable.

**Second Girl**: And my name is K'ou Pai-men, "White Gate."

**Hou**: You truly deserve it.

**Third Girl** [*a clown*]: And I'm Cheng T'o-niang, "Lady Safety."

**Hou**: You certainly look quite safe.

**Chang:** I'm afraid I don't agree.

**Shen:** Why not?

**Chang:** She would never be safe, from her husband's point of view.

**Cheng:** You should be ashamed of yourself. If I had not stuck to my job, you would never have grown so fat on overfeeding! [*General laughter.*]

**Pien:** Since the bridegroom is ready, let us ask Fragrant Princess to join him. [***Mistress Li** leads **Fragrant Princess** in.*]

**Shen:** We should welcome the bride with music.

> [***Chang, Ting,** and **Shen** play music on the right side of the stage.
> **Bride** and **Groom** greet each other.*]

**Cheng:** It isn't the custom in our houses to perform the ceremonies of worship, so we can go straight to the celebration wine.[4]

> [***Bride** and **Groom** take their seats, center; the **three singing-girls**
> sit near, at left. The **Maid** brings wine, which is served from the left.*]

**Hou** [*sings*] :
> In the company of famous flowers and willows,
> Daily I write of love in jewelled rhymes,
> Like Tu Mu of Yangchow,[5] clad in silken robes,
> Entirely given to painting my beauty's eyebrows
> And teaching her perfection on the flute.
> This very moment spring begins anew;
> My fevered thirst will soon be quenched.
> But oh, how slowly sinks the setting sun!
> Meantime I'll drink another cup of wine.

**Fragrant Princess** [*sings*] :
> Flowers tremble on the terrace, curtains flutter.
> My lord, so handsome and so elegant,
> Withholds no mark of favour;

---

4. See above, Scene 2, n. 2. Since Hou and Fragrant Princess have not performed the ceremonies of obeisance to Heaven and Earth and the ancestors, their "marriage" is more an expression of intention than a strict legal contract. This is why the girl can later be urged to "marry again" – without need of divorce from Hou Fang-yü.

5. Tu Mu, 803-852, T'ang poet famous for the number and beauty of his concubines and singing-girls.

I shall be wife, not slave-girl, in his eyes,
And worthy must I prove;
A random flower still lovely,
A wild herb no less fragrant.
Under the glow of many scarlet lanterns,
Tonight I am to be the chosen bride.
Even adepts in the art of love would quail —
How fearful then a virgin's trepidation!

**Ting**: Now that the red sun is swallowing the mountains and the crows are choosing their roosts, we should escort the young couple to their chamber.

**Shen**: Why such haste? His Honour Hou is a distinguished man of letters who has won the heart of an exceptional beauty. He has celebrated his happy union with wine, but poetry should not be neglected.

**Chang**: You are right. I'll fetch ink and paper to wait upon his inspiration.

**Hou**: I need no paper, since I have a fan. I shall write a poem on it for Fragrant Princess to keep as a lifelong token of my love.

**Cheng**: Marvelous! Let me hold the ink-slab for you.

**Li**: Such a freak is only fit to remove His Honour's shoes.

**Pien**: Fragrant Princess should hold the ink-slab.

**All**: That is correct.

> [*Fragrant Princess does accordingly, while Hou writes on the fan. All chant the words of his poem.*]

**All** [*chanting*]:
On a path between two rows of crimson towers,
The lucky Prince advances in his chariot.
From the magnolias he turns aside
To gaze in rapture at the breeze-blown peach blossoms.

**All**: What an exquisite poem! Fragrant Princess, mind you keep it carefully. [*Fragrant Princess puts the fan in her sleeve.*]

**Cheng**: Though we may not be as pretty as peach blossoms, why should he call us magnolias?

**Chang**: Don't worry; the magnolia withers, but returns to life in the spring.

**Cheng**: That's as may be, but who will water my blossom?

**Maid** [*entering with a scroll*]: His Honour Yang has sent you these verses.

**Hou** [*takes it and reads aloud*]:
Lady Fragrance was born with a beauty to overwhelm cities,
Yet how demurely she yields to her lord's embrace!
In his arms she is like the goddess of the twelve Magic
    Mountains,
Appearing in a dream to the King of Ch'u.

**Hou**: That old gentleman shows a profound understanding of love. His verse is admirable.

**Chang**: It is a fine evocation of Fragrant Princess's slender grace. She reminds me of the jade pendant of a scented fan.

**Cheng**: Well, what's a jade pendant worth, anyway? At least I'm an amber one! [*All laugh.*]

**Ting**: Let us have more music to inspire the young couple to drink.

**Cheng**: And excite them all the more to enter the love nest.

[*Wine and music follow.*]

**Hou** and **Fragrant Princess** [*singing a duet*]:
These golden cups create a thirst for wine,
And friendly voices urge us on to drink.
The hour is late; we droop with drowsiness,
Furtively clasping hands, our eager eyes
Look forward to a night of endless bliss,
Longing to loosen our hibiscus clothes.
Burn out, oh candles! Let the feast be done
Ere the palace water-clock its course has run!

**Ting**: The second watch is announced; it is growing late. Let the banquet be cleared away.

**Chang**: But we have not finished all the dishes. It would be a pity to remove them.

**Cheng**: I haven't eaten enough, either. Please wait awhile.

**Pien**: Stop fussing. Let us escort the young couple with music to their chamber.

**All** [*singing*]:

To the strains of pipes and flutes we descend the stair,
Swaying to the lilt of songs under glowing lamplight.

3. Hou Fang-yü (sings):
"Burn out, o candles, let the feast be done
Ere the palace water-clock its course has run!"

On yonder heavenly terrace the comely pair
Will enter the 'broidered haven of scented curtains
While others knit their brows with envy. Lo,
How beautiful their wine-flushed self-abandon!
Such love as this was certainly predestined.

[*Exeunt* **Hou** *and* **Fragrant Princess** *hand in hand.*]

**Chang:** Let us divide into couples and all go to bed together.

**Cheng:** Old Chang, you'd better not delude yourself. I'll take
nothing less than hard cash for favours. [**Chang** *hands her ten
coppers and she counts them.*]

**All** [*singing in chorus*]:
The misty moon above the Ch'in-huai River
Abides forever,
Yet how much powder and rouge are washed away
Day after day!
Irrevocably love's supreme delight
Is lost each night.

**Ting:**
South of the river grow the flowers, the current flows fast
     away.

**K'ou:**
All who live on the river's banks are debonair and gay.

**Shen:**
Though your home be distant many a league, through
     clouds of dust and spray,

**Pien:**
Here ballads of love are sung till break of day.

# The Rejected Trousseau

1643, THIRD MONTH

**Maid** [*a clown, entering with a chamberpot, sings.*] :
  Turtle-piss, turtle-piss,
  Little turtles come of this;
  Tortoise-blood, tortoise-blood,
  Turning into tortoise brood.
  Mixing, mating, copulating,
  Wholly undiscriminating,
  Never know who fathered who;
  Wouldn't matter if they knew.

  Ha ha, hee hee! Yesterday Fragrant Princess lost her maiden-
  head and I lost half a night's sleep. Today I must rise early to
  empty the chamberpot, but who knows how late the lucky
  lovebirds will slumber on? [*She scrubs out the pot.*]

**Yang**: [*enters and sings*] :
  They sleep serene behind the willow screen.
  Flower-vendors cry outside the door, "Come buy!"
  Yet they dream on; the curtains never open.
  At last you hear the tinkling of jade hooks;
  All spring is wrapped within those folds of silk.

  [*Speaks*] : I have returned to congratulate His Honour Hou,
  but the doors are closed and nobody seems to be stirring.
  They must be fast asleep. [*Calls*] : Maid, please run to the
  young couple's window and tell them that I have come to
  congratulate them.

**Maid**: They retired very late; I doubt if they have risen. Would
  you mind returning tomorrow?

**Yang** [*laughing*] : Nonsense, you do as you're bid.

**Li** [*from inside*] : Maid, who is there?

**Maid**: It's His Honour Yang come to offer congratulations.

**Li** [*still inside*] : Once heads touch pillow, how short the spring
  night seems! Then comes a knock at the door, always some-
  one to interrupt! [*Greeting Yang*] : I must thank Your
  Honour for arranging this match.

**Yang**: Don't mention it. Where are the young couple?

Li: Please sit down while I call them. They have not risen yet.

Yang: Pray don't disturb them. [*Exit Mistress Li. Yang sings*] :

Young love's like liquid honey fresh from flowers,

So beautiful, so innocent and pure,
Gently distilled in a dark world of dreams.

[*Says*] : Thanks to myself [*again singing*] :

Pearls and emeralds glow
And silken dresses flow,
And every precious toy
Is here for lover's joy.

Li: It was as pretty as a picture. The two of them were buttoning each other's clothes and gazing at each other's reflection in a mirror. They have just finished dressing. Will Your Honour step through to call them out for a cup of wine?

Yang: I am sorry to have interrupted their sweet dreams. [*Exeunt.*]

[*Hou and Fragrant Princess enter, dressed in their finest and singing together.*]

Hou and Fragrant Princess [*singing*] :
Cloud after cloud and shower after shower —
Desire fulfilled without satiety!
Who comes to rouse the lovebirds at this hour?
The scarlet quilt is rolled into a billow;
Scent lingers on the coverlet and pillow;
Throbbing with joy we rise as from a trance.

[*Enter Yang and Mistress Li.*]

Yang: So at last your have succeeded in rising! Congratulations! [*Sitting down*] : How did you like the poem I sent last night?

Hou [*bowing*] : It was a splendid composition. My only criticism is that Fragrant Princess, slender as she is, deserves to be kept in a house of pure gold.[1] How could I keep her under these sleeves of mine?

---

1. A reference to the Han Emperor Wu-ti, 140-87 B.C. (see Scene 6, n. 1), a great patron of literature and student of Taoism. When he fell in love with his future consort A-chiao, he remarked, "If I could only win A-chiao, I would build a house of gold to keep her in."

**Yang**: I expect you were also inspired to write poetry last night.

**Hou**: I merely improvised a little stanza.

**Yang**: Where is it?

**Fragrant Princess**: On this fan [*drawing the fan from her sleeve*].

**Yang** [*examining it*]: White silk, and what a graceful shape, what a subtle aroma! [*He chants the poem inscribed on it, and then recites*]:

Like Tso Szu, your verse
Sends up the price of paper in Loyang;
Like P'an Yueh,
Your carriage draws all eyes.[2]
Beauteous and fragrant are the peach and apricot blossoms;
Their very souls are captured on this fan.
But of outer storms and treacherous winds beware!
Preserve it under your sleeve with tender care!

[*Looking at **Fragrant Princess**, he says*]: You are even lovelier since your nuptials. [*To **Hou**]: How fortunate you are to have won such a prize.

**Hou**: Fragrant Princess was destined to be the beauty of her age, but today the pearls and emeralds in her hair and apparel display her charms to perfection.

**Frangrant Princess** [*to **Yang**]: Thanks entirely to your munificence! [*Sings*]:

You gave me the fillets to weave in my hair,
And a casket of a hundred precious stones,
Jewelled tassels for my curtain, and silver candlesticks,
Lanterns of silk to shine all through the night,
And golden cups for the wine that flows with song.

[*Speaks*]: And then, coming so soon to greet us like this! [*Sings*]:

You have treated me as a daughter of your own,
Having filled my wardrobe, you come to bless my union.

[*Speaks*]: Though related to General Ma, you are a stranger

---

2. Tso Szu and P'an Yueh won renown for their elegant *fu*, "rhapsodies," in the last decades of the third century. There were so many purchasers for copies of Tso Szu's "Rhapsody on the Three Capitals" that — according to the oft-quoted hyperbole — the price of paper soared. On P'an Yueh's handsomeness, see Scene 2, n. 9.

in this region. Why should you have incurred such expense for people like us? I feel deeply embarrassed, since you have been so extravagant without any apparent motive. Please explain, so that I may make amends in future.

**Hou:** Fragrant Princess's question is opportune. Brother Yang and I chanced to meet like duckweed floating on water. These lavish gifts have made me quite uneasy.

**Yang:** Since you ask, I'll be candid. The dresses and banquet cost over two hundred taels of silver, all of which came from Huai-ning.

**Hou:** How do you mean, "from Huai-ning"?

**Yang:** From the former Minister Juan Ta-ch'eng, who is from Huai-ning.

**Hou:** Why should he have done this for me?

**Yang:** He is anxious to gain your friendship. [*Sings*]:

He admires your talent and reputation,
The fame of which is spreading far and wide.
Since you sought a fair companion on the banks of the
    Ch'in-huai River,
Hibiscus wardrobe and mandarin duck quilts were
    indispensable.
These were presented by Master Juan,
Your good neighbour from the south.

**Hou:** Old Juan was a classmate of my father's, but I have always despised and avoided him. I am puzzled why he should show me such kindness now.

**Yang:** He has various private troubles, and thinks you may be able to help him.

**Hou:** What is the matter?

**Yang:** Juan was originally associated with our comrades. He only joined the eunuch Wei Chung-hsien's faction to protect his friends of the Eastern Forest Party, never dreaming that these would treat him so shockingly since Wei's downfall. The Revival Club launched a campaign against him, and he was attacked and reviled by all its members. It is just like a family feud. Juan's old cronies are so suspicious that none will step forward in his defence. In his utter dejection, he keeps on saying: "That old friends should fall out like this is deplor-

able. Only Master Hou can save me." Hence his anxiety to
gain your goodwill.

**Hou:** Now I understand. If he is in such distress as to need my
help, I pity him. Although he belonged to Wei's faction, he
has repented of it since. I disapprove of such violent extremes. Wu and Ch'en are both close friends of mine. If I see
them tomorrow, I shall try and explain the situation to them.

**Yang:** That would be doing him a great kindness, and it would
benefit all concerned.

**Fragrant Princess** [*indignantly to Hou*]: How can you say such
things, my honoured lord? Juan Ta-ch'eng shamelessly supported the traitors; even women and children would gladly
spit in his face. Yet when others justly attack him, you
propose to defend him. Consider how this will affect your
own position. [*Sings*]:

How can you make such promises
So thoughtlessly?
Though you wish to save that creature from ruin,
You must also bear in mind
How others will judge yourself!

[*Speaks*]: Merely because he has done you a personal
favour, you forget the commonweal. Can't you see that I am
indifferent to all this finery? [*She removes her headdress and
outer gown, singing*]:

I care not whether I seem poor,
Of lowly birth and station;
In humble homespun I may win a virtuous reputation.

**Yang:** Dear me, what a fiery temper!

**Li:** The pity of it, the pity of it! Fancy throwing such precious
things all over the floor! [*She picks them up.*]

**Hou:** No! No! This is well done! Fragrant Princess has shown such
excellent judgment that I feel she is my superior in this. She
is a friend to be looked up to with respect and trembling!
[*To Yang*]: Please do not blame me, elder brother. Much as I
should like to oblige you, I am afraid I would be scorned by a
woman if I did so. [*Sings*]:

Though frivolous her profession,
How keen her sense of justice and propriety.

Shame on those
Who belong to the Academy and the Emperor's Court,
Yet cannot distinguish between blue and yellow!

[*Speaks*]: In the past I have won the respect of my colleagues on account of my firm convictions. If I compromised
with a traitor, I would become a target myself. Why should I
defend such a villain? [*Sings*]:

One should never risk losing
One's character and reputation.
The serious and the trivial
Must be clearly distinguished.

**Yang:** But old Juan has taken such pains to please you. I beg you
not to send him a flat refusal.

**Hou:** I may be foolish, but I won't throw myself into a well on
his behalf.

**Yang:** Then I had better say goodbye.

**Hou:** All those things in the wardrobe belong to old Juan. Since
Fragrant Princess will not use them, please take them away.

**Yang:** This is a bitter disappointment. [*Exit, while **Fragrant Princess** stares angrily after him.*]

**Hou:** My Fragrant Princess was born a great beauty without
jewelled ornaments, and she is even lovelier without her satin
gown.

**Li:** All the same, it was a pity to lose those valuable gifts. [*Sings*]:

When gold and pearls are in your hand,
Heedless you let them slip away
Daughter, you fail to understand
All that your mother had to pay.

**Hou:** Those trifles are not worth worrying about. I shall find
others for her.

**Li:** That will be ample compensation. [*Sings*]:

For the cost of powder and rouge do have a care.

**Fragrant Princess:**
I do not mind what simple clothes I wear.

**Hou:**
Only such beauty could have such wisdom rare.

4. Madam Li Chen-li: "The pity of it!
Fancy throwing such precious things all over the floor!"

**Fragrant Princess:**
Distinction's free from fashion's passing flare.

---

SCENE 8

# A Riverside Occasion

1643, FIFTH MONTH

*[Enter Ch'en Chen-hui and Wu Ying-chi.]*

**Ch'en** [*sings*] :
Hard by the examination halls
Is the Ch'in-huai pleasure-quarter.
Young candidates compete
At once for honours and for softer charms.

**Wu** [*sings*] :
Double Fifth,[1] the gay Summer Festival
Is over in a twinkling.
The charms of Nature endure,
But local celebrities are soon forgotten.

**Ch'en:** Life at the inn has been so lonely that we came to the river to enjoy the festival. So far we have seen none of our friends; I wonder why.

**Wu:** I suppose they have all gone boating. Ting Chi-chih's water pavilion lies yonder; let us go there. [*They enter the pavilion, which has been erected on stage and festooned with lanterns.*]

**Ch'en** [*calling*] : Is old Master Ting at home?

**Boy Servant** [*enters reciting*] :
The pomegranate flower is red as flame,
The artemisia leaves are blue as mist.

---

1. Double Fifth, i.e., the fifth day of the fifth lunar month, is *Tuan-yang* a summer festival when the dragon, symbol of fructifying rain, is much in evidence. The day is commonly associated with the death of the poet Ch'ü Yuan, whose works form the core of the *Elegies of Ch'u* (see Scene 1, n. 3). Ch'ü Yuan was slandered at court, went into exile, and drowned himself in the Mi-lo River about 288 B.C.. Offerings were made during the festival to appease his spirit, and the dragon-boats which ran races for prizes commemorated the search for his body.

[*Speaks*]: Oh, it's you two gentlemen! My master has gone to the Dragon-boat Festival, but he has prepared refreshments here for any friends who wish to come in and enjoy the view.

**Ch'en**: How kind of him!

**Wu**: Yours is a very hospitable master.

**Ch'en**: It will be enjoyable so long as there are no tiresome intruders. We must contrive to keep such people out. [*Calls*]: Boy, bring me a lantern. [*Servant produces one; Ch'en proceeds to write on it, reading out*]: "The Revival Club is holding a meeting. Outsiders are not admitted." [*Servant hangs it up.*]

**Wu**: But if any fellow members arrive, we must invite them in.

**Ch'en**: Of course.

**Boy Servant**: Do you hear the drums and flutes? That's the dragon-boat approaching. [*Ch'en and Wu peer over the balcony. Hou, Fragrant Princess, Liu Ching-t'ing, and Su K'un-sheng enter in a boat, playing musical instruments.*]

**Ch'en** [*sings*]:
Black scholar's cap and crimson skirt appear to strains
    of music,
How full of grace against the setting sun
By yonder willow bank! Poet and beauty,
Companions in natural harmony,
As a handsome boat should sail near handsome houses.
The sight of this heavenly pair
Has warmed my soul in the cool evening air.

[*He points and says*]: There goes Hou Fang-yü, unless my eyes deceive me.

**Wu**: As he's a member of our club, we should ask him to join us.

**Ch'en**: His companion must be Fragrant Princess. Should we ask her too?

**Wu**: She snubbed bearded Juan by returning his gifts, so she's a friend. Of course we should invite her.

**Ch'en**: The two musicians are Liu Ching-t'ing and Su K'un-sheng, who abandoned Juan, so they should also be treated as friends.

**Wu**: I'll beckon to them. Brother Hou!

**Hou:** Ch'en and Wu are calling us from the water pavilion. Friends, how do you do!

**Ch'en:** Why don't you all come in and celebrate with us? Ting Chi-chih has prepared a feast.

**Hou:** That sounds very tempting. Let us go up. [*They do so, playing their instruments.*]

**Hou** and **Fragrant Princess** [*singing*]:
　　The dragon boat is moored,
　　The painted oars at rest
　　Under the scarlet tower among the reeds.
　　With music of the flute and drum,
　　High into wreaths of cloud we come.

　　　　[*All exchange greetings.*]

**Ch'en:** Now that you four have joined us, the Revival Club can open its meeting.

**Hou:** What is this about?

**Wu:** Look! [*pointing to the notice on the lantern*]

**Hou:** I knew nothing about it, but it seems we have arrived at an opportune moment.

**Liu:** I see that outsiders are not admitted. I fear we are intruding.

**Wu:** Since you spurned Juan's patronage, we consider you as members of our group.

**Hou:** Does the same apply to Fragrant Princess?

**Wu:** Her refusal of Juan's gifts was an act which few of our members could emulate.

**Ch'en:** From now on we should appoint her the club's honorary sister-in-law.

**Fragrant Princess** [*laughing*]: I'm unworthy of such a distinction.

**Ch'en:** Boy, bring us wine. We'll celebrate this festival.

　　　　[*All take their seats on either side of the stage.*]

**Ch'en** and **Wu** [*singing*]:
　　Great talent and great beauty meeting,
　　The room resounds with joyous greeting.

**Liu** and **Su** [*singing*]:

Pay no more heed to bygone sorrows
Than to the twittering of the swallows.

**Hou** and **Fragrant Princess** [*singing*] :
Like flame the pomegranate flower
Flickers against the scholar's tower.

**Boy Servant**: The procession of dragon-boats is about to pass. Look at the throng, like a mountain, a sea of faces! They are clustering round the illuminated dragon. Make haste if you want to see it.

[*All peer over the balcony. A dragon-boat with many coloured horn lanterns is brought in, to loud drumming and piping. It passes across the stage several times before it is removed.*]

**Liu**: See their finery in that boat, all nobles and officers of the court!

[*Another dragon-boat is brought in, this one with silk lanterns and to an accompaniment of large gongs. It crosses the stage several times and is removed.*]

**Su**: These are rich merchants, yamen secretaries, and so on — a fine sight.

[*A third dragon-boat, now with paper lanterns and to the accompaniment of small cymbals, crosses the stage several times and is removed.*]

**Ch'en**: The party in this boat are all famous members of the Imperial Academy.

**Wu**: Compared to them, we are very small fry.

**All** [*laugh and then sing together*] :
Look how the golden waves
Reach to the rim of Heaven! What a festive scene!

**Hou**: Now that night is falling and the dragon-boats have passed, let us compose some poetry to justify our name.

**Ch'en**: Good; what subject shall we choose?

**Wu**: I suggest "Sorrow on the Hsiang River."

**Hou**: Let each contribute a couplet. We may thus continue indefinitely.

**Ch'en**: Splendid! But who is to begin?

**Hou**: Of course you should, elder brother.

**Liu**: Are the rest of us just to sit here and doze while you three gentlemen spend the night composing poetry?

**Ch'en**: Never fear, we shall find you an occupation.

**Su**: What service can we render?

**Ch'en**: At the end of each stanza, you can play for us while we swallow a cup of wine.

**Hou**: Delightful! A blend of poetry, music, wine, and song.

**Ch'en**: Pardon my presumption if I take the lead. "Enjoying the festival from a pavilion on the Ch'in-huai River, we exchange hearts at a famous actor's abode."

**Wu**: "The willow leaves are burnished gold, the pomegranate blossoms flaming red."

**Hou**: "As for the magic sword of the season[2] — we need not put its sharpness to the proof. The heart of the sunflower never fails to warm us."

**Ch'en**: "While escaping the disasters of war, we have made a happy love-match. To ward off evil spirits, I have brought the philosopher's stone."

> [*While the poets drink,* Liu *plays cymbals,* Su *the "moon guitar,"* and Fragrant Princess *the pipes.*]

**Wu**: "The mirage is distant and ethereal. We see the sloping curve of a rainbow bridge."

**Hou**: "Lanterns evoke the chariot of the Sun God, and the boats resemble dragons."

**Ch'en**: "The stars rise over the sea; the crystal vault glitters as if it had come from the goddess's crucible."[3]

**Wu**: "Light streams from the Milky Way; shadows of clouds float over the red city."

---

2. At the time of the Double Fifth (see n. 1), leaves of calamus and mugwort were hung up beside gateways to avert misfortune, in a survival of an ancient belief that the mugwort leaf resembled a tiger and the calamus leaf a sword.

3. The goddess is Nü Kua, sister and successor of the legendary Emperor Fu Hsi. She had a human head on the body of a serpent and helped to arrange marriages. It was she who mended the visible Heaven, after a celestial revolt, by melting down stones.

[*More wine, more music.*]

**Hou**: "The Jade Tree melody is out of tune; the Yü-yang drum is pounded without rhythm."

**Ch'en**: "The flutes and pipes are piercing shrill; the lute and harp are plucked incessantly."

**Wu**: "The boats are moored by a thousand silken ropes; lanterns at windows, myriad gleaming eyes."

**Hou**: "The pawns are slowly moved across the chess-board, while tea is poured from lustrous porcelain."

[*More wine, more music.*]

**Ch'en**: "The fireworks resemble an ancient palace burning. The clamour swells like war-cries in mid-battle."

**Wu**: "Thunder and lightning vie to vanquish night. Where are the jewels put away unworn?"

**Hou**: "Fireflies illuminate forsaken courtyards; through empty office buildings caw the crows."

**Ch'en**: "Let us remain till the crowd disperses; then we may write an elegy for genius cut off in youth."[4]

[*More wine, more music, then All rise.*]

**Ch'en**: That was a fascinating exercise. We have finished sixteen couplets. Tomorrow they can be sent to the printers.

**Wu**: We have all combined to express our deepest emotions, and the musicians have chimed in with harmonious accompaniment. But I doubt if those on the river could understand us.

**Su** [*to Liu*]: As we old storytellers say: festive times are few and all too brief. Let us have more songs and ask Masters Ch'en and Wu to pour wine. We wish the young couple in our midst to enjoy themselves.

**Liu**: I'll be glad to entertain them.

**Ch'en**: Since Brother Wu and I were the first to arrive, we should act as hosts.

---

4 The allusion is to Chia Yi, second century B.C., precocious poet and essayist who became a Doctor of the Imperial Academy, but was so young that colleagues refused to consult him, whereupon the Han Emperor Wen-ti transferred him to the Privy Council.

**Wu**:  Then let us take our seats accordingly.

> [*Hou and Fragrant Princess sit in the center. Ch'en and Wu
> on the left, Liu and Su on the right.*]

**Hou** [*to Fragrant Princess*]:  Since our friends have so graciously
seated the two of us in the center, we should share a loving-
cup according to the old custom. [*They drink together.*]

**Su** and **Liu** [*sing*]:
The song has just begun;
The lamps are burning bright;
The stillness of the scene is deepened by the night.
A poem is written down when wine-cups touch the lips;
The dialogues of love this poet's rhymes eclipse.

**Boy Servant**:  The dragon-boats are returning.

**Ch'en**:  But it is already midnight. Why are they coming now?

> [*They peer over the balcony. Juan Ta-ch'eng enters slowly, seated
> in an illuminated boat with soft singers and musicians.*]

**Su**:  Let us listen carefully: this must be some inveterate old rake.

**Juan** [*standing on the prow of his boat*]:  I hired this boat to take
me down the river with my players. I had intended to come
earlier and enjoy the festival, but I was afraid of being
molested again by those young featherbrains, so I had to wait
till midnight. How maddening! But I see a few lights in Ting's
water-pavilion. Boy, run and find out what is going on there.

**Boy** [*jumps to the bank and returns to report*]:  There is a notice
on the lantern: "The Revival Club is holding a meeting. No
outsiders admitted."

**Juan**:  Mercy on us! Stop playing at once and put out all the
lights.

> [*The lights are extinguished, the music stops, and the boat glides
> off the stage.*]

**Ch'en**:  That was a perfectly handsome boat, I wonder why the
music stopped and it vanished so suddenly.

**Wu**:  How strange! We should investigate this mystery.

**Liu**:  There is no mystery. Juan was on board. My old eyes
detected him.

**Su:** I fancied I recognized his musicians.

**Ch'en:** What impudence the scoundrel has to parade in front of this house. Who does he think he is?

**Wu:** I'll go and pull his whiskers.

**Hou** [*restraining him*]: Since he has fled, we need not take violent action.

**Ch'en:** Don't you realize, Brother Hou, that unless we take violent measures, he will?

**Liu:** By now his boat is far away. It is too late to catch him.

**Wu:** He is lucky to have escaped in time.

**Fragrant Princess:** It is so late we should be retiring.

**Liu:** Fragrant Princess is thinking of her mother. Let us escort her home.

**Ch'en** and **Wu:** We shall be spending the night here.

**Hou:** Farewell then. Our boat will take us back.

**Ch'en** and **Wu:** Farewell!

**Hou, Fragrant Princess, Liu,** and **Su** [*embark, singing*]:
The merrymakers have departed.
Love speeds our homing oars;
We glide through bowers of sleeping flowers
Until we reach our doors.          [*Exeunt.*]

**Hou:**
The moon has set; dense mist enfolds the land.

**Fragrant Princess:**
Whose is the small red solitary window?

**Liu:**
We have rowed a full league down the Ch'in-huai River.

**Su:**
A spring breeze wafts the beauty home at midnight.

## SCENE 9

# The Troops Mollified

### 1643, SEVENTH MONTH

[*Two military Officers enter, followed by four Soldiers.*]

**All** [*sing*] :

As soon as the banner unfolds, we warriors appear.
When we shoot arrows o'er the waves, the whales and sharks
    take fright.
With bows and swords we lead the cavalry,
While drum and pipe resound until the sunset.

[*Speak*] : We serve under the Commander-in-Chief, His Excellency Tso Liang-yü, who garrisons Wuchang city. The General will be attending today's roll-call. We shall await him here.

> [*Flourish of trumpets and drums. Tso Liang-yü enters in full uniform.*]

**Tso** [*sings*] :

Seven-foot stature,
Tiger's brow and swallow's beak,
Boldly all over the world I stride,
Meeting all manner of men,
Solving every problem in my path.
The winds and clouds move at the sound of my voice;
I pour out my blood in the service of my country.

[*Recites quatrain*] :

After a flourish of trumpets, all is hushed
While I march to the platform to take the salute;
I have given my heritage to win the hearts of men,
Leaving only my sword to serve the Emperor.

[*Speaks*] : I was brought up in Liao-yang, where for generations my family held high office; but being in reduced circumstances, I began my career as a common soldier. Fortunately I met General Hou Hsun, who recognized my merits and gave me a chance to distinguish myself in battle. Within a

[71]

year I commanded a division. I led successful campaigns in
the north and south and was rewarded with numerous titles.
Now I am garrisoning Wu-ch'ang with a large army. [*Strikes
an attitude*]: Behold me, Tso Liang-yü. I have been trained
since childhood in the arts of war; I can bend the stoutest
bow and shoot to the left or right with equal precision. It
should not have been difficult to repress the rebellions of
such bandits as Li Tzu-ch'eng and Chang Hsien-chung, but we
lacked a wise statesman to direct our strategy. Many a fine
opportunity was lost. Hsiung Wen-ts'an and Yang Szu-ch'ang
failed because they were too self-seeking; Ting Ch'i-jui and Lü
Ta-ch'i through negligence. Only my kind patron General
Hou had sagacity and courage equal to the task, but he
incurred the jealousy of an evil faction, and was forced to
retire soon after his promotion. My blood boils within me.
How vile to be denied the chance of serving my country!
[*Stamps his foot.*] So be it, so be it! This large area round
the Tung-t'ing lake may still be held as a strategic position.
Fresh opportunities may favour us. [*He sits down. There is a
sound of shouting from soldiers behind the stage.*] What is
that noise outside the gate?

**Officers:** All is quiet, Your Excellency.

**Tso** [*angrily*]: Do you think I am deaf? What was that I heard?

**Officers:** That is no ordinary noise. It is an angry protest from the
starving soldiers.

**Tso:** Impossible! During the past month we have received thirty
full boatloads of provisions. Have these been consumed in so
short a time?

**Officers:** The troops in this city have been increased to three
hundred thousand, Your Excellency. How could the provisions we have received suffice for so many?

**Tso** [*pounding on the table*]: This is becoming a thorny problem.
[*Sings*]:

Tigers and leopards run rampant all over the empire.
Though every eye is fixed on the Dragon Throne,
Who would raise a banner to defend His Majesty?
Veterans to lead the armies are lacking;
High officials behave like infants.
A single man is unequal to so mighty a task.

Then battle looms, and supplies run short.
The soldiers stamp their feet and shout in protest;
How can I answer them?
Listen! a noise like a swarm of angry bees.

[*He sits down. There are noises from backstage, and* **Tso**
*says*]: Louder and louder, like a warning of mutiny. [*To
officers and soldiers around him*]: Now hear me! [*Sings*]:

Do not be so unjust
As to blame me for this crisis.
We are all His Majesty's subjects;
Three centuries his dynasty has protected us.
We should beat our breasts and examine our conscience,
Not beat at the gate and cry in rage.
Would you loot the treasury,
Destroy your barracks?
Eyes strain towards the east;
Will supplies never reach us?

[*Tso sits down and throws the arrow of command on the floor.*]

**Officers** [*picking up arrow of command and shouting towards
backstage*]: His Excellency the Commander-in-Chief's
orders: All three armies at attention! Supplies have run short
not because of incompetence, but because so many regiments
have come to reinforce us. This is a sign of strength rather
than weakness. Be loyal to the Emperor, obey the Commander, and keep discipline! There will be fresh supplies
from Kiangsi within a day or two; listen to us now, and quit
this hubbub. [*They report back to Tso*]: We have passed on
your orders to the men. [*Renewed murmurs from backstage.*]

**Tso:** Why does the noise continue? It is drawing nearer and
nearer. Repeat my orders to them. [*Stands and sings*]:

Control your hunger for tonight.
Supplies are due from Kiangsi;
Urgent dispatches have gone to Nanking,
With pleas for transfer to regions less distressed.
Once we move east,
Our needs will be supplied.
There men and horses may earn a rest,
Relaxing on barges under the Swallow Cliff.

**Officer** [*towards backstage*]: The Commander-in-Chief's orders: All three armies at attention! If the supply boats arrive in time you shall have your provisions at once. But if they are delayed, you will not be left to starve. We shall soon withdraw from Hankow and find quarters in Nanking. There we shall enjoy a life of plenty without fear of hunger. Keep calm! No more shouting and yelling!

**Voices from backstage**: Good, good, good! Let us start packing. We shall soon be on our way towards the east.

**Officer** [*to Tso*]: Your Excellency's order has restored confidence. The troops have withdrawn from the gate in better humor.

**Tso**: For the time being, there is nothing else we can do. We must fix a date to move the garrison and prevent their morale from collapsing. [*Ponders*]: But wait! If I lead my troops east without an explicit order from the government, though His Majesty might be so generous as to pardon me, I shall expose myself to suspicion. This puts me in a quandary. I might be condemned by popular opinion. [*Sings*]:

To appease my troops and silence their complaints,
I had to promise to remove the garrison.
But wherever I move my heart is like the sunflower,
Turned towards the sun.

> [*Tso exits, followed by four **Soldiers**. The gate is closed behind them.*]

**First Officer**: Brother, I should like to hear your opinion on a particular matter. Our armies in Wuchang are the strongest in the land. Tomorrow we shall be sailing eastward down the river, and we shall meet with no resistance along the way. Why not persuade our Commander to seize control of Nanking, hoist a yellow flag, and then turn north to Peking?

**Second Officer**: Our General Tso is the most loyal of officers. This wild idea of yours should not be repeated. In my opinion we should only think of going where the army can be fed.

**First Officer**: Don't you realize that we shall cause unrest as soon as we enter Nanking? Even if we do not take Peking, we have lost our reputation anyway. [*They sing the next quatrain*]:

**Second Officer:**
Every officer and man is anxious to move eastward.

**First Officer:**
In every camp under the willows the evening bugle blows.

**Second Officer:**
Heroes of every age must stand on guard.

**First Officer:**
This eastern drive may wreck a whole career.     [*Exeunt.*]

SCENE 10
# The Letter
### 1643, EIGHTH MONTH

**Liu Ching-t'ing** [*enters, reciting quatrain*]:
I'm a proud old rover of the lakes and rivers,
Who lives by telling tales of past and present.
Loathing the patronage of profiteers,
I would sooner sit in the street and drink cold tea.

[*Laughs and says*]: Homeless since childhood, I have wandered in many places. Though a minstrel by profession, I never eat or drink without rendering some service to mankind.

[*Bowing to audience*]: Whom do you gentlemen think I resemble? I think I resemble Yama, God of the Underworld, who keeps such a bulky account-book. The names of innumerable ghosts are recorded in it. Perhaps I also resemble the Laughing Buddha. All the vanities of this world have been digested in this belly of mine. When I beat my drum and clappers, I seem to sway wind and thunder, rain and dew. Days, months, and seasons are bodied forth when I move my lips and tongue. I avenge the wrongs of filial sons and loyal ministers who suffered death unjustly, and make their spirits rejoice. To villains who led happy lives on earth I mete out the punishment their crimes deserve. My power, however limited, is genuine, and serves good causes well.

[*Laughs again*]: I, pock-marked Liu, invent all sorts of tales as they spring to mind, and they thrill all kinds of people. Yesterday Master Hou of Honan sent me some tea-money and made an appointment to hear my stories this afternoon. I shall practise on my drum and clappers till he comes.

[*Beats drum and clappers, and sings*]:
I say whatever I please, and at my leisure.
Each word I utter has a message, bitter or sweet.
A hundred and eighty thousand years have passed since
    the world's creation,
Yet time has ever sped like the wings of a swan.
Fierce tempests come and go,
And strife is endless in this world below.
Only the Sleeping Immortal[1] knows true peace.

**Hou Fang-yü** [*enters and says*]: I search for powder and rouge in the fragrant grass, and talk of heroic deeds in the setting sun. I have come to listen to old Liu's stories. Already I hear the sound of his drum and clappers. He must have an audience gathered around him. [*On seeing **Liu** alone, **Hou** bursts out laughing and says*]: There is no audience. Pray, whom are you entertaining?

**Liu**: Story-telling is my vocation. You play on your lute and chant poetry alone in your study. Why then should I require an audience?

**Hou**: Well spoken; you are right.

**Liu**: Which dynasty do you wish me to tell of today?

**Hou**: I do not mind, so long as the tale's exciting.

**Liu**: You may not realize that excitement produces depression. Pleasant events are mingled with unpleasant. Perhaps it would be better to tell of the decline of empires and shed compassionate tears over orphans and loyal ministers who died frustrated.

---

1. Ch'en T'uan, died 989, semi-legendary poet and profound student of the *Book of Changes* who wrote a treatise on the elixir of life. Failing to obtain a degree, he retired to the Wu-tang mountains in Hupeh for over twenty years. Five supernatural beings were said to have transported him to the Hua mountain in Shensi, where they taught him the art of hibernating so that he could sleep for a hundred days at a time.

**Hou** [*sighing*] : Alas, I had no idea that you, too, had reached this conclusion!

**Yang Wen-t'sung** [*enters in haste, reciting couplet*] :
Don't let the iron chain sink in the depths of the
      river;[2]
The flag of surrender may fly on the city wall.

[*Speaks*] : I have a matter of extreme urgency to discuss with Brother Hou. Having sought him everywhere else, I suspect he may be here.

**Hou**: You are just in time. Sit down with me and listen to Liu's stories.

**Yang** [*impatiently*] : In times like these, how can anyone listen to stories?

**Hou**: Why are you so upset?

**Yang**: General Tso Liang-yü is leading his armies towards the east. They will probably pillage Nanking and then march north to seize the capital. The local commander Hsiung Ming-yü feels utterly helpless, and he has asked me to beg a favour of you.

**Hou**: What can I do for him?

**Yang**: We heard that your noble father had been a beloved patron of General Tso. If your father sent him a personal letter, his advance could be stopped. What is your opinion?

**Hou**: I am sure my father would gladly do this, but he is living in retirement. Moreover, he is a thousand leagues away and this emergency calls for immediate action.

**Yang**: I have always admired your courage. Faced with this national calamity, you cannot keep your hands in your sleeves. Why don't you write a letter on your father's behalf? You could explain the facts to him later, and he will certainly not blame you for it.

**Hou**: The case warrants me to act as you suggest. I'll go home and draft the letter, and then we'll discuss whether it is suitable.

**Yang**: We have no time for discussion. Even if the letter is sent at once, it may arrive too late.

**Hou**: Then I'll write it here and now.        [*Sings*] :

---

2. In naval warfare, iron chains were strung across rivers just below water level to "lower the boom" on enemy ships.

"Senile and foolish as I am,
I have words for your attention.
Halt your standards awhile;
An army marching without clear goal
Can only arouse suspicion.
The Imperial tombs and parks
Still honour the capital;
Who would dare lead his horses
To trample them under foot?
Though your troops lack supplies,
Still take thought for their provision,
But do not let your heart turn from its loyalty."

[*Hou hands the letter to Yang.*]

**Yang** [*examining it*]: This is both persuasive and forcefully expressed. It is bound to influence him, and is further proof of your literary skill.

**Hou:** Even so, it should be submitted to General Hsiung for correction.

**Yang:** That is needless. I shall report to him later. But there is yet another problem to be solved. We have the letter, but who is to deliver it in the shortest possible time?

**Hou:** I have only two servants, and they are too young for so important a mission.

**Yang:** It should be delivered by a man we trust implicitly.

**Hou:** What are we to do?

**Liu:** Don't worry, gentlemen. I'll be glad to undertake this mission.

**Yang:** There is nobody else we trust so completely as you, most honoured Elder. But you will have to endure many cross-examinations on the way, and it will be hard to deal with all of them.

**Liu:** My wits are always ready, and my arms are sturdy despite my age.

**Hou:** I have heard that General Tso's camp is very closely guarded and that no travellers are allowed in that zone. With your distinctive appearance, how will you manage to gain admittance to him?

Liu: You are saying this as a challenge. My story books have taught me how to cope with such situations. If I believe I can reach him, I shall do so.     [*He rises and sings*]:

Eloquent words are marshalled by your pen,
While subtle plans are hatched within my breast.
My tongue will be my weapon;
Do not underrate my abilities.
Like famed Liu Yi[3] of yore,
I'll dive to the bottom of the sea;
Shedding my feigned simplicity,
I shall exploit my mother-wit.
Quietly I go; in triumph I'll return,
Winning the plaudits of a myriad men.

Yang: I never doubted your skill. I trust you will explain the gist of this letter persuasively to the General, and ensure the success of our plan.

Liu [*sings*]:
To explain the letter would be a waste of breath.
Even if I went empty-handed, your aim would be achieved.
I'll stop his cavalry with the tip of my tongue,
And make them withdraw eight hundred leagues away.

Hou: What will you say?

Liu [*sings*]:
Since he is defending the country against bandits,
Why should he risk being taken for one of them?

Hou: Excellent. Your words will be more effective than my letter.

Yang: Please get ready while I fetch your journey money. You had better leave tonight.

Liu: Of course. Excuse me now.     [*He bows and exits.*]

Yang: I did not expect this Liu to be so resourceful.

Hou: I have always said he's as good as any of us. Story-telling is only one of his talents. [*sings*]:

A letter is merely the envoy of our wishes,
On the wit of Liu Ching-t'ing we must rely

---

3. Liu Yi was the hero of a T'ang story which describes his visit on a mission of chivalry to the undersea palace of the Dragon King.

To stop the rash Commander before dawn,
And ensure the safety of the state by sunset.

**Yang:**

That sheet of paper was worth several battles.

**Hou:**

No warships must sail hither from the West.

**Yang:**

The left bank of the Yangtze may rightly boast of its
native talent.

**Hou:**

With a pen-stroke I prevent a national crisis.

---

SCENE 11

# A Visit to Headquarters

1643, NINTH MONTH

[*Enter two Soldiers*]

**First Soldier:**

We say we fight the bandits,
But we merely collect their baggage.
We say we protect the people,
But we requisition their houses.
The officials are only concerned with hoarding grain;
One soldier seeks to devour the rations of three.

**Second Soldier:** That version of the song is no longer correct.

**First:** You sing the correct one then.

**Second:**

The bandits are too wily to leave their bags behind them.
The people escape; their vacant homes remain.
The officials are too poor to possess a granary,
And a thousand soldiers have not enough rations for one.

**First:** So there is starvation ahead of us!

**Second:** That is almost certain.

**First**: The other day when we made a mass protest, the General was so alarmed that he promised to move to Nanking. But there has been no sign of moving yet. He must have changed his mind.

**Second**: If he has, we shall repeat the protest. That is simple enough.

**First**: Let us not waste time here. Come along to the gate and see what is happening. Unless we're threatened with starvation, we should not break the rules. [*Exeunt.*]

**Liu** [*enters, his baggage-roll on his back, and sings*]:
I come from the empty wood where only the dead leaves
    whisper,
Pale reeds and tawny bracken all the way,
With my bamboo hat and broadsword and whiskers flowing,
Who would recognize the old jester who scoffs at the
    world?

[*Speaks*]: Through wind and rain I have travelled along the river without seeing a single soldier search for food. All this must be hearsay. Now that I have reached the suburbs of Wuchang city, I'll change my clothes in this meadow. Before delivering the letter I must make myself presentable. [*He proceeds to change.*]

**Two Soldiers** [*enter and sing*]:
After the morning rain the hungry rooks are cawing,
The paths in all directions are deserted,
The camp is only half a league away.     [*They point.*]
Our flags and banners flutter in the wind —
How feeble sound the bugle and the drum!
The gate lies just ahead; let us quicken our pace.
How hard it is to bear an empty stomach!
Even so, we must attend the roll-call.

**Liu** [*saluting*]: May I ask Your Excellencies where is the General's headquarters?

**First** [*whispering to Second*]: This old fellow sounds like a northerner. If he's not a deserter, he must be a prowling spy.

**Second**: Let us get some money out of him to buy food.

**First**: A good idea. [*To Liu*]: Are you looking for the General's headquarters?

**Liu**: I am, sir.

**First**: I'll show you the way. [*He throws a rope around Liu's neck.*]

**Liu**: Why do you arrest me?

**Second**: We are soldiers on patrol in Wuchang city. Of course we must arrest you.

**Liu** [*knocks both soldiers down and laughs, saying*] : How starved you two blind beggars must be to fall at a single push!

**First**: How do you   know that we're starved?

**Liu**: If you weren't, I should not be here.

**Second**: So you are the official who is bringing our provisions?

**Liu**: Who else could I be?

**First**: Forgive us, forgive us; we are blind indeed! We'll carry your bags and lead you to headquarters.

**Liu** [*sings*] :
Behold the town above the rolling river,
The lofty Yellow Crane Tower, Parrot Island,[1]
But even the dogs are scarce — all is still,
The chimneys void of smoke, the market empty . . .
As if wolves and leopards had been feasting there —
The noble vista of a river town reduced to a mere sketch.
Only a clamor of shouted orders,
The rolling of the drums to fill the ears,
And whinnying of mail-clad steeds.

**Second** [*pointing*] : Here is the General's headquarters. Please wait while I report. [*Beats the drum.*]

**Orderly** [*enters and recites*] :
Behold the awesome might of our Commander,
Whose powers to punish or behead
Rival the ruler himself.

[*Speaks*] : What is so urgent that you beat the drum? Answer me at once.

**First**: We caught a stranger in the suburbs. He says he is an official

---

1. The town is Wuchang, and Yellow Crane Tower and Parrot Island are famous local beauty spots.

to deliver supplies, but we don't know whether it is true. Consequently we brought him here for your inspection.

**Orderly** [*to Liu*] :  If this is your mission, where are your papers of identity?

**Liu**:  I only have a letter.

**Orderly**:  That looks suspicious. [*Sings*] :
Your purpose in coming here
Must be made clear.
You will need more than a letter in evidence.
How can supplies come out of nowhere?
Obviously you are trying to deceive us.
Either you are a deserter or a bandit.

**Liu**:  You are mistaken. Why should a deserter or bandit seek the General's headquarters?

**Orderly**:  That sounds sensible. Hand the letter to me and I'll take it to the General.

**Liu**:  But it is strictly confidential. I must deliver it to the General in person.

**Orderly**:  This looks even more suspicious. You wait outside while I report to the General.

[*Exeunt Liu and two Soldiers. A flourish of trumpets and drums. Six armed guards enter and stand at each end of the stage. Tso Liang-yü enters and recites the conventional quatrain.*]

**Tso** [*recites*] :
I guard the most famous city on the river,
The commonweal of the empire depends on me.
But my army's sustenance has become a pressing problem,
Not one for carefree gesture to resolve!

[*He sits down and says*] :  Yesterday my troops were clamouring for food, and there was almost a mutiny. To humour them, I promised a move to Nanking, but I'm sure it is unwise to move troops for the sake of provisions. Instead, I should explore every means of procuring fresh supplies. I am still hoping that those contributed by the people of Kiukiang will arrive. There will be no roll-call today. Let everybody return to his post until the distribution of rations.

**Orderly**:  Yes, Your Excellency. [*He exits, to re-enter shortly.*]

The order has been proclaimed. All the men have returned to their posts.

**Tso:** Have you anything new to report?

**Orderly:** Nothing, except the arrival of a stranger who claims that he has come to deliver supplies. He wishes to see you personally.

**Tso:** So the supply boats have arrived! Thank Heaven! But has this man brought any official documents?

**Orderly:** He has only a private letter for Your Excellency.

**Tso:** That is odd. There may be something shifty about him. Guard him carefully and order him to approach on his knees.

> [*Orderly summons* **Liu**. *The* **Guards** *form a lane with weapons raised.*]

**Liu** [*stooping low to enter, merely bows, saying*]: I salute Your Excellency the Commander-in-Chief.

**Tso:** How dare you address me so impudently?

**Liu:** I am a mere commoner. I had no intention to be rude. [*Sings*]:
I belong to the class of fisherman and woodcutters
Who seldom stray far from the rivers and mountains.
How should I know that princes are so high and their
      guests so low?
When I saw the long spears and broadswords at your gate,
They seemed like the trees of a jungle,
The abode of tigers and foxes.
Why such a display of might
To alarm a lone traveller with no hope of escape?
When I saluted you with a bow, it was not impudence.

[*He bows again, and says*]: Forgive my ignorance of military etiquette. [*Laughing*]: You are still vexed, but here is a letter for you.

**Tso:** Who sent it?

**Liu:** It comes from old Master Hou of Honan, who sends you his regards.

**Tso:** The former Minister Hou was my beloved patron. How do you happen to know him?

5. General Tso Liang-yü (to storyteller Liu Ching t'ing):
"How dare you address me so impudently?"

**Liu:**  I too have been a guest in his house.

**Tso** [*bowing*] :  I apologize for my rudeness. Where is the letter? [***Liu** presents the letter.* ***Tso** orders the doors to be closed and is left alone with **Liu**.*] Please sit down, honoured sir. [***Liu** sits while **Tso** reads the letter and sings*] :

Thanks, venerable Master,
For your sincere and affectionate message!
How kindly he gives me advice,
As if I were his son!

[*Speaks*] :  Though the letter is written with such delicate discretion, his purpose is clearly to dissuade me from going to the capital. [*Sighing*] :  My beloved Master, how could you fathom my true motives from such a distance! [*Sings*] :

Heaven bears witness that my heart is loyal.
Never will I oppose your wishes,
Nor prove unworthy of your respect!

[*To **Liu***] :  What is your name, my honored guest?

**Liu:**  Liu Ching-t'ing is my humble name. [*Tea is served.*]

**Tso:**  Since the bandit Chang Hsien-chung and his rabble have pillaged and burned this city of Wuchang, nine houses out of ten are vacant. Though ordered to garrison the place, I have never had enough provisions for my army. Night and day they are clamouring for food. I begin to despair of controlling the situation.

**Liu** [*angrily*] :  Why talk like that, Your Excellency? As the ancients put it, soldiers can move only when their commander leads them. No general should follow the soldiers' lead. [*Sings*] :

You command over a million men;
You wield the power of the dragon and the tiger,
And your strength can move mountains.
Now the hungry soldiers wish to invade the capital;
Instead of restraining them you let them run wild.
How can you escape blame for this?
It is wrong to pretend
That a general cannot control the movements of an army.

[***Liu** dashes his teacup on the floor.*]

Tso [*angrily*]: Your manners are extraordinarily offensive. Why did you break that cup?

Liu [*laughing*]: I had no intention to break it, but in the heat of the moment it fell from my hand.

Tso: Do you mean that your mind cannot control your movements?

Liu: If the mind were a good general, the hand could not have made a mistake.

Tso [*laughing*]: You are quite right, but the fact remains that my troops are hungry. It is difficult to restrain them.

Liu: Oh, I've travelled such a distance that I am hungry too. Why didn't Your Excellency inquire about my stomach?

Tso: I'm so sorry! I forgot. I'll have a meal prepared for you at once. [*Gives orders.*]

Liu [*rubbing his stomach*]: Oh, I'm starving. I'm simply starving!

Tso: How useless the servants are! Why don't they hurry up?

Liu [*rising*]: I really cannot wait. May I go to your private quarters and find something to eat?

Tso: Certainly not. They are out of bounds.

Liu: But I'm absolutely famished.

Tso: However hungry you may be, you cannot go where it is strictly forbidden.

Liu: So Your Excellency realizes that there should be no trespassing on forbidden ground, despite the pangs of hunger.

Tso [*laughing*]: What a satirist you are! How neatly you have exposed my failings! You are the very person I need here in my camp. [*Sings*]:

Though but a wanderer over lakes and rivers,
I recognize a celebrated wit.
He is a consummate master of riddles,
Of biting admonitions and parables.

Liu: Your Excellency overrates me. My tricks are trivial. They have earned me no more than a modest livelihood in my roamings.

Tso: It is evident that you have associated with men of culture, and that you are extremely gifted yourself.

Liu: My education has been neglected since childhood, and I am
sadly aware of my defects. I have only a smattering of crude
fiction and historical legends. I tell stories as they come to
mind, and though I have known several worthies, I have never
been intimate with people of genuine culture. [*Sings*]:

I express my sentiments in quaint legend and rustic song.
Wandering in the wilderness,
I have often had to drink the bitter pine-sap wine.
My feeble hand trembles
When I beat my drum and sound my clapper.
But when I sing of loyal ministers and filial sons,
Every word resounds like the dragon's voice and the
     tiger's roar.
The tip of my tongue
Is like a sharp dagger drawn from its sheath.
Even amid the noise of thunder and cannon,
I can blame as well as praise.
I require no writing-brush
To persuade misguided heroes to change their plans.

Tso: Your talk is very stimulating and delightful. I hope you will
stay with me, so that I can benefit from your valuable
experience. [*Sings*]:

From now on I shall reap knowledge
From your talk of the past and present.
Your words will be like wind and rain to nourish my mind.
With your witty tongue and my sharp arrows,
We may yet save the country from calamity.

Liu: Thanks for the compliment, but may I ask what was Your
Excellency's purpose in moving the armies east?

Tso: Perhaps only Heaven knows the loyalty in my heart. I
appreciate your argument and the advice in my patron's
letter. But there is no real need for either. [*Sings*]:

My conscience is clear as water reflecting the brilliant
     sky.

Liu:

Though His Majesty be distant, his face is as near as we
     are from each other.

**Tso:**

I shall remain the pillar of this southwest corner of his
Majesty's realm.

**Liu:**

Then turn not east towards the ocean's tide.

---

SCENE 12

# The Lovers Parted

### 1643, TENTH MONTH

*[Enter Yang Wen-ts'ung in official dress.]*

**Yang** [*sings*]:

In the 'broidered land of southeast China,
Many a glorious kingdom has passed away.
Heroes have striven for its possession;
The grief of Chou Yü[1] echoes louder than before,
But the river flows ever on towards the east.

[*Speaks*]: Yesterday General Hsiung ordered me to procure
a letter from Brother Hou to General Tso, to prevent him
from marching north. Liu Ching-t'ing was sent to deliver it
and, since we feared it might not suffice, a memorandum was
sent to the Imperial Court, recommending General Tso's
promotion and honours for his family. All the local governors
and officials have been summoned to a conference, to discuss
the dispatch of provisions as soon as possible. We have done
our utmost under the circumstances. Juan Ta-ch'eng and I are
attending the conference, though it is a long time since either
of us has been active in politics.

**Juan** [*enters in official dress and recites*]:

I can see the black and white of events as on a chessboard;
Brushing my eyebrows and beard again, I shall play a role
in the drama.

---

1. Chou Yü, 174-218, generalissimo of the Three Kingdoms period, who destroyed
Ts'ao Ts'ao's fleet at the Red Cliff on the Yangtze River.

[*Says to* **Yang**]: Greetings, Wen-ts'ung. Since we are called to the conference, we should offer some fresh proposals. One should never be silent on such a momentous occasion.

**Yang**: But a very serious matter is to be discussed. People like ourselves, who have been out of office, had better listen quietly to others' opinions. It is enough that our presence be noticed.

**Juan**: What do you mean? [*Sings*]:

This is His Majesty's concern.
Remember what is at stake:
The safety of this holy city,
Founded by the First Emperor.
Naval invasion threatens, and we should guard
Against treachery from inside the city walls.
Bugles and drums may shake the bastions,
While ships sail down the river as if blown by the wind.
Traitors may secretly plot to open the gates.

**Yang**: There is no evidence of treachery. Please say no more about it for the present.

**Juan**: But I have received news from reliable sources. How can I keep silent?

**Clerk** [*enters and recites*]:
Everywhere the situation grows more tense.
Day after day more conferences are held.

[*Says to* **Yang** *and* **Juan**]: Your Honours! The Governor General of Huai-an, His Excellency Shih K'o-fa, and the Military Governor of Feng-yang, His Excellency Ma Shih-ying, have both arrived.

[*Yang and* **Juan** *advance respectfully to meet them.* **Shih** *has a white beard,* **Ma** *a grey shaggy one; both wear official dress.*]

**Shih**: All our military supplies depend on a single line of communication. I dread failing in my duty.

**Ma**: The positions of the Imperial tombs foreshadow the fortunes of the dynasty. My hair and beard are thinned with anxiety about the war. [*Mutual greetings are exchanged.*]

**Shih**: Where is the garrison commander, General Hsiung?

**Clerk**: His Excellency has been ordered to review the troops on the river.

**Ma:** Then we cannot hold the conference. What a pity!

**Shih** [*sings*] :

>The yellow dust rises,
>The Imperial light fades.
>Even with the magical feather-fan of Chu-ko Liang,[2]
>I would find it hard to pacify this turmoil.
>Urgent dispatches have been sent like meteors,
>While a fleet of ships comes sailing down the river.
>Kuan Chung[3] of old — where are you in our time of need?
>Words were impotent against the disasters
>That struck down the southern dynasties.
>Now I would gladly sacrifice
>This worn-out body of mine.

**Yang:** Please do not worry so much. Tso Liang-yü is a former subordinate of old Master Hou. We have sent a letter to stop him. I think he is bound to obey.

**Shih:** I had heard about that. Although it was General Hsiung's idea, you deserve credit for carrying it out.

**Juan:** I cannot prove it yet, but I have heard that Tso's troop movements have been prompted by one who is going to abet him from inside the city.

**Shih:** Who is it?

**Juan:** The son of old Hou Hsün, a classmate of mine. His name is Hou Fang-yü.

**Shih:** Fang-yü stands in the same relation to me as he does to you. I am well acquainted with him. He is a prominent member of the Revival Club. Your accusation is incredible.

**Juan:** Your Excellency may not realize that he and Tso are intimate friends who have been continually in secret correspondence. Unless we nip this young Hou in the bud, he will certainly help Tso from inside.

**Ma:** You are right. Why hesitate to sacrifice an individual at the risk of losing the city?

**Shih:** But this statement is without foundation. Master Juan has no right to make it under the circumstances. [*He turns to leave, reciting*] :

---

2. Chu-ko Liang, 181-234, was an outstanding strategist of the Three Kingdoms wars and minister of Liu Pei. Credited with supernatural powers, he used a magic fan as wand.

3. Kuan Chung, died 645 B.C., a minister of state famed for political sagacity.

No good can come from an evil tongue.
His public utterance involves a private interest.          [*Exit.*]

**Juan** [*to Ma*]: Why should General Shih depart so brusquely?
What I said was entirely supported by facts. Recently pock-
marked Liu was sent to deliver Hou's personal letter to Tso
Liang-yü.

**Yang:** But this is most unjust. I persuaded Liu to take the letter. I
was actually present while Hou wrote it, and could appreciate
the sincerity of his effort to stop Tso. Why should you
suspect him?

**Juan:** You fail to realize that the letter was written in a secret
code prearranged between them. How could you understand
what he really meant?

**Ma** [*nodding his head in approval*]: That is quite possible. Such
people must be eliminated. I shall go back and have him
arrested. [*To Yang*]: Brother-in-law, are you coming with
me?

**Yang:** Please go ahead. I will join you later.

**Juan** [*to Ma*]: Your brother-in-law and I are as close as twins and
I am always telling him of my admiration for Your Excellency. I was lucky indeed to have met you here today, as I
have some confidential news for you. Could I see you in
private?

**Ma:** The admiration is mutual. I should be glad to have a quiet
chat. [*Exeunt.*]

**Yang:** What does this mean? Though I have not watched Brother
Hou's every movement, I know all about this affair of sending the letter. [*Sings*]:

How can this wrong be righted?
He is being accused of a crime he has never committed.
I cannot stand idly by
While this faithful friend is branded a regicide.

[*Speaks*]: I had better warn him so that he can escape in
time. [*Sings as he walks along to Mistress Li's house*]:

In the soft spring night,
He sleeps blissfully with his mate among the flowers,
Heedless of the cruel blow which will sever the lovebirds.

[*Speaks*]: Here is the house of Mistress Li.

[*Yang knocks at door. Singing is heard from behind stage.
Su K'un-sheng enters.*]

**Su**: Who's there?

**Yang**: Open the door at once.

**Su** [*opening it*]: Ah, it is Your Honour! You have come at an
unusually late hour.

**Yang**: Pray where is Master Hou?

**Su**: Fragrant Princess has been singing a new medley of lyrics. We
have all been listening to her upstairs.

**Yang**: Please ask them to come down quickly.

[*Su goes and calls **Mistress Li**, **Hou Fang-yü**, and **Fragrant
Princess**, who enter accordingly.*]

**Hou** [*recites*]:
Love is continual intoxication.
Even in the chill of night, flowers bloom beside the curtain.

[*Says to **Yang***]: Brother Yang, I'm so glad you can join our
festive party.

**Yang**: Evidently you're not aware of the danger threatening you.

**Hou**: What do you mean?

**Yang**: At today's conference, Juan told everyone that you are a
close confederate of Tso Liang-yü, that you have been in
secret correspondence with him and will help him to invade
the city. Your arrest is being considered.

**Hou** [*in surprise*]: There has never been a serious breach between
Juan and myself. Why should he wish to ruin me like this?

**Yang**: Perhaps your refusal of his gift offended him, and his
resentment turned into rancour.

**Li**: You must not delay. It would be wiser to leave at once, lest
others become implicated.

**Hou**: You are right. [*Grieving*]: But it is cruel for a loving couple
to part so soon.

**Fragrant Princess**: A brave man like my lord should not be
swayed by personal sentiment like ordinary folk.

**Hou**: That is true, but where can I go? [*Sings*]:

I have parents,

But I never hear from them.
The war clouds rise,
And my home is half destroyed.
I long to return,
But the journey is hard and dangerous;
Straying about the world,
Where can I hide myself?
Every road is stopped,
The sky turns dark,
The earth is wrapped in gloom.

**Yang**: Please don't despair. I have a suggestion. His Excellency Shih and Governor Ma, my brother-in-law, were both present at today's meeting. My brother-in-law was prejudiced against you, and your arrest was only delayed because His Excellency Shih defended you so stoutly. He also said that he was a friend of your family.

**Hou**: Yes, of course. He was my father's pupil.

**Yang**: Then why don't you follow him to Huai-an and wait there until you hear from home?

**Hou**: Perhaps that is the best expedient. Thanks for your advice and for the timely warning.

**Fragrant Princess**: Let me pack for you. [*She packs and sings*]:

A blissful union will now become the memory of two hearts.
We must endure the bitterness of parting.
I knit my brows to keep the tears from falling.
Last night's perfume lingers on the feather quilt;
I roll it tightly into a bundle, wetting it with my tears.

[*Servant comes in for the luggage.*]

**Hou** [*to Fragrant Princess*]: We part now, but it will not be for long.

**Fragrant Princess** [*weeping*]: Everywhere the smoke and dust of war is rising. When shall we meet again? I cannot be sure. [*Sings*]:
Separation and union, sadness and joy —
All pass in a twinkling.
When shall we meet again?

**Li**: Patrols have probably been sent to search for you. You should leave without delay.

**Hou** [*sings*] :
> We are blown apart with the speed of the west wind.
> We are not granted a moment's respite.

[*Speaks*] :  But where does His Excellency Shih reside?

**Su**:  When he visits the capital, he usually stays in the hermit's garden near the marketplace. I'll be glad to show you the way.

**Hou**:  Thank you kindly. [*Exeunt Hou and Su.*]

**Li**:  As Your Honour brought this trouble upon us, you must find a way to protect us. What shall we do if they come tomorrow to arrest him?

**Yang**:  Don't worry, Mistress Li. Once Hou has gone, you will not be molested. [*Sings*] :

> Union and separation can never be foretold.

**Fragrant Princess** [*sings*] :
> While the quilt is still warm, the wine cup is dry;
> The song is over.

**Li**:  A flower cannot rest in peace alone with its shadow.

**Yang**:  You must bolt your doors against tomorrow's storm.

---

SCENE 13

# Lament for the Emperor

### 1644, THIRD MONTH

**Orderly** [*enters and sings*] :
> Across the river lie the misty forests;
> The green hills lurk in shadow, men are dwarfed.
> Alas, the nobler landscape of the west
> Is ever screened by dust of galloping horses.

[*Speaks*] :  I am an orderly under General Tso Liang-yü. Since the General recaptured Wuchang, Imperial favours have showered upon him. Yesterday he was given the new title of Grand Guardian of the Heir Apparent, and his son Meng-keng has been made an honorary general. His Honour Huang Shu, the Imperial Herald who bestows titles, is still in the General's residence. Today the Governor of Kiukiang has sent us thirty shiploads of grain. Our Commander-in-Chief is so delighted that he has ordered a banquet to entertain our distinguished guests at the Yellow Crane Tower. Under the trees beside the limpid river, and in the flowery fields, the citizens and soldiers are all rejoicing. What a scene of peace and prosperity! Now I hear voices cheering. His Excellency the Commander-in-Chief must have arrived. I must see that the banquet is ready.

[*A tablet inscribed "Yellow Crane Tower" is set up on stage. The orderly arranges seats. A band of **musicians** enter, followed by Tso Liang-yü in uniform.*]

**Tso** [*sings*]:
Wherever we go, the colours of spring pursue us,
The brilliant sunlight dazzles our eyes,
And banks of endless green slope toward the river.
The music of flutes from the tower seems to scatter the
    plum blossoms.
Friends bearing dainties enjoy the scene with loosened
    garments.
Who dare mock me as a soldier while I cherish
The subtle refinement of accomplished scholars?

[*Speaks*]: I am giving a banquet at Yellow Crane Tower for Their Excellencies Yuan and Huang. I expect them to appear at any moment. [*Commands*]: All my captains and guards wait downstairs for their arrival. [*Exeunt. **Tso** walks upstairs, saying*]: The mutations of spring are reflected in my heart. The wind and smoke of a myriad miles I assimilate at a glance. [*Gazing out*]: Behold the vast expanse of Tung-t'ing Lake and the blue peaks of Dreaming Cloud Mountain! This southwestern country has great strategic importance. It is a glorious thing for me to garrison so famous a district. [*He sits down and calls the **orderly**, who enters and kneels before him.*] Is the banquet ready?

**Orderly**: Aye, aye, Your Excellency.

**Tso**: Why have our two guests of honour not arrived?

**Orderly**: We have sent messengers repeatedly. His Excellency the Governor is supervising the shiploads of supplies on the river bank, and His Excellency Huang, the Imperial Inspector, is receiving guests at the Dragon Flower Temple. They will not be here till evening.

**Tso:** So long a wait will be tedious. Send for Master Liu.

**Orderly** [*kneeling*] : Master Liu is downstairs.

**Tso:** Ask him up at once.

**Liu** [*enters, reciting*] :
My spirit broods over the marshes;
My voice makes high towers tremble.

**Tso:** What brought you here to await my summons?

**Liu:** I knew you would be feeling lonely.

**Tso:** That's curious. How did you guess that?

**Liu:** There is a saying, "Scholars assembling will not sit, till all the candles have been lit," for scholars are never punctual.

**Tso:** Too true. It is still early in the afternoon. How long shall we be kept waiting?

**Liu:** If you like, I shall continue the story of Ch'in Shu-pao [1] which I began last night.

**Tso:** That would be delightful. Have you brought your drum and clappers?

**Liu:** It is said that an official never leaves his seal behind, and I always carry my stock-in-trade. [*He produces them.*]

**Tso:** Servants, prepare tea and fetch me an easy chair. I wish to enjoy the story thoroughly. [*A couch is moved and tea is served, while Tso changes his clothes. A servant massages his back. Liu sits down and proceeds with the story.*]

**Liu** [*recites*] :
The mighty river rolls towards the east,
And many a fabled bank is washed away.
When we count the heroes of history on our fingers,
Though few lived long, regret for them still lingers.

[*Speaks*] : After this new poem, the old story continues. The rarest of happy moments in this life is when those who are near and dear to each other meet after long separation and

---

1. Ch'in Shu-pao or Ch'in Ch'iung rose to high office under the first T'ang Emperor in the seventh century, after a successful military career under the Sui dynasty.

hardship in time of trouble. North or south, on earth or in
Heaven, time passes and all things change, in wars and
famines men scatter like duckweed across a pond. Ch'in
Shu-pao was arrested and led to the General's residence in
chains. He was about to be cross-examined when his aunt
crept down the stairway behind a curtain. On seeing him, she
clasped him in her arms and wailed aloud. He was given fresh
raiment and entertained as a member of the family. A prisoner on the verge of execution thus became like a prince. As
the old saying has it, "In misfortune, even gold becomes
valueless. But when fortune smiles, the cheapest metal
glitters." [*He strikes mallet on the table.*]

Tso [*deeply moved*] :  I have experienced this myself.

Liu:  To continue: The General, who turned out to be Ch'in
Shu-pao's uncle, inquired about his proficiency as a soldier
and was gratified by his qualifications. To give him a chance
of distinguishing himself that day, the General ordered his
troops to parade in battle formation. Ten thousand troops
were spread over the plain in two divisions. General Lo
looked so majestic in their midst that Ch'in Shu-pao stood
beside him full of awe and admiration. And he said to
himself: "That is how a man should live." [*Liu strikes the
table again.*]

Tso [*proudly*] :  I, too, have not lived in vain.

Liu:  General Lo gazed at Ch'in Shu-pao and asked him aloud:
"Ch'in Shu-pao, you look tall and strong, but what of your
military skill?" Ch'in promptly prostrated himself before him
and answered: "I can wield a pair of maces." The General
then ordered his attendants to fetch a pair of silver maces.
Now the total weight of these was sixty-eight catties,[2] but
they were only half as heavy as the iron maces which had
belonged to Ch'in. Being accustomed to heavier weapons, he
flourished these like toys. He demonstrated all kinds of
movements and struck out in every direction, till the maces
resembled white serpents emitting thousands of sparks round
his body, or a couple of silver dragons whirling so quickly
that they seemed like a full moon. The General shouted
"Bravo, bravo!" and his ten thousand troops echoed him like
thunder shaking the mountains. [*Liu roars in illustration.*]

---

2. Catty or *chin* is a weight equivalent to one and one-third pounds avoirdupois.

You could hear them from miles away. [*He strikes the table again.*]

**Tso** [*looking into a mirror and stroking his whiskers*]: I have fought valiantly on the frontiers and won victory after victory. The whole world has admired me as a great warrior. But alas, my hair will turn white before all the bandits are exterminated!

**Orderly** [*entering*]: Your Excellency, the guests of honour have arrived.

[*Tso changes his clothes. A servant removes the couch and lays the table. **Yuan Chi-hsien** and **Huang Te-kung** enter in official dress, their retainers preceding them with shouts of "Clear the way!"*]

**Yuan** [*recites*]:
The sunset over the river looks sublime
As we gaze homeward from the Yellow Crane Tower.

**Huang**: Our host is as famous as one of the Immortals. Our cups are overflowing with delight.

**Tso**: What an honour it is for me to entertain you with wine on the river in spring.

**Yuan**: We have admired you so long that today's meeting is the greatest event in our lives. [*They sit down and are about to drink wine when a courier rushes in, hot and dishevelled.*]

**Courier**: I must quickly report this cataclysmic event to those who loyally serve His Majesty's empire. [*To Tso*]: Your Excellency the Commander-in-Chief, calamity, direst calamity!

**All** [*rising*]: What has happened?

**Courier** [*rapidly*]: A great horde of bandits rushed north and surrounded His Majesty's capital. Three days passed and no army came to his rescue. The gates were secretly opened, the palaces set on fire, and there was terrible slaughter. [*Stamps his foot on the ground and wails.*] Woe for His Majesty, the Sage Emperor Ch'ung-chen. He hanged himself from a tree upon Coal Hill.

**All**: Incredible! When was this?

**Courier** [*panting and stuttering*]: It was the, the ... nineteenth day of the third month.

[*All kowtow in the direction of the north and wail aloud.*]

**Tso** [*rising and wringing his hands*]: My Emperor, my Imperial Master! Your orphaned servant Tso Liang-yü being far away could bring no troops to your rescue. I deserve ten thousand deaths! [*Sings*]:

Below in the Yellow Springs,
The first ancestor of our dynasty
Cannot know the Imperial house is ruined,
The sacrificial vessels broken,
The dragon descendants adrift
As rootless weeds upon the water.
His Majesty Ch'ung-chen
Endured the trials of seventeen turbulent years
And neither Heaven nor the Imperial Ancestors came to his
      aid.
With none to defend him,
A strip of white silk
Brought despair to the nation.
He honoured Coal Hill
By sacrificing himself for his people and for the world.

[*All wail aloud.*]

**Yuan** [*shouts, waving his hands*]: Let us restrain our grief for the moment. There are urgent matters to discuss. Now that Peking is lost, the central power has sunk to its lowest ebb. Unless Your Excellency raises a standard as a symbol of order, the whole country will fall into chaos.

**Huang**: That is true. This area is the vital center of the southwest. If we lose it, the plight of the country will be hopeless.

**Tso**: Since I am in command of so many armies, I cannot escape responsibility, but I shall require the support of both Your Excellencies in guarding this area.

**Yuan** and **Huang**: Of course we shall do our utmost.

**Tso**: Let us all change into white robes of mourning and bewail the death of our Emperor. We must invoke his soul in Heaven and swear to put forth our most strenuous exertions. [*To servants*]: Fetch us white robes of mourning.

**Orderly:** At such short notice we shall have to borrow some in the neighbourhood. [*All don mourning.*]

**Tso:** Let all the armies kowtow together with us. [*Cries out*]: My Emperor! [*Sings*]:

The empire collapsed when your chariot departed.
Civil officials panic;
Your warriors are demoralized.
Your mountains have fallen today, your rivers run low.
This tower above the moonlit waves
Is shaken with our cries of lamentation.
How can such a wrong be avenged?
Let Heaven be our witness.
We shall put forth all our strength
To avenge the country and recover His Majesty's capital.

[*Speaks*]: After swearing this oath together, we are as brothers. Your Excellency Yuan will direct the strategy of the army, and Your Excellency Huang will maintain discipline. I shall undertake the training of the troops. Let us guard this area stubbornly. When one of the princes succeeds to the Throne, he may lead us north to recover the central plain. Then our present decisions will not be unavailing.

**Yuan** and **Huang:** Your orders will be obeyed.

**Orderly:** Your Excellency the Commander-in-Chief, the whole city is in turmoil. A riot is likely to break out at any minute. Please come down and tranquillize the people. [*All descend together.*]

**Tso:** Where shall you two go?

**Yuan:** I must proceed to Kiukiang.

**Huang:** And I to Hsiang-yang.

**Tso:** Farewell for the time being. [*As they retire, he calls*]: One moment, please! In case of emergency, let us all meet here again.

**Yuan** and **Huang:** You have only to send us word. We shall come at once. [*Exeunt.*]

**Tso:** Alas, that Heaven and Earth should be overturned this day! The shock has almost killed me. [*Sings*]:

Before the wine can be enjoyed, amid the blossoms,
A message alarms the assembled guests.

By the time the weeping ceases in Yellow Crane Tower,
The river darkens, the moon sinks low, the third watch
    sounds.

---

SCENE 14

# The Traitor Blocked

1644, FOURTH MONTH

**Hou Fang-yü** [*enters and sings*]:
    My distant home is torn by strife;
    How can I even write for news?
    I have cried to high Heaven till my throat is choked
        with blood.
    My country's shame, my longing for home
    Make all else trivial in comparison.

[*Speaks*]: Last winter I fled from sudden disaster and travelled at night to join His Excellency Shih. I accompanied him
to Huai-an, and half a year went by. Recently the Minister
for the South, Hsiung, was summoned to the capital, His
Excellency Shih succeeded him in office, and I accompanied
him south of the River. All this time he has treated me like a
member of his family. My constant hope was that we should
move to Nanking, but communications are cut and the whole
country is divided by the question of Imperial succession.
Our troubles are endless. I'll wait for His Excellency and see
if there is any news. [*Exit.*]

    [*Enter Shih K'o-fa, followed by Servant. Shih shows great
    distress.*]

**Shih** [*sings*]:
    While mountains heave and rivers are in spate,
    The pale-faced scholars wag their tongues and vainly
        speculate.
    Our national plight is as uncertain as a game of chess.
    Gazing towards the capital, I long for a genuine
        successor to the Throne.

[*Speaks*] : A native of Honan, I was educated in Peking and obtained a doctor's degree during the reign of His Majesty Ch'ung-chen. For over ten years I have held office in and out of the capital, and throughout this period I have never slept in peace. From Director of Grain Transport in Huai-an, I was promoted to President of the Board of War in Nanking. This national disaster descended on us when I had held the post barely a month. Were I to die ten thousand deaths, I could see no immediate redress. Fortunately, the strategic position afforded by the Yangtze River protects our provisional capital. But the country has been without an Emperor for a month, and alarm is spreading among the people. Opinions differ every day as to who should succeed to the Throne. While reviewing my troops on the river bank this morning, I received some news from the north. I shall have to discuss it with Brother Hou.

**Servant** [*calling*] : Master Hou, His Excellency wishes to see you.

**Hou** [*entering*] : Have you tidings from the north, venerable sir?

**Shih**: Today there is good news. According to this, His Majesty was not harmed after the loss of Peking, but escaped by sea and sailed towards the south. The Heir Apparent is reported to have gone east, but I don't know whether this is reliable.

**Hou**: If true, this is fortunate for the whole country.

**Young Messenger** [*entering, recites*] :
When there is no Emperor to issue decrees,
Generals and ministers have rumours to seize.

[*Speaks*] : Ho, is anybody there?

**Servant**: Where do you come from?

**Young Messenger**: I'm from the office of the Governor of Feng-yang. His Excellency Ma sends a letter, requesting a prompt reply.

**Servant**: I'll take it in for you. [*To Shih*] : Governor Ma has just sent Your Excellency this letter.

**Shih** [*opening it with a frown*] : Old Ma has his own ideas about a successor to the Throne. [*Sings*] :

Three conferences in this Hall of Pure Discourse
Produced nought but frowning and gazing at the ceiling.
Depressing each other with long-drawn sighs,

We were dumb and utterly downcast.
Alas, the affairs of a nation
Can never be dealt with lightheartedly!
I would hesitate to express my own views,
Yet here is a man most eager to win credit for himself.

[*Says to Hou*] : He expresses his partiality for Prince Fu; he also repeats that His Majesty hanged himself on Coal Hill and that the Heir Apparent cannot be found anywhere. If this is true, and I disagree with his proposal, he may act independently. Moreover, according to the law of primogeniture the Prince would not be too unsuitable a successor. I can see no alternative but to suggest that we meet tomorrow and join him as one of the sponsors.

Hou: I fear that you are mistaken, venerable Master. My home was in Prince Fu's fief. I am familiar with his reputation, and am convinced that he should never be Emperor.

Shih: Why not?

Hou: He has three unpardonable vices.

Shih: What are they?

Hou [*sings*] :
Prince Fu has inherited his mother's defects,
For the Empress Cheng was an unscrupulous wanton.

[*Speaks*] : It was she who plotted the murder of the Heir Apparent, to appoint her son successor. [*Sings*] :

Had there not been loyal ministers on guard,
The claim to the Throne would already have been usurped.

Shih: That is most reprehensible. What other vice has he?

Hou [*sings*] :
Avarice:
He carried off cartloads of gold,
Half emptying the Imperial treasury.

[*Speaks*] : Yet when the bandits besieged Honan, he would not contribute a single coin to relieve the starving troops. Now that the country is ruined, all his wealth remains to fill the bandits' pockets.

Shih: That is just as bad. What else is there against him?

Hou: When a close kinsman was killed by brigands, he left the corpse exposed without burial. He fled, and in the general disorder debauched the wives and daughters of commoners. [*Sings*]:

Without the slightest virtue to fit him for the Throne,
How could he be trusted for so high a mandate?

**Shih**: These three vices are unforgivable.

**Hou**: Apart from these, there are five other positive reasons why he should not be elected.

**Shih**: What are they?

**Hou**: First, [*sings*]:

We have no proof
Whether His Majesty is in Heaven or still on earth;
Never can two suns rule the same sky.

[*Speaks*]: Secondly, though His Majesty may have become a national martyr, the Heir Apparent may still be alive. [*Sings*]:

Why should we forsake the Heir Apparent
To seek another outside the direct line?

[*Speaks*]: Thirdly, during a national crisis it is not necessary to select a new Emperor by order of primogeniture. [*Sings*]:

For such a heroic Emperor as Kuang-wu of the Han[1]
Was brought to the throne by virtue and brilliance.

[*Speaks*]: Fourthly [*sings*]:

Beware the rival claims of other ambitious princes.

[*Speaks*]: Fifthly, certain villains [*sings*]:

Will take advantage of his weaknesses.

**Shih**: Your views are sound, and I agree with them entirely. I have heard from several who share them, but none have expressed their reasons so clearly as you. I'll ask you to write a reply stating the three vices and five causes why he should not be appointed successor to the Throne.

**Hou**: I shall do so.

---

1. Kuang-wu, 4 B.C. – A.D. 57, in A.D. 25 after bloody battles placed himself on the throne as first Emperor of the Eastern Han dynasty.

[*A candle is lighted, and Hou writes the letter.* **Juan**
*Ta-ch'eng enters with a young servant carrying a lantern.*]

**Juan**: To select an Emperor is like choosing the most profitable
merchandise. One should act quickly, before rivals stake a
claim. I have been to Chiang-p'u and interviewed Prince Fu.
After travelling all night, I have returned here. General Ma
and I have decided to elect the Prince immediately. Our only
fear is that Shih, President of the Board of War, may object,
so we sent him a letter soliciting his consent. In case that
fails, I have come in person at this late hour to knock at his
door and try to convince him. [*Seeing the* **messenger** *he had
sent still waiting,* **Juan** *asks*] : You seem to have been here an
age. What about the reply?

**Messenger**: I am still waiting for it. It is a great relief that Your
Honour has arrived. Perhaps you will obtain a ready answer.
[*Calls out at the gate*] : Are you there, old brother?

**Servant**: Yes, I am here. [*He sees* **Juan** *and performs a mockingly
elaborate bow.*]

**Juan**: Please report that Master Juan wishes to see His Excellency.

**Servant**: Master Juan — *juan* meaning "soft"? Let me feel you, see
whether you're soft or hard.

**Juan**: Stop making fun of me, do me a favour and tell him I'm
here.

**Servant**: I'm afraid it is too late. His Excellency must have retired.
I doubt if he will see anybody.

**Juan**: Please tell him that the matter is urgent. I *must* see him.

**Servant** [*enters and reports to* **Shih**] : Master Juan wishes to see
Your Excellency.

**Shih**: Which Juan?

**Hou**: I suspect it is that soft villain with the beard.

**Shih**: Why should he come at this hour?

**Hou**: Doubtless he wants to discuss the next Emperor.

**Shih**: Oh, whiskered Juan! He is the one who slandered you
recently at the conference. He was one of Wei Chung-hsien's
clique; I'll have nothing to do with him. Tell him I can't see
him, steward.

**Servant** [*goes out and says angrily to* **Juan**] : I told you that it was too late. His Excellency will see nobody. Now please go home.

**Juan** [*slapping his shoulder familiarly*] : You should know, my friend, that urgent matters must be discussed even in the dead of night. They are not for the light of day.

**Servant**: Well, since you are so insistent, I'll try again.

**Juan**: I'll see that you reap your reward.

**Servant** [*re-entering, to Shih*] : Your Excellency, Master Juan insists on seeing you for a minute. He says he has something urgent to discuss. He declares it is a topic of the greatest interest.

**Shih**: Stuff and nonsense! When the whole country is on the brink of ruin, what does he mean by his interesting topic? Drive him away and slam the door in his face.

**Servant**: What am I to tell Governor Ma's messenger, who is waiting for an answer?

**Hou**: Here it is. Will Your Excellency please read it through?

**Shih** [*sings while reading it*] :
"From the two founding Emperors,
Through the line of their descendants,
The glories of our dynasty passed
To our present Lord, who laboured to maintain them.
Suddenly he is gone, and who shall succeed?
Set out herein
Are three crimes and five objections
Which proclaim Prince Fu unworthy of the Throne.
The successor of our choice
Must be a truly virtuous heir to the Imperial line."

**Shih**: I think the facts are sufficiently clear in this letter. After reading it, they are not likely to make this foolish move. [*To servant*] : Hand this to the messenger and shut the door. Don't let anyone disturb me. [*He stands and says*] : His Majesty's orphaned servant has turned grey from grief.

**Hou**: Under the lamplight, the lone traveller laments long separation from his love. [*Exeunt Shih and Hou.*]

**Servant** [*goes out and calls*] : Where is Governor Ma's messenger?

**Messenger**: Still waiting.

**Servant:** Here is the reply. Now take it away with you. I'm going to lock up.

**Messenger:** But you can't lock up yet. His Honour Juan is expecting to see the General.

**Juan** [*to servant*]: I spoke to you not long ago. Have you forgotten?

**Servant** [*pretending not to recognize him*]: Who are you?

**Juan:** I am that "Juan the Soft."

**Servant:** What, still soft, and it's nearly midnight? You wouldn't be much use in bed! [*Pushes him*]: Go on, off with you! [*He finally shuts the door.*]

**Messenger:** I shall take this reply to the Governor. [*Exit.*]

**Juan** [*furiously*]: This is outrageous! He has locked me out. Ah well, that's that! Ten years ago I had to suffer similar affronts for the sake of my career. [*Rubs his hands*]: This time I shall let nothing stand in my path, but Shih K'o-fa holds the highest office as President of the Board of War. One of the most important seals of the government is in his grasp. If he objects to Prince Fu, there is nothing we can do about it. But how stupid of me! Since even the Emperor's seal has disappeared, what is the use of his? [*Pointing towards the gate*]: Old Shih, old Shih, I came to offer you a precious gift, full of meat and nourishment, yet you refused to touch it. Now I shall take it elsewhere. You needn't blame me henceforth! [*Recites quatrain*]:

When you reach the end of the road, you will taste my spite.
Any hand can grab an empire without a master.
I have a precious gift to offer luck's favourite;
You never know where luck will fly the faster.

# The Coronation

**Ma Shih-ying** [*enters in official dress and sings*] :
The capital is lost, now all are "chasing the stag."
Furiously the ministers compete for the highest rank!
By putting a new Emperor on the Throne, I shall hold
    power in the nation.

[*Speaks*] : I, Ma Shih-ying of Kweiyang, Kweichow, obtained
the doctor's degree in the year 1619 and currently hold
office as Governor-General of Feng-yang. It is lucky for me
that the country is in such turmoil. People of my sort have
golden opportunities at present. Recently I wrote to Shih
K'o-fa, asking him to support Prince Fu as prospective
Emperor. In his reply he stated three sins and five reasons
why the Prince should not succeed to the Throne. Juan
Ta-ch'eng went to sound him personally, and was refused
admittance. It looks as if Shih's mind is determined, and he
wields the supreme military power. In deference to his opinion, other high officials might hesitate to agree with me, and
this would create difficulties over the succession; so I sent
Juan to the commanders of the four chief outposts who are
susceptible to influence. I also sent him to various members
of the Imperial household and eunuchs likely to cooperate. I
hope he returns with a favourable report; I burn with impatience.

**Juan** [*enters and recites*] : When I have a perfect plan in mind, I
fear no adverse wind. Here is Governor Ma's study. I'm all
agog to see him.

**Ma:** So you're back, old Juan! How did everything go?

**Juan:** All the commanders were delighted with your proposal.
They promised to be ready for the ceremony on the twenty-
eighth of the fourth month.

**Ma:** Excellent. What did they say: Kao, Huang, and the two Liu?

**Juan** [*sitting down, sings*] :
> They said,
> "Dukes and earls of the Yangtze region,
> Remote from the capital, we still are anxious to serve.
> Now that the capital is lost,
> How can we stand idle at our posts?
> We will lead our valiant troops down the river
> To welcome the new Emperor and avenge the old.
> This is no time for wavering."

**Ma:** Who else is prepared to join us?

**Juan:** The Duke of Wei, Hsü Hung-chi; the Imperial Director of Ceremonies, Han Tsan-chou; Li Chan of the Civil Service; and the Grand Censor, Chu Kuo-ch'ang.

**Ma:** That's gratifying. What did they say?

**Juan** [*sings*] :
> They said, "Since His Excellency Ma takes the lead,
> How dare we Imperial servants hang back?
> We shall all subscribe our names.
> Let us make a public petition
> To support the new Emperor and revive our national life.
> When we pay homage to our new master in the Dragon Tower,
> Our efforts will be rewarded with promotions and fresh
>     favours."

**Ma:** Perfect. But my official post is outside the court, and those commanders are not in the cabinet either. How can we make our list of names look more impressive?

**Juan:** That's easy enough. We can procure a directory of nobles and officials and add their names to our list.

**Ma:** That is all very well, but if only a handful of us appear to welcome the new Emperor on his arrival and the majority fail to turn up, it will seem a practical joke.

**Juan:** I have noticed that few officials hold a definite opinion on the subject. As soon as the Imperial chariot arrives, I am sure they will all rush out to fawn on the new Master.

**Ma:** That's quite ingenious. The appeal is drafted, so we had better find the directory and put down all the names.

**Secretary** [*enters with the directory and says*] : Here's the Directory of Officials published by Hung's Bookstore on West Riverbank. [*He exits.*]

**Juan:** I'll copy them out, but they should be inscribed in the most formal style. My eyesight is not good enough. What shall I do? [*He takes up a pair of spectacles and puts them on while he copies.*] The Minister of Public Affairs, Kao Hung-t'u . . . My hand is shaking and the case is urgent. What shall I do?

**Ma:** Get the clerks to copy them.

**Juan:** But there is still the matter of selection. They are bound to bungle it.

**Ma:** Not if you supervise them personally. [*He summons* **clerk**, *and* **Juan** *gives the necessary directions.* **Ma** *remarks*]: It is said that in chasing the stag on the central plain, one should be the fleetest of runners. We must not lag behind. Let us pack at once and leave the city today. [*Steward comes in to help him pack.*]

**Juan:** What clothes should I wear for the occasion?

**Ma:** Naturally, you should wear your official cap and gown.

**Juan:** But I have lost my official rank.

**Ma:** Of course — I had forgotten! I shall appoint you the official bearer of the petition, though the post is far beneath you.

**Juan:** That will have to suffice. When a man has vaulting ambition, he must swallow certain indignities in the beginning.

**Ma** [*laughing*]: Sad but true.

**Juan** [*changing into robes of a minor official, sings*]:
I feared my career was a heap of cold ashes,
Today I rejoice that a dried-up sea is to flow again.
A golden tortoise is baited on my hook;[1]
With one flourish of my fishing rod,
I shall enjoy fame and riches forever.
What boots it if I must swallow my pride for the nonce?
A minor post may prove stepping-stone to Prime Minister;
Others may mock, but I need feel no shame.

**Clerk** [*entering*]: The list is completed. Please examine it, Your Honour.

**Juan** [*doing so*]: It is correct. You may put it in my dispatch case. I shall have to carry it on my back. [*The* **clerk** *and* **steward** *strap the case on* **Juan's** *back.*]

---

1. Allusion to Chiang T'ai-kung (see Scene 1, n. 4). Legends describe him as engaged in fishing in the River Wei when he was recruited to become founding minister of the Chou dynasty.

**Ma** [*laughing*] :  Old Juan, this is indeed a fine service you are
  performing.

**Juan** [*seriously*] :  Please do not scoff. One day my portrait will
  hang in the Hall of Meritorious Ministers, so I do not mind
  appearing in this humble role. [*Horses are led in by the
  steward.*]

**Steward**:  It is growing late. The horses are ready for Your Excellencies.

**Ma**:  For this grand occasion, I cannot take many attendants [i.e.,
  to the new Emperor's audience], but I shall take both of
  you.

**Juan** [*to* **clerk** *and* **steward**] :  You are in luck. Your names will be
  placed on record.

  [*All mount horses, and exeunt, singing together.*]

**All** [*singing*] :
  Before sunset the rain stopped over the southern hills.
  We spur our horses past many a misty station;
  We crack our golden whips beside the shore,
  As we hasten to the rising glory across the river.
  All the heroes of the age
  Rush forward like tigers and dragons.
  Oh, that we had wings
  To be first in paying homage to the new Emperor!

**Ma**:  Where shall we find lodging on the journey?

**Juan**:  Does Your Excellency expect to sleep on the way? No, let
  us hurry on. [*They apply their whips and sing*] :

**Ma**:
  Vapours rise from the river and mist from the hills, as twilight
    gathers.

**Juan**:
  Along the highroad our horses gallop madly.

**Ma**:
  Let us not be the last to arrive!

**Juan**:
  Tomorrow we'll meet the noblest man alive.

# The New Regime

## 1644, FIFTH MONTH

[*The Emperor Hung-kuang enters, preceded by two eunuchs. Formerly Prince Fu, he has assumed the Throne and now wears the Imperial robes.*]

**Emperor** [*sings*]:
Behold this ancient palace
Built by our Imperial Founder!
For the first time after many years,
The gates are opened again.
New purple clouds arise;
A mountain of ten thousand feet screens the walls from
    view.
I shall make the virtue of my ancestors shine again,
And enjoy the veneration of my subjects;
They will raise me to the bluest Heaven.
As a curtain is lifted, the clouds clear from the sky.
How majestic, this misty land of the southeast!

[*Recites*]:

I dreamt I lay in a royal bed, borne aloft by a yellow
    cloud;
On waking, I felt doubtful of reality.
Without fighting a single battle, I have mounted the
    Throne in this crisis.
No sooner is the dust washed from my face than I don my
    Imperial robes.

[*Speaks*]: I am the grandson of Emperor Shen-tsung, and the son of His Highness the Prince of the Fu Palace. Since childhood I have been Junior Prince of Te-ch'ang. Last year the bandits captured Honan and my father fell, a martyr for his country. I contrived to escape to Chiang-p'u. Now that the capital is lost and His Majesty has gone to Heaven, the people and officials of Nanking have supported my ascent to the Throne. This is the first day of the fifth month in the year Chia-shen,[1] and I have just returned from a pilgrimage

---

1. The Chinese had a binary notation system which yielded sixty possible combina-

to my ancestral tombs. I shall wait in this wing of the palace
for my officials.

[*Enter Shih K'o-fa, Ma Shih-ying, Huang Te-kung, and Liu Tse-ch'ing
in court attire, with ivory tablets and jade girdles.*]

**Subjects** [*reciting in unison*]:
Day dawns again on royal pageantry;
The palace is re-opened with new splendour.
The golden vessels are still intact,
The jade candlesticks newly supplied.

[*Speaking*]: We ministers and officials have escorted His
Majesty to the palace, after accompanying him to the Imperial Tombs. Though our names and titles have all been regis-
tered in the Imperial record, we have not yet paid formal
homage to His Majesty on his ascension of the Throne. [*All
kneel to present the petition, saying*]: Your servants beseech
Your Majesty to mount the Throne and adopt a new reign-
title, in response to the deepest desire of all your people.
[*They sing*]:

For an age Your Majesty has hidden like a dragon in your
    palace.
Your noble aspect is that of your grandfather, His
    Majesty Shen-tsung;
Your reputation for wisdom and benevolence has won
    universal acclaim.
All look up to you as to the wisest monarchs of antiquity.
The most precious branch of the golden Imperial tree,
You are appointed successor to the Lord of the Empire;
We implore you to ascend the Throne,
That the continuance of rule may be delayed no longer.

**Emperor**: Although a member of the Imperial family, I lack the
talent and virtue to undertake so formidable a task. It is only
in response to the earnest prayers of my people and ministers
that I have come to reside in the palace of the first Emperor.
But until the deaths of His late Majesty and my father are
avenged, I have not the temerity to mount the Throne
formally. For the present I should prefer to act as regent and

---

tions for naming years. There is thus a sixty-year cycle before the same year-name comes
round again. *Chia-shen* here is 1644. In other contexts it could be used for 1584, 1704,
etc.

retain the reign-title of Ch'ung-chen.[2] Let all records be dated accordingly. Persuade me no longer, oh loyal ministers, for it would only increase my sense of unworthiness. [*Sings*]:

Cease persuading me.
Disaster overwhelms the central plain;
The Imperial family beg by the riverbank,
Living among the fens or in the wilds,
Surrounded by dust and sand,
While in Loyang the flowers bloom as before.
The end of calamity is not in sight.
Tombs and monuments are levelled to the ground;
Dead warriors grip their swords, with none to bury them.
How shall I have the heart to wear the Imperial robes
And face south to receive universal acclaim?

**Subjects**: [*kneel and cry out*]: May the Emperor live ten thousand years. Your Majesty has pronounced the wisest words of a benevolent reign. How dare we disobey? But the dynasty must be avenged as soon as possible; the central plain must be recovered; and new generals and ministers must be appointed. We offer these proposals for your Imperial consideration. [*They sing*]:

Auspicious omens have appeared;
Lucky mists and clouds of blessing have arisen.
The empire will be built up again;
No bandits can share the same sky with us.
We shall eat gall and sleep on faggots to remind
    ourselves of the immediate task.
Let us appoint patriots to recover the central plain,
Skilled officials of every rank to direct our national
    policy.
These should be chosen now.

**Emperor**: We appreciate your very loyal proposals. Regarding appointments, we have made our choice. [*Sings*]:

First, a Prime Minister and National Commander.
Those who laboured most strenuously to enthrone the
    Emperor shall lead,
For they travelled with the petition all night
And escorted the Imperial chariot on its return.

---

2. See Prologue, n. 1.

They never faltered in their duty
Until they had invested us with the yellow robe,
Cheering us so vociferously
That we could not refuse the Imperial seal.
We are cognizant of those who deserve the highest rewards,
And shall appoint them in order of merit.

[*Speaks*] : Our loyal ministers, please retire for the present.
Await our orders at the Gate of Noon.

> [*Exeunt Emperor with eunuch attendants.  Shih, Huang, Ma and
> Liu step back and stand at attention.*]

**Shih**: Among those who worked hardest on His Majesty's behalf,
you, General Ma, stand foremost. Of course the highest
appointment should be yours.

**Ma**: Being only an outside official, I cannot expect such promotion. Now that the country is torn by war, you as Minister of
War should also be appointed Prime Minister. [*Turning
round*] : But you, commanders of the four outposts, have
been most dutiful in escorting His Majesty. You must be
ennobled instantly.

**Liu** and **Huang**:  We thank you, beloved patron.

> [*The Grand Eunuch enters with the Imperial decree.*]

**Eunuch**: Hearken to the Imperial decree! The Governor of Feng-
yang, Ma Shih-ying, who was first to meet His Majesty, is
deemed the most meritorious. He is appointed Prime Minister
and Minister of War concurrently. The Minister of Public
Affairs, Kao Hung-t'u; the Minister of Ceremonies, Chiang
Yüeh-kuang; and the Minister of War, Shih K'o-fa, are all
promoted to Vice Premiership, while retaining their former
titles. Kao Hung-t'u and Chiang Yüeh-kuang will both cooperate with the Premier in the Cabinet; Shih K'o-fa will
proceed north of the river and assume command of the army.
Other officials in all the ministries and departments will be
promoted three grades. Vacant posts will be filled by those
who took part in escorting the Imperial chariot, and the
military commanders of the four outposts[3] are awarded
earldoms. Give thanks for the Imperial favour!

**Subjects**: [*prostrating themselves*] :  We thank His Majesty's Impe-

---

3. The "Four Guardian Generals," Huang Te-kung, Kao Chieh, Liu Tse-ch'ing, and
Liu Liang-tso.

rial favour. May the Emperor live ten thousand years. [*They rise.*]

**Shih**: [*to Huang and Liu*] : I am so anxious to recover the central plain that I am overjoyed to command the armies north of the river. I shall expect Your Excellencies at Yangchow on the tenth day of the fifth month. We shall hold a conference to discuss our future strategy. Let there be no delay.

**Huang** and **Liu**: We hear and obey.

**Shih**: Now I must return to my duties. [*Recites*] :

Truly,
As when an enlightened prince restored the Eastern Han,
So now I am commissioned to recover the central plain.

> [*Exit Shih. Huang and Liu are about to withdraw when Ma detains them.*]

**Ma**: Wait a minute, generals. [*He clasps the hands of both.*] Now that, thanks to our efforts to enthrone the new Emperor, he has promoted us to high ranks, you and I are firm friends. From now on we must keep in close contact and always exchange notes to help each other maintain our wealth and power.

**Huang** and **Liu**: For all these advantages, we are indebted to you. Of course we shall do as you say. [*Exeunt.*]

**Ma** [*chuckling*] : Who would have expected me to become Prime Minister! What a happy day for me! [*Juan Ta-ch'eng creeps in. Ma, about to leave, stops and says*] : But hold! Since a new court is being established, everything is in disorder. I must take care that the three Vice-Premiers do not gain too much power. There is no hurry for me to go home. I had better investigate conditions in the cabinet.

> [*As Ma is about to leave, Juan approaches him with a quiet greeting.*]

**Juan**: Congratulations, my venerable Lord Prime Minister.

**Ma**: Where have you sprung from?

**Juan**: I was hiding outside the hall to hear what was being settled.

**Ma**: This place is out of bounds. You're dressed as an ordinary clerk and should not be here at all. Please retire quickly.

**Juan**: But I have something of importance to tell you. [*Whis-*

*pers*] : Now that you are Prime Minister, my venerable lord, do you remember the little services I rendered, especially as keeper of the petition appointed by yourself?

**Ma:** It has just been announced in the Imperial decree that all vacant posts will be filled by those who escorted the Imperial chariot, and you are included among them.

**Juan:** Wonderful, wonderful! Thank you, thank you!

**Ma:** It is only proper that you should be rewarded. [*Ma turns again to leave.*]

**Juan:** There must be many details requiring immediate attention. Let me be Your Excellency's private secretary until you can find me a suitable post in the cabinet.

**Ma:** True, this is the first time I am in charge of cabinet affairs. I may require plenty of assistance from you, but you must walk warily.

**Juan:** Of course I shall. [*Follows Ma obsequiously, carrying his tablet of office for him.*]

**Ma** [*sings*] :
After long service outside the Yellow Gate,
I am become Prime Minister.
I stride with lofty steps and my spirit leaps with joy;
How magnificent I must appear!

**Juan** [*sings*] :
Pray don't forget your plodding old adviser.

**Ma:**
The palace roofs slant towards the east, and the morning
    mist is yellow.

**Juan:**
A newly appointed courtier has cause to be elated

**Ma:**
All those who went to the river return as minions of the
    dragon.

**Juan:**
I too shall climb the golden stair, holding an ivory
    tablet.

# The Matchmakers Resisted

1644, FIFTH MONTH

**Yang Wen-ts'ung** [*enters and sings*]:
Now that an Emperor in the prime of life is enthroned,
We shall revive the festive spirit of the southern
   dynasties.
Forget the dust of war beyond the river:
Rare perfume becomes the most popular merchandise.

[*Speaks*]: Having won credit for escorting the Imperial
chariot, I have been appointed a Councillor in the Ministry of
Ceremonies. My sworn brother Juan has become a member of
the secretariat, and my fellow countrymen Yüeh Ch'i-chieh
and T'ien Yang have also received good posts. We have all
won these appointments on the same day — a day of rejoicing
for each of us. T'ien Yang should receive the vacant post of
Director of Military Supplies. He has just sent me three
hundred silver *taels* with a request to find a lovely singing-girl
to take along with him. The most eligible beyond any doubt
is Fragrant Princess. I'll go and ask her. [*Calls
out*]: Steward!

**Steward:** Though I have memorized the entire directory of nobles
and court officials, I am called upon to trudge the brothel
district. What are Your Honour's orders?

**Yang:** You are to summon the musician Ting Chi-chih and Mistress Pien Yü-ching to my study.

**Steward:** But I'm a respectable steward, Your Honour. I am only
familiar with the residences of ministers and officials. I don't
know the abodes of vagabonds and harlots.

**Yang:** Let me enlighten you. [*Sings*]:

Everywhere is a bustle for the Summer Festival,
But most seductive is the Water Pavilion,
Where young gallants can find red skirts
More easily than Oxherd crosses the River of Heaven![1]

---

1. Weaving Maid and Oxherd are star lovers, condemned to a single annual meeting
across the Milky Way.

**Steward**: If Your Honour refers to the Pavilion on the Ch'in-huai River, I think I can find it.

**Yang** [*pointing, sings*]:
    There, where a gauze of almond blossoms
    Shows beneath flowering dates,
    You should make discreet enquiries.

> [*Enter the three poet-musicians **Ting Chi-chih, Shen Kung-hsien**, and **Chang Yen-chu**.*]

**Musicians**: The brothel harbours the old and idle; the court attracts the young and brisk.

**Ting**: Here is His Honour Yang's mansion. I'll knock. Hey, is anybody there?

**Steward** [*opening*]: Who are you?

**Ting**: I'm Ting Chi-chih, and these are my good friends Shen and Chang. We wish to see His Honour. Please announce us.

**Steward** [*delightedly*]: What a happy coincidence. I was just about to look for you.

> [*As the musicians enter the house, the three courtesans **Pien Yü-ching, K'ou Pai-men**, and **Cheng T'o-niang** appear.*]

**Courtesans** [*recite*]:
    Why are the purple swallows here so early?
    It seems the orioles come too late.

**K'ou**: Will you three gentlemen wait for us? We might as well enter together.

**Ting**: Oh, it's you, sisters. What brings you here?

**Cheng**: We must have all caught the same disease. You're afraid of being teachers, and we're afraid of being apprentices.

> [*Visitors enter together.*]

**Yang**: How providential! I was hoping to see you.

**Visitors**: We should not have ventured to intrude if we had not an urgent request. We came to ask Your Honour a favour, but first let us pay our respects. [*All kowtow.*]

**Yang** [*politely restraining them*]: Please sit down and tell me what's troubling you.

**Ting**: Is it true that the newly promoted Secretary Juan is an intimate friend of Your Honour's?

**Yang**: It is indeed.

**Ting**: We have heard that he has presented four plays of his own invention to His Majesty, and that the Emperor is so delighted, especially with *The Swallow Letter,* that he has ordered many copies to be made. It is rumoured that we are to be taken to the Inner Court to be trained for the various roles. Has Your Honour also heard this?

**Yang**: I have; and it should be a fine performance.

**Chang**: To be frank, nearly all of us have families of at least eight mouths to support with our own two lips. If we are taken to the Inner Court, we shall never see them again and they will starve.

**Cheng**: We too have eight mouths depending on two strips of flesh.

**Yang**: You need not worry on that account. When the Imperial decree is issued, there will be plenty of boys and girls to choose from. I'll see that you are exempted.

**Visitors**: We shall be grateful for Your Honour's protection.

**Yang**: I'll send a special request to Master Juan. You may rest at ease about it.

**Visitors**: We thank Your Honour. [*All sing together*] :

In this city, the misty waters are ever beguiling,
But there must be melody and damsels smiling
To enhance the fiery glamour of the sunset . . .
If we are all transferred to the Inner Court,
Only gloom and rain will hide the landscape;

On the pleasure-boats, behind the blue curtains,
There will never be the same gaiety.
Your Honour must protect
The charm of the Ch'in-huai River;
Then the hills themselves will retain
Their glow of joyous life.

**Yang**: I have a favour to ask you in return.

**Ting**: What is Your Honour's wish?

**Yang**: A kinsman of mine, T'ien Yang, will soon be promoted to

Director of Military Supplies. He has sent me three hundred
silver *taels* to procure him a concubine.

**Cheng**: Wouldn't I be suitable?

**Chang**: You can't go — if you did, this place would lose its
rhythm.

**Cheng**: How "lose its rhythm"?

**Chang**: There'd be no one left for me to strum!

**Cheng**: Pah!

**Ting**: Has Your Honour any particular girl in mind?

**Yang**: I have, but I must ask you to negotiate.

**Pien**: Who is the lucky choice?

**Yang**: Fragrant Princess.

**Ting** [*shaking his head*]: I doubt if that can be arranged.

**Yang**: Why?

**Ting**: Remember, she is contracted to Master Hou. [*Sings*]:

The notes of her flute as she sits in her tower are full
    of fond memories.
Though the willows are three springs older,
She pines behind closed doors for her absent love,
And hears the swallows twittering in vain.
There's little hope of persuading her to yield;
She's not the fickle kind.

**Yang**: But her union with Master Hou was a temporary arrangement. Now that he is far away, I doubt if he gives her a
thought. In any case, the attempt is well worth making.

**Pien**: Ever since Master Hou's departure, Fragrant Princess has
remained faithful to him. She has never entertained another
guest, and I am sure she would never remarry. The attempt
would be hopeless. [*Sings*]:

She is like a swan who has lost its mate.
Alone she lingers by the shore,
Cries to the passing clouds;
And when the moon shines on her desolate tower,
Her powder and rouge are washed away,
Her ornaments thrust aside.
The voice that used to sing is silent now.

She is like a nun who spends all her time embroidering
    Buddha's image,
Lest the dusty world pollute her.

**Yang:** Even so, if she were offered a mate more suitable than
Master Hou, I think she would accept him.

**Ting:** As her mother is an old friend of Your Honour's, you might
be able to cajole her by that means.

**Yang:** Since I arranged the match with Master Hou, I would be
embarrassed to broach this second one. It would be more
becoming for you to do so. You shall be amply rewarded for
your pains.

**Chang** and **Shen:** In that case we'll go too.

**K'ou** and **Cheng:** If it is a flesh-and-blood transaction, we are
quite as efficient as any of you.

**Yang:** Stop arguing. If Mistress Pien and Master Ting don't succeed, the next chance will be yours.

**All:** Your Honour's will be done. We beg to take our leave.

**Yang:** Excuse me for not accompanying you to the door. [*Recites*]: I have jesters to amuse me, and other men's affairs to
keep me busy. [*Exit.*]

**Ting** and **Pien:** We must do our best to oblige His Honour, since
he has done so much for us.

**Shen** and **Chang:** That goes without saying.

**Ting** [*to the others*]: You others might as well go home while we
visit Fragrant Princess and see if she can be persuaded.

**Cheng:** If you get any money out of this, we must share and share
alike.

> [*Exeunt Chang, Shen, K'ou, and Cheng, laughing and joking.
> Ting and Mistress Pien walk together.*]

**Ting:** When Master Hou was united to Fragrant Princess, we were
also intermediaries. [*Sings*]:

Not long ago a banquet was spread
For the betrothal of a genius to a radiant beauty.
How lovely the flowers were,
How brilliant the decorations!
Flutes and viols filled the air with joyous modulations.

[*Speaks*]: And now we are helping another to obtain her. What a shame! [*Sings*]:

We are like grooms at posting stations, receiving
One traveller after another as they come and go.

**Pien**: Supposing we don't comply?

**Ting**: If we don't, I'm afraid that the new official will use coercion.

**Pien**: What is the most prudent course, then?

**Ting**: Let us be ambiguous. When we get there, speak noncommittally, express our sympathy, and see how the wind blows. [*Sings*]:

Let us imitate the leisurely bee,
Which flies among flowers without apparent aim.

**Pien**: That seems the most sensible approach.

**Ting**: Oh, here we are. Let's go in. [*Calls*]: Mistress Li!

**Fragrant Princess** [*enters reciting*]:
In my silent empty tower I sit alone,
And doze in sickness through the weary days.

[*Calls*]: Who is downstairs?

**Pien**: Master Ting and I would like to see you.

**Fragrant Princess**: Please come up.

**Ting** and **Pien**: Where is your mother?

**Fragrant Princess**: She has gone to a hamper party. May I offer you some tea?

**Pien**: You seem to be always alone with nothing to do. Does nobody ever keep you company?

**Fragrant Princess**: Dear aunt, you cannot conceive my state of dejection. [*Sings*]:

The spring is ending, yet I am solitary.
Sometimes I sing "The Lament of White Hair"
Until the tears soak my handkerchief.

**Pien**: Have you never thought of finding another mate?

**Fragrant Princess**: I'm pledged to Master Hou. My heart will never change.

**Ting:** Of course we understand your feelings. However, His Honour Yang told us that a high official has offered a large sum of money for you and we came to consult your opinion on the matter.

**Fragrant Princess** [*sings*]:
> You were utterly mistaken,
> You were utterly mistaken.
> The crimson silk which bound me to my love
> Is worth far more than the largest sum of money.

**Pien:** The decision rests with you. If you are unwilling, we shall have to seek elsewhere.

**Fragrant Princess** [*sings*]:
> There are bevies of beauties in this pleasure resort
> Whose smiles are for sale.
> It was not my destiny
> To enter the rich man's gate.

**Pien:** Then we shall refuse this proposal on your behalf.

**Ting:** But when your mother returns she may be tempted by so large an offer.

**Fragrant Princess:** My mother is too fond of me to force my hand.

**Ting:** We need not worry then. I admire your resolution. [*He stands up and says goodbye.*]

**Chang, Shen, K'ou,** and **Cheng** [*running in, recite*]:
> Love binds two people a thousand leagues apart,
> But money may sever the bond betwixt heart and heart.

**Chang:** Let us hurry. If the others succeeded in cajoling her, we shall lose our reward.

**Cheng:** Even if they have swallowed the money, I'll make them cough it up.

**Chang** [*to Fragrant Princess*]: We have come to congratulate you.

**Fragrant Princess:** What for?

**K'ou:** Two matchmakers have called on you at the same time. Isn't that a reason for congratulation?

**Fragrant Princess:** Are you referring to T'ien Yang's proposal?

**Chang:** Precisely.

**Fragrant Princess:**  I have already rejected it.

**Shen:**  His Honour Yang was kind enough to recommend you. How can you be so ungrateful as to disappoint him? [*Sings*]:

> Since you were born a rare pearl,
> Waxing in beauty like flowers under the moon,
> He has found you a mate
> Renowned for elegance and fabulous wealth.

**Fragrant Princess:**  I have no inclination for either. Say no more.

**Ting** and **Pien:**  We have discussed it with her, and she has decided not to marry again.

**K'ou:**  So she's being obstinate, eh? But if she's dragged off to the Inner Court, she will never have a chance of seeing another man. [*Sings*]:

> After each performance,
> She will be locked in a gloomy den.
> Night and day,
> She will live to regret it.

**Fragrant Princess:**  Why should it be so hard to remain alone all one's life?

**Cheng:**  Three hundred *taels* of gleaming silver! What more do you expect, you drivelling child?

**Fragrant Princess:**  If you're so fond of silver, go and marry him yourself. Why bother me?

**Cheng:**  You little idiot, how dare you talk to me like that? You have so provoked me, I shall die of rage here and now. [*She bumps her head in a clownish attempt at suicide, singing*]:

> You cheap little low-born hussy,
> How dare you wag your tongue
> To abuse your elders and betters?

**Chang:**  You brazen strumpet, remember that His Honour Yang is now a high official in the Ministry of Ceremonies, and you and your sort come under his jurisdiction. Tomorrow he can send you to the magistrate and have your thumbs cracked. [*Sings*]:

> In his anger he may send a thunderstorm
> To destroy all our peaches and willows.

**Fragrant Princess**: Threaten as much as you please, my mind is determined.

**Pien** [*to others*] : Don't regard her as a child. Young as she is, she knows her own mind.

**Ting**: It is useless threatening her. Let us go.

**Cheng**: I was on the verge of suicide. Didn't you notice it? Why did nobody try to stop me? I'm disgusted with the lot of you. As for the wench, if she keeps on refusing, why not carry her off if we have to drag her downstairs? [*Sings*] :

Stick her in a two-wheeled cart,
Stick her in a two-wheeled cart,
Break her jewelled hairpins,
Tear her silk robes apart.

**Ting**: Remember the proverb: No matter how rich you are, you cannot buy what is not for sale. Both threats and coercion are useless. Let us go.

**Shen** and **K'ou**: We never wanted to come in the first place. It was old Chang and Cheng T'o-niang who dragged us into this unpleasant situation. [*Sing*] :

Let's be off.
Save ourselves a little face,
Say no more of this disgrace.

**Chang**: We had better go, too. It has all been a waste of effort.

[*Exeunt Chang, Shen, K'ou, and Cheng.*]

**Pien** and **Ting**: Don't worry, Fragrant Princess. We'll explain everything to His Honour Yang, and nobody will trouble you again.

**Fragrant Princess** [*bowing*] : Thank you, thank you!

**Ting**:
Matchmakers like butterflies and bees:

**Fragrant Princess**:
They swarm at my window to disturb my peace.

**Pien**:
None can ever touch your fragrant heart.

**Fragrant Princess**:
But where is he from whom I had to part?

SCENE 18

# The Rivals Struggle

1644, FIFTH MONTH

**Hou** [*enters and recites*]:
Victory and defeat are as uncertain as a game of chess:
What the next move should be I dare not say.
But the Yangtze cannot be allowed to cut off north from
  south;
Here in midstream we swear to recover what is lost.

[*Speaks*]: Recently I drafted a letter for His Excellency
Shih, and in the heat of the moment I stated Prince Fu's
three cardinal sins and the five reasons against his succession
to the Throne. But now he is Emperor, and Ma Shih-ying has
become Prime Minister. All those who escorted his chariot
have been promoted to high office. Though His Excellency
Shih is also a member of the cabinet, he has been sent to
command the army north of the river. Their purpose was to
brush him aside, but he does not care. On the contrary, he is
glad of a chance to grapple with the bandits. I am proud to
help him, for I admire his courage and loyalty more and
more. Today he has invited the commanders of the four
outposts to confer about the strategic defence of the
river. . . . where is the steward?

**Servant** [*entering*]: Oh, Master Hou, so you have arrived. Let me
announce you.

**Shih K'o-fa** [*enters and sings*]:
I stand firm on the banks of the river.
Amid the leaping of dragons and roaring of tigers,
I forget my aging body and whitening hair . . .

[*Speaks*]: Brother Hou, the commanders of the four outposts will soon be here for the conference. At last there is
hope of uniting our armies and avenging His Majesty.

**Hou**: That is encouraging, but General Kao Chieh, who garrisons
Yangchow and Tungchow, poses something of a problem. He
has been very arrogant, and his troops are unruly. The three
other garrison generals are often incensed at his behaviour.

[128]

Everything should be done to placate them at today's conference, for their disputes will only benefit the foe.

**Shih**: This is good advice. I'll do my best to pacify them.

**Steward**: The drums are beating at the gate. The generals of the four garrisons have arrived.

> [*Exit* **Hou**. *A flourish of drums and trumpets. Guards enter and stand at both ends of the stage. Enter the four generals* **Kao Chieh, Huang Te-kung, Liu Tse-ch'ing,** *and* **Liu Liang-tso,** *in full armour.*]

**Generals**: Though the northern capital lacked a stout defender, a great statesman-general commands the left of the Yangtze. [*Entering the hall, they salute* **Shih**.] Greetings to the Commander-in-chief!

**Shih**: Generals, I bid you welcome.

**Generals**: [*standing at both sides of the platform*]: We await Your Excellency's orders.

**Shih**: As Cabinet Minister in command of the armies, I have been authorized to direct the general strategy. By His Majesty's decree, all officers in this area are my subordinates.

**Generals**: Aye, aye.

**Shih**: You generals of the four garrisons are not mere officers, but noble earls. I am aware of the impropriety of giving you subordinate seats, but it is important to proceed with the conference as quickly as possible.

**Generals**: Your Excellency is too courteous.

**Shih**: As Commander-in-Chief, I order you to be seated.

> [*The four* **generals** *bow and obey.* **Kao** *promptly takes the seat of honour.* **Huang** *frowns at him.*]

**Shih** [*sings*]:
Protected by noble rivers on every side,
This region is of high strategic importance.
Battle formations can be massed like heavy clouds,
With clustered hosts numerous as the willow branches.
Our iron-mailed cavalry will roar in the wind as they
    gallop forth:

The whizzing arrows of our infantry will startle the
    rushing tide.
We should try to emulate the great strategists of yore,
And reform the nation with a single heart.
Your portraits, in full armour,
Will soon adorn the Hall of Fame.

**Huang** [*angrily*]: I don't wish to cause trouble, but this Kao
Chieh was only a bandit who surrendered to us. By what
superior merit does he take the seat of honour?

**Kao**: I was among the first to be promoted after my surrender.
Besides, I am the most advanced in age, and could not sit
below you.

**Liu Tse-ch'ing** [*to Kao*]: This is your own garrison area, whereas
we are guests. How can a good general betray such ignorance
of etiquette?

**Liu Liang-tso**: His head is swollen after revelling in the luxuries of
Yangchow. But it should be our turn now.

**Kao**: If ever you dare set foot in Yangchow, I might yield my seat
to you.

**Huang**: So you think I dare not? [*Rising*]: Will the brothers Liu
join me? I shall fight a duel with him. [*Exit.*]

**Shih** [*to Kao*]: You should not offend the majority. Let us try to
be more modest.

**Kao**: I would rather die than yield to their arrogance.

**Shih**: You are wrong in this. [*Sings*]:

How brave you four generals appear!
The recovery of the northern capital depends chiefly
    on you;
You should be like brothers, fighting shoulder to
    shoulder.
Why gnash your teeth about a chair?
Dignity and decorum are thrown to the winds.
One, eyes glaring, starts a battle in a quiet room;
Another, blazing with rage, stirs a storm from tranquil
    waters.
Long before your valour shines forth in battle,
Already your talons are in each other's flesh.
Since such hot-blooded youths have been promoted,
His Majesty's decree is laughed to scorn.

[*Speaks*]: I did not expect you brave generals to behave to foolishly. I called this conference with the highest hopes. Now they are cold as ashes. Alas, I have no alternative but to send the three other generals back to their posts until further notice. [*To Kao*]: Since this is your district, I appoint you Commander of the Vanguard. Hearing of this extra duty, the others may be less jealous.

**Kao**: Thank you, Commander-in-Chief.

> [**Shih** *writes his order and hands it to* **Kao**. *A hubbub sounds from backstage.* **Kao** *walks out of the camp without a word. In the meantime* **Huang** *and the* **Liu brothers** *enter shouting with drawn swords.* **Kao Chieh** *meets them.*]

**Kao**: Heaven and sun above! How dare you shout and shake your swords at me. Is this a mutiny?

**Huang**: No, but we want your life.

**Kao**: We are still before the gate of our Commander-in-Chief. Have you forgotten who you are, you savages? [**Huang** *and* **both Lius** *advance to kill* **Kao**, *who runs into the gate calling*]: Help, help, Your Excellency!

> [**Huang** *and the* **Lius** *fight their way into the camp, still shouting and cursing.*]

**Shih** [*standing astonished, sings*]:
I fancied the northern cavalry had come to attack us,
So fierce the cries for blood;
Yet the war is inside our own camp.
When we should be united, our ranks are torn by discord.
An evil plant has taken root,
Which bodes ill for this campaign.
It is easier to quell bandits than to pacify
    quarrelsome generals.

[*Speaks*]: Ask Master Hou to come here. [**Steward** *goes to call him.*]

**Hou** [*entering in haste*]: What now, Your Excellency?

**Shih**: I want you to exert your skill in appeasing the turbulent officers, so that my order is carried out. Here it is in writing. Take it and expound it to them.

**Hou**: I obey. [*Takes the order with him and leaves the camp,* *saying*] : Greetings, Your Excellencies. The Commander-in-Chief has charged me to explain to you that in spite of the new succession to the throne, the mission of punishing the bandits still lies before us. This is a time when we should grasp our spears and prove our patriotism. No personal grudge should interfere with our purpose. When the central plain is recovered, an Imperial banquet will be given to celebrate the victory. Naturally, the seats will be arranged according to court etiquette. Those with the finest record in the campaign will be the most highly honoured. Now that we should devote all our energy to the struggle, this is no time to grumble about points of punctilio. Please be reasonable. Since Earl Kao Chieh's garrison is in this area, he will stay here to command the vanguard. Earl Huang and the two Earls Liu will return to their garrisons until further notice. The discipline of the army must be maintained. To preserve the dignity of command, there will be no leniency for offenders. Such is the order.

**Huang**: We only want to kill that wretched brigand. We have no intention of breaking discipline.

**Hou**: To threaten the life of a general in our own camp is an intolerable breach of discipline.

**Liu Tse-ch'ing**: In that case, we shall give no further alarm to our Commander. We shall withdraw for the present.

**Huang**: But tomorrow we shall beard Kao Chieh in his den. To avenge the country is a noble duty; but personal revenge demands immediate action. [*Exeunt.*]

[***Hou** re-enters the camp and reports to **Shih**.*]

**Hou**: The three garrison commanders retired after hearing the order, but they are determined to continue the feud.

**Shih**: How can we curb them? [*Pointing at **Kao Chieh**, sings*] :

General Kao, you are responsible for this mischief.
Why be so blinded with false pride?
By grabbing the seat of honour,
You have drawn jealous swords against you.
No tongue, however eloquent, can restrain them;
Till my throat were dry, I could not shóut them down.
The future is ominous:
Our mission is endangered.

**Kao**: Never mind, Commander-in-Chief. I shall settle accounts with them tomorrow. Then all the cavalry under their command will be brought under mine. United, I shall lead them to victory. The recovery of the central plain will then be an easy matter.

**Shih**: You talk without sense. The bandits are reported to be crossing the Yellow River. General Hsü Ting-kuo at the front is unable to hold out against them. He has been sending urgent messages for reinforcements. I had called this conference to discuss our defence of the river. How can I muster enough troops in time, when you are all fighting among yourselves?

**Kao**: The three of them are against me only because Yangchow is wealthy and flourishing. They are jealous and want to seize it for themselves. Why should I yield to oblige them?

**Shih**: This is even more absurd. [*Sings*]:

As one against three,
You will be crushed like an egg under a mountain.
All yours are the twenty-four bridges of Yangchow,
The flutes playing on moonlit nights;
But they too would like to stroll on your Sui embankment,[1]
Boast of the bygone glories of your gardens.
Who would not choose Yangchow for his personal heaven?
I only fear that their envy, by tomorrow,
Will drown the torrent of your river in murderous cries.

[*Speaks*]: Alas, so be it! I have racked my brains to no purpose. Brother Hou, I shall have to count on your ingenuity.

**Hou**: Perhaps we should wait before making a decision.

[*Exeunt **Shih** and **Hou**. Drums and trumpets resound. The gate is closed.*]

**Kao**: I am as brave as any man. Why should I wait to be slaughtered without striking a blow? Tomorrow I shall muster my troops on the Yellow Dyke for the counter-attack. [*Recites*]:

---

1. One of the glories of Yangchow, built during the Sui dynasty, 589-618, which unified China when it overcame the Ch'en, last of the "southern dynasties."

Like dragons and tigers we fight to prove our prowess.
Instead of exchanging wine-cups, we cross swords.
I shall not stop to consider the fortunes of war:
Even if my head be struck off I shall not yield.

---

SCENE 19

# The Pacification Attempt

1644, FIFTH MONTH

[*General Huang and both Generals Liu with attendants and soldiers enter shouting. They are armed to the teeth and carry banners.*]

**Huang:** Brothers, we shall have to be cautious. I have heard that Kao has mustered his troops to attack us at the Yellow Dyke. Let us split into three columns and advance in serried ranks.

**Liu Liang-tso:** I have not brought enough soldiers, so I had better just challenge him and leave it to you to support me.

**Huang:** My strongest champion T'ien Hsiung is absent, so I will take the second column and ask Liu Tse-ch'ing to head the main column.

**Liu Tse-ch'ing:** Agreed. Forward march! [*Exeunt shouting.*]

**Kao Chieh** [*entering with armed guard*]: Men, take up your positions and await the foe.

**Scout** [*entering*]: Your Excellency, the foe are advancing towards us.

**Liu Liang-tso** [*enters with a big halberd, shouting*]: Come out, old Kao! Let us see who is the better warrior!

**Kao** [*waving his spear*]: Cease bragging, upstart booby!

[*A fight ensues to the beating of drums.*]

**Kao:** Catch him alive, boys. [*Soldiers join in. Exit Liu.*]

**Huang** [*entering with a pair of whips, to Kao*]: Knowing my strength, you should kneel and beg for your life.

**Kao:** I never liked that phiz of yours. Now I shall chop your head

6. General Kao Chieh (waving his spear
at General Liu Liang-tso): "Cease bragging, upstart booby!"

off. [*Drums are beaten. The fight continues.*] Join the battle, boys!

**Huang** [*angrily*]: A general should fight a general, a trooper a trooper. That has always been the rule. But an old brigand like you knows nothing of rules. I withdraw. [*Exit, defeated.*]

**Liu Tse-ch'ing** [*entering with a pair of swords, followed by soldiers*]: Cease bragging, Kao Chieh. I too have soldiers. Let us fight a full-fledged battle.

**Kao**: I'm known as the Heaven-upsetting Hawk, and am utterly fearless. Fight any way you please, but kill, kill, kill!

> [*A general melee ensues. Hou enters and walks up to an adjacent peak, his guards beating gongs. The battle ceases. All look up to him.*]

**Hou** [*flourishing his arrow of command*]: His Excellency the Commander-in-Chief's orders! This rioting among the armies of the four garrison generals amounts to open mutiny, and the Commander-in-Chief assumes full blame for it. He bids you come and kill him at his own headquarters, whereupon you may go to Nanking and loot the palace. You need not fight here and endanger the lives of harmless citizens.

**Liu Tse-ch'ing**: This is no mutiny. We merely wish to punish Kao as he deserves. After settling this matter, we shall report to His Excellency.

**Kao**: As Commander of the Vanguard, I am no rebel. Since the others came to kill me, I was compelled to fight in self-defence.

**Hou**: You have disobeyed orders by fighting among yourselves, and you should all be considered rebels. A memorial to that effect will be sent to His Majesty. If you have anything further to add, you may say so in His Majesty's presence.

**Liu Tse-ch'ing**: His Majesty was raised to the Throne by us, and the Commander-in-Chief was appointed by His Majesty. Since our disobedience of this order has been interpreted as rebellion against the Emperor, we should kneel in chains before His Excellency and plead for pardon.

**Hou**: What has General Kao to say?

**Kao:** I'm His Excellency's slave. Let my disobedience be punished as he thinks fit.

**Hou:** Then the two other garrison commanders should come to headquarters and apologize.

**Liu Tse-ch'ing:** The other two were defeated. They have returned to their garrisons.

**Hou:** No personal grudge should exist between the generals in control of neighbouring areas. Why should you pay attention to others' intrigues? Now come before the Commander-in-Chief and await his verdict. [*Hou descends from his peak, accompanied by Liu and Kao.*]

**Hou:** Here we are at headquarters. You generals please wait outside while I announce you. [*Exits and re-enters, saying*]: Hear the Commander-in-Chief's order: This quarrel among the four garrison generals was a serious breach of discipline, but since it was provoked by General Kao's disregard of etiquette, he should be the first to apologize. The matter will thus be settled without a court-martial. [*Sings to Kao*]:

General, think for yourself.
Punishment means disaster;
Your only course is to shoulder a load of thorns
And bow in contrition.

**Kao** [*furiously*]: Though I am a close subordinate of the Commander-in-Chief, His Excellency asks me to apologize instead of offering me his protection. I am too mortified to do so. Enough, enough! This can only mean that His Excellency has no further use for me. I shall lead my troops independently across the river. [*Sings*]:

I cannot endure such cruel humiliation.
I shall cross the great river
And my deeds will shake the world.

[*Calls*]: Soldiers, follow me! [*His soldiers enter with banners and leave the stage, shouting.*]

**Liu:** Alack, alack! If he crosses the river, his numerous henchmen on the other side will join him. They will return with reinforcements to attack us. I had better warn the other garrison generals so that our troops are ready to meet him on the spot. [*Sings*]:

How foolish of him to fly off in such a tantrum!
Even the Yangtze could not wash away his shame.
Surely he must return to do more violence. [*Exit Liu.*]

**Hou:** An unexpected crisis — how can I resolve it? [*Sings*] :

Mountains and streams slip and slide —
How to rebuild this land?
Men's hearts split apart like loosened tiles,
As they forget old friendships.

[*Gazing south, he says*] : Kao Chieh has really become a
rebel. [*Sings*] :

Proudly he crosses the river,
His banners disrupting its flow
As he sails for Chenkiang.

[*Gazing north, he says*] : And Liu Tse-ch'ing rushes north to
assemble the troops of the three garrisons for battle. [*Sings*] :

Dust and smoke will cover the earth,
While the Commander-in-Chief scratches his head,
And his adviser wrings his hands.

[*Speaks*] : I shall report to His Excellency and try to help
him find a solution. [*Sings*] :

The Commander-in-Chief, mighty above all generals,
Is charged with a mission of vital import;
But towered warships and iron-clad steeds
Converge with covetous speed on the delights of Yangchow.

---

SCENE 20

# The Defence Assignment

1644, SIXTH MONTH

**Kao Chieh** [*enters with armed guards and sings*] :
Where now shall I spur on my mount?
The river is sealed, its cities guarded
By companies of fierce bowmen.

Sound the retreat
For the safety of Yangchow's walls.

[*Speaks*]: After crossing the river with my troops, I wished
to capture Soochow and Hangchow, but Governor Cheng
Hsüan blocked my advance with armed ships and a powerful
cannonade, so I had to return to Yangchow. I wonder where
my enemies of the three garrisons are at present?

**Messenger** [*entering*]: Your Excellency, all the regiments of the
three garrisons are marching south to attack us. Their
advance patrols have reached this neighbourhood.

**Kao**: Alas, this is appalling. I can neither go north nor south,
neither forward nor backward. Enough, enough, I shall have
to return to the Commander-in-Chief and implore his aid.
[*Walks and sings*]:

I hasten to beg his forgiveness,
But what shall I say in my shame?
I have invited my doom:
Heaven seems to will my death.        [*Exit.*]

**Shih K'o-fa** [*entering with guards, sings*]:
The situation worsens:
What help is there?
I have lain awake night after night;
Sleep has forsaken me.

**Hou** [*entering, sings*]: All my talents, alas, seem limited to paper.

**Shih**: Kao Chieh retired without a word, and the other generals
refuse to obey my orders. Our troops are too few to defend
the north of the river. The skies are falling upon us. What
shall we do?

**Hou**: I have just heard that Governor Cheng Hsüan has blocked
Kao's advance and prevented him from going south. He has
returned to Yangchow.

**Shih**: What of the other garrison generals?

**Hou**: On discovering his return, they have mustered all their
forces to attack him here. Their patrols are already in the
vicinity.

**Shih**: This makes matters even worse. [*Sings*]:

A dynasty of three hundred years

Has sunk to this.
How can I, single-handed,
Support the falling skies?
I am reduced to words to ward off trouble.

**Shih** and **Hou** together [*singing*]:
Smoke and dust fill the eye;
Across the meadows corpses lie,
While on a single column we rely.

[*An Orderly beats a drum; Shih's attendant asks him the reason.*]

**Orderly**: General Kao is standing with his soldiers outside the gate. He asks to see the Commander-in-Chief.

**Shih**: So the worst is true. Tell him to come straight in. I'll hear what he has to say.

[*Shih mounts a platform, and the gate is opened. Guards stand on either side.*]

**Kao** [*rushing in*]: Your Excellency's humble servant Kao Chieh, having relinquished his post without orders, deserves ten thousand deaths. I crave Your Excellency's most generous pardon.

**Shih**: You were formerly a bandit, but His Majesty most graciously accepted your surrender and even promoted you to an earldom. Why did you rashly desert and become a rebel? Since you were unable to cross the river, you have returned to me. This wavering between rebellion and surrender is an outrage to military discipline. You deserve the severest punishment, but since you have repented so soon, you are pardoned for the present. [*Kao kowtows and rises. Shih continues*]: What else have you to say?

**Kao** [*kneeling*]: I left my post because I was unwilling to apologize. Now that the three garrison generals are aware of my return, they wish to renew the attack. Though my army is strong, I doubt if it is equal to such odds. I hope Your Excellency will vouchsafe me protection. [*To Hou*]: Your Honour Hou, please say a word in my favour.

**Hou**: Since you were so stubborn then, how can the Commander-in-Chief protect you now?

**Shih**: Precisely. At this juncture I do not see how I can protect you. [*Sings*]:

After a quarrel over a seat,
You rashly resorted to arms.
Now there are three to one;
The future of your army hangs upon a thread.

[*Shih* and *Hou* repeat the previous duet.]

**Kao:** If Your Excellency spurns me, I may crack my head open at your gate, but I shall never yield to my foes.

**Hou:** This is very unlike your boast at the Yellow Dyke.

**Kao:** But then they had fewer troops. Now that they have mustered three whole garrisons, I have not the nerve to meet them.

**Hou:** I have a plan, if you will agree to it.

**Kao:** I shall agree to any plan except apology.

**Hou:** The bandits are rushing south; they will soon be on this side of the Yellow River. General Hsü is no longer able to hold them back, and has asked most urgently for reinforcements. The Commander-in-Chief is anxious to send them. Why not volunteer on his behalf? By marching to Kaifeng and Loyang, you will relieve General Hsü and pave the way for greater tasks in future. The other garrison generals will have no further excuse for fighting you. What do you think of this?

**Kao:** I shall have to consult my staff.

[*Sounds of shouting from behind the stage.*]

**Shih:** I hear war-cries outside the city.

**Messenger** [*enters to report*]: The three garrison generals are leading their troops to challenge General Kao.

**Kao** [*greatly alarmed*]: I shall obey the Commander-in-Chief.

**Shih:** In that case I'll order the garrison generals to withdraw. [*Shih throws down his arrow of command.* **Orderly** *kneels to pick it up.*]

**Shih:** Kao's insubordination deserves punishment; but since reinforcements are required at the front, and he was among those to escort the Imperial Chariot, he is pardoned. He will be sent to defend the Yellow River area so that he may redeem himself with a worthy task. The three garrison generals should forget their feud and concentrate on operations of national importance. They are to return to their posts pending further orders.

**Orderly**: Your Excellency shall be obeyed. [*Exit.*]

**Shih** [*to Kao*]: Oh General Kao, beware of your own temper. [*Sings*]:

> The Yellow River cannot be your sole defence,
> Your plans must have a beginning and an end.

[*Speaks*]: Bear in mind that General Hsü is not easy to deal with. [*Sings*]:

> Be cautious on convivial occasions;
> A quarrelsome tongue is disastrous as spear or sword.

[*Says to Hou*]: The defence of the Yellow River is essential. Since General Kao has more energy than intellect, I shall be responsible if anything goes wrong. He is proceeding to your native province of Honan, and you have long been anxious to visit your family; only the dangers of the journey have deterred you. Now, if you accompany his army, you will fulfill your wish while supervising the campaign. Furthermore, you will be able to protect your home.

**Hou**: I thank Your Excellency for this wise proposal. I shall bid farewell and make instant preparations to accompany General Kao.

**Kao** [*bowing*]: I shall also take leave of Your Excellency.

**Shih** [*to Hou*]: Since you are accompanying him, I feel as if I were defending the river in person. But unforeseen difficulties may arise. Please take every precaution. I hope to receive good news from you. Truly, a man has no say over victory or defeat, only Heaven will ordain his rise or fall.

> [*Exit Shih. Flourish of trumpets and drums. The gate is closed after Hou and Kao walk through.*]

**Kao**: Master Hou, do you hear the war-cries? I fear they will stop to challenge us.

**Hou**: Never mind. They know that you have been sent to the front, and this should appease them. Besides, they will have to take the eastern route when they withdraw. We had better march out through the Northern Gate. By travelling through

T'ien-ch'ang and Liu-ho districts, we are not likely to be molested.

[*Soldiers enter with banners.*]

**Kao:**  Let us proceed.

**Hou** [*sings*] :
  It is so long since I have heard from home.
  Like a lone lost raven, I have dreamt of that distant
    garden.
  Now I return with fellow-travellers, like a floating cloud;
  The yearning of three years is about to be assuaged.

**Kao** [*sings*] :
  At the head of our great army,
  We shall pass many a misty town and willow-clad station.
  I must dissemble my ancient pride,
  While we creep through perilous gorges.

**Hou** and **Kao** together [*singing*] :
  Looking back, we no longer see
  Level hills and desolate temples.

**Kao:**
  Over the trees, the setting sun glows on our waving banners.

**Hou:**
  Northward bound, I shall tread familiar ground.

**Kao:**
  I shall defend the mighty river's bend.

**Hou:**
  Though this may prove to be our journey's end.

---

Interlude (Supplementary Scene):

# A Quiet Chat

### 1644, SEVENTH MONTH

[*Gongs, drums, and war-cries are audible behind the stage. An* **old** *man in white cap and hempen clothes enters, a bundle on his back.*]

**Old man:**
> When will the warring host stop galloping?
> I am alone in this vast universe,
> A white-haired traveller by the riverside,
> My sleeves all drenched with tears of crimson blood.

> [*He pauses and wails aloud. A **young man** dressed as a mountaineer
> enters with baggage on his back.*]

**Young man:**
> Smoke hides the village in the fading sunlight,
> And rainclouds loom over the cold dark river.

> [*A **merchant** also enters with baggage on his back.*]

**Merchant:**
> Every year I have travelled on this road,
> But war has made it hazardous and strange.

**Young man:** Greetings! As we are both going to Nanking, we had
better keep company, for the hour is late.

**Merchant:** Yes, during bad times like these, with battles raging
and soldiers running amok, the road has become dangerous.
We had better stick together. Why does that old gentleman
stand weeping and wailing apart?

**Young man** [*to **old man***]: Are you lost, sir, or is a member of
your family missing?

**Old man:** No, no. I have come all the way from Peking. While
passing through Honan I fell in with the troops of Kao Chieh,
a frightful rabble. It was very hard to slip past them. Though
I have safely crossed the river, I am haunted by tragic
memories. Seeing so many refugees on the road flying for
their lives, I could not help weeping. [*Wipes his tears.*]

**Young man:** So that is what upsets you. It is indeed lamentable.

**Merchant:** I long to hear about recent events in Peking. Let us
find an inn for the night so that we may rest and discuss
them.

**Old man:** Right willingly. My legs are getting weak. I need an
early rest.

**Young man:** Yonder there's an inn whose walls still seem to be
standing. We might try that.

[*They enter, deferring to each other.*]

Old man [*looking up*] :  That's a fine bean trellis.

Young man:  Let us set down our baggage and sit beneath this bean trellis for a comfortable chat.

Landlord [*entering*] :  The inn is newly plastered, but I don't get any younger. Do you want any supper, gentlemen?

All:  No thanks!

Young man:  Please bring some wine with pickled beans and melon. [*To others*] :  Let me be your host.

Old man:  I should not put you to such inconvenience.

Merchant:  All men are brothers within the four seas. Let's accept his hospitality, and take our turn later.

[*Landlord brings wine and refreshments. The three sit drinking.*]

Old man:  We have met by chance, and I should be glad to learn your honourable names and your errands in Nanking.

Young man:  My name is Lan Ying, and I'm a painter by profession. I'm going to Nanking to visit some friends.

Merchant:  My name is Ts'ai Yi-so, and for generations my family have been booksellers in Nanking. Having collected some debts in this neighbourhood, I'm on my way back. May I know your honourable name? What made you leave Peking in so desperate a plight?

Old man:  I was an officer of the Imperial Guard in the old capital. Chang Wei is my name.

Ts'ai:  Forgive me for not realizing that Your Honour was an officer.

Lan:  Please tell us why you have travelled so far south.

Chang:  On the nineteenth day of the third month, the bandits entered Peking. His Majesty, the late Emperor Ch'ung-chen, hanged himself on Coal Hill, and the Empress Chou took her own life, the blessed martyr. On climbing down from the city wall with a few of my guards, we discovered their mortal remains and carried them outside Tung Hua Gate, where I performed a simple funeral ceremony. I myself guarded the sacred tablets.

Lan:  But where were all the high ministers and officials?

**Chang**: Not one was to be seen. When the bandit chief Li Tzu-ch'eng was searching for court officials to procure supplies for his men, he found me and put me in prison under prolonged torture. At last, when I had surrendered all my family possessions, I was allowed to wear mourning and tend the sacred tablets. All other officials had fled or gone into hiding or been imprisoned or killed. In some cases individuals were sacrificed, in others whole families were martyred.

**Lan**: Such loyal officials are worthy of the highest admiration!

**Chang**: But many turned traitor and paid homage to the bandit usurper.

**Ts'ai**: Such curs deserve no mercy.

**Chang** [*weeping*]: How heart-rending that the coffins of the Emperor and Empress should be buried by the road with none to tend them! [*All burst into tears.*] Finally, on the third of the fourth month, the Ministry of Ceremonies obtained permission to move the coffins to the Imperial Mausoleum. I led the procession with the funeral banner. Fortunately, on reaching Ch'ang-p'ing district, a local official collected three hundred strings of cash to re-open the old tomb of Lady T'ien and bury the coffins there, while I remained to look after the burning of incense. When summer began, the bandits were driven from the capital. Funds were raised, and the memorial hall, monuments, walls, and causeways were built for the Emperor Ch'ung-chen's tomb, like those of the other twelve Emperors. That surpassed all expectation; in my relief I did not wait till the buildings were completed. With my own hand I wrote inscriptions for the monument and the sacred tablets. Then I started on my journey south to make a report to the people and government in Nanking.

**Lan**: Well done, well done! If you had not been there, sir, the Emperor Ch'ung-chen would have had no one to watch over his tomb!

**Ts'ai**: What happened to the Heir Apparent and his two brothers?

**Chang**: There has been no news of the two princes, but I heard that the Heir Apparent travelled south by sea. Perhaps he was killed on the way. [*Weeps.*]

**Lan**: I heard that a message was sent from Peking to Minister Shih K'o-fa, censuring the ministers and generals of the fallen regime for making no effort to attend the burial or to avenge his late Majesty. Minister Shih wrote a reply and sent the high official Tso Mao-ti in deep mourning to Peking to pay homage to the late Emperor.

Chang: I met Tso on the way. We clasped hands and nearly cried our hearts out.

[*Loud thunder and wind offstage.*]

Landlord [*entering with a lamp*] : A storm has risen. You had better come quickly indoors.

All [*cover their heads with their long sleeves and rush indoors, exclaiming*] : What a violent downpour!

Chang: Now that it is evening, I shall have to burn incense.

Ts'ai: For whom will you pray?

Chang: His Majesty has not been dead a year, so I am still in mourning. Every day and night I burn incense, kowtow, and bewail him. [*He produces incense burner and incense, places them on a bench, washes his hands before lighting the incense, and kneels facing the north, bowing twice. While kneeling, he says*] : Great Emperor and most sage Majesty! On this fifteenth day of the seventh month, your orphaned servant Chang Wei prostrates himself and offers you incense.

[*Wind and thunder offstage;* **Chang** *prostrates himself and cries aloud.*]

Lan [*to Ts'ai*] : Come, we two from the outer wilderness should also join in worship and lamentation.

[*All kneel and cry together, then prostrate themselves, rise, and bow twice.*]

Lan: Old Master, you must be exhausted after so long a journey. You should retire to rest.

Ts'ai: Let us do likewise.

[*All unpack their baggage.*]

Lan: The rain and wind continue. We may be prevented from travelling tomorrow.

Chang: It rains or shines according to Heaven's will. Man cannot foretell.

Ts'ai: Does Your Honour remember the names of those martyred officials you mentioned?

Chang: Why do you ask this?

Ts'ai: I should like my bookshop to publish some popular ballads to celebrate their patriotic deeds.

Chang: That is a fine idea. I have kept their names in a notebook. Tomorrow I shall give it to you.

Ts'ai: Thank you kindly.

Lan: But those who surrendered to the bandits and became their tools should be exposed to public execration.

Chang: I have noted their names also; you shall have them tomorrow.

Ts'ai: I'll be duly grateful.

> [*All fall asleep. Ghosts moan behind the stage. Chang wakes up and listens.*]

Chang: How strange. There are sounds of moaning and wailing in the midst of the storm. What can they be? [*Several hideous ghosts enter, leaping and howling. Chang peers through the window, exclaiming*]: Terrible, terrible. The ghosts of those who died in battle, some without heads and others without feet. But why are they here? [*Exeunt ghosts. Chang falls asleep. Soft music behind the stage. Chang wakes and listens*]: I hear music outside the window and the galloping of horses. [*He opens the door and sees a procession, first the dead Emperor and Empress in chariots, followed by ministers and officials with banners on horseback. The soft music continues. Chang goes out and kneels*]: Long live Your Majesties! Your orphaned servant Chang Wei is here to salute you. [*Exit the whole procession. Chang rises and calls aloud*]: Your Imperial Majesties, why cannot your orphaned servant follow your retinue? [*Bows and weeps. Lan and Ts'ai wake up.*]

Lan and Ts'ai: Already it is dawn. Why does Your Honour cry out? Is it time for burning incense?

Chang [*tearfully*]: It was extraordinary. While asleep, I heard sounds of lamentation. Looking through the window, I saw the ghosts of those who died in battle.

**Lan**: Last night was All Souls' Festival.[1] They must all have wandered abroad in hope of salvation.

**Chang**: But something even stranger occurred.

**Ts'ai**: Pray, what was that?

**Chang**: I heard cavalry, drums, and trumpets, and soft music. On opening the door I could see the late Emperor and Empress going east with a procession of martyred officials, as if on their way to Heaven. I lingered by the road until they vanished, and I could not repress my tears.

**Lan**: It is only natural that their Majesties should go to Heaven, but it was entirely owing to Your Honour's great loyalty that they revealed themselves to you.

**Chang**: I have made a solemn vow to hold a memorial service in a beautiful part of Nanking on the fifteenth day of the seventh month next year. A sacrifice will be offered to their Majesties, and a prayer for the salvation of all martyrs. Would you two gentlemen contribute toward the service?

**Ts'ai**: Of course I'll share the expenses with you.

**Chang**: Good man, good man! When I buy books and paintings in Nanking, I'm sure I shall see more of you.

**Ts'ai**: I hope so.

**Lan**: Now let us pack and continue on our journey.

**All** [*recite*]:
The rain has washed the trees a brighter green;
In the chill dawn, we start beside the river.
The crows caw on and on over desolate tombs,
Sophora petals fall from palace ruins.
Why is the spirit of the Imperial heirs so feeble?
Why are the heads of the generals bowed?
Leaving the central plain, through battlefields,
We totter weeping on our weary way.

---

1. All Souls' Festival or *Chung-yuan*, fifteenth day of the seventh month, when sacrifices were made to the ancestors and ancestral graves were swept.

# PART II

## Prologue to Scene 21

### 1644, EIGHTH MONTH

[*Enter the old **Master of Ceremonies** in a broad robe and felt cap.*]

**Master of Ceremonies** [*sings*] :
> The rain-swept autumn streets now glitter clean,
> And crimson leaves adorn the urban scene.
> Who has an extra pot of rouge to spare,
> To give to the actresses as they prepare?

[*Recites*] :

> All done with family cares,
> In this garden, cup in hand,
> I relish the days of peace
> And watch *The Peach Blossom Fan*.

**Voices from backstage**: Venerable Sir, are you returning to see this play at the Garden of Tranquillity Theatre?

**Master of Ceremonies**: Indeed I am.

**Voices**: You saw the first part yesterday. What did you think of the performance?

**Master of Ceremonies**: It struck me as both pleasurable and painful. It made me laugh aloud for no special reason, and weep copiously without knowing why, as if it had been written by Ssu-ma C'hien[1] and interpreted by that prodigious actor Tung Fang-shuo.[2] Changes in time and space have blurred the

---

1. For Ssu-ma Ch'ien, see Scene 1, n. 6.
2. Tung Fang-shuo, born 160 B.C., semi-legendary wit who was appointed Censor by the Han emperor Wu-ti. "On one occasion he drank off some elixir of immortality which belonged to the Emperor, and the latter in a rage ordered him put to death. But Tung-fang Shuo smiled and said, "If the elixir was genuine, your Majesty can do me no

significance of some episodes, and prejudice may blind a few
to the underlying truth. [*Sings*] :
Time whizzes like an arrow: yet again,
Cicadas chirp in willow groves, and lotus pools
    waft fragrance.
Idly I stroll beside the stream, in flimsy garments
    clad,
After a rainy night in the festive Northern City.[3]
Again the soul drifts from the sleeper's pillow
To the shady yard or hamlet, where I hear
The washerwomen pounding with their mallets,
And the hum of autumn insects from the moss,
Gripping the heart, as I saunter with my stick
Along paths all strewn with leaves and fallen
    wisteria.
A wrinkled skin covers my bony limbs,
Too oft exposed to bitter frost and snow;
The hair is silver-white upon my brow.
Steeped in autumnal sadness, the vagrant's gloom,
Yet still alive in this resort of pleasure,
I almost begrudge this ancient body of mine.
Family cares, desire for fame and profit,
Are as floating clouds or a running brook to me.
The fury of lords, the rage of ministers,
Are as withered weeds that rustle in the sunset.
I gaze at spring unseeing; like wind-blown ashes
Are the pictures of Han palaces I recall . . .
When the chess-game's played, and all the guests
    are scattered,
Who cares which won the victory, white or black?
Historic tombs and temples lie in ruins,
And hills crumble, though fragile flowers return.
All men are gone; the darkening mist descends.
With whom shall I discourse of doughty deeds?
The red sun rolls away the yellow dust,
And even poetry is engulfed by time.
The lawn where dancers of Wu swayed to and fro,
Whirling their sleeves with memorable ease,

---

harm; if it was not, what harm have I done?" (H. A. Giles, *Chinese Biographical
Dictionary*).
   3. The traditional theatre district since the Sung dynasty.

Is gone like Hsuan-tsung of T'ang[4] without a
   trace.
The loftiest poets lay down their pens and sob.
Before the sweetest melodies are sung,
Barely an inch remains of the dripping candle;
Before another scene begins,
Costumes and makeup must be changed again.
Writing is not reality; acts are vain.
He only is wise who knows the very instant
When he should raise the wine-cup to his lips.
Susceptible, despite my load of years,
I steal an amorous glance at crimson skirts,
Heedless if peach flowers mock me from the fan.
In bygone years, reality was the play;
The play becomes reality today.
Twice have I watched its progress: Heaven
   preserves
This passive gazer with his cold clear eyes.

[*Speaks*] : Now here comes Ma Shih-ying; please watch closely.

[*He bows and exits.*]

SCENE 21
# The Invented Match
1644, TENTH MONTH

[*Enter Ma Shih-ying with steward and retinue.*]

**Ma** [*sings*] :
   I devote all my care
   To the Imperial vessels in the temple hall,
   Distributing favours and penalties
   To suit my varied interests.
   I cling tenaciously to office,
   Striking sparks from dry timber to kindle cold
      ashes.

4. Hsuan-tsung or Ming-huang, the "Illustrious Emperor," reigned 713-756 over the most brilliant court of the entire T'ang dynasty.

[*Speaks*] : As Prime Minister, I wield the greatest power in the land. The new Emperor prefers to do nothing, so I let him wallow in every luxury. I do whatever I please, since half the court are at my beck and call. I have given much thought and skill to winning fresh honours and confounding my foes. Those who say that too many breeds of horses raise too much dust do not realize that I can grant life or death at will, since the Emperor is my ward. [*He laughs.*] These last few days have been uneventful, and the plum flowers are in bloom. I'm giving a banquet in the Garden of Myriad Jades. The greater the number of guests, the greater my prestige. Life was meant to be enjoyed. Gather riches and fame while you may! [*Calls*] : Steward, remind me who has been invited.

**Steward**: The guests are all fellow provincials of Your Excellency. They include Councillor Yang Wen-ts'ung, Censor Yüeh Ch'i-chieh, the new Director of Military Supplies T'ien Yang, and your adviser Juan Ta-ch'eng.

**Ma** [*dubiously*] : But Juan Ta-ch'eng is not my fellow-provincial.

**Steward**: He has been telling people that he is closely related to Your Excellency.

**Ma** [*laughing*] : In a sense, that may be true. Since the party consists of old friends, let the banquet be served in the Plum Studio. It is already well past noon. Where are my guests?

**Steward**: They have been awaiting your call in the antechamber. [*Calls*] : His Excellency is ready to greet his guests.

**Yang** and **Juan** [*enter, reciting*] :
A steward's voice may bear prodigious weight
When it resounds within the Premier's gate.          [*They
    greet Ma.*]

**Ma**: Why do you behave like strangers? Brother-in-law Yang, you're a near relation of mine. Why didn't you enter at once?

**Yang**: Even close relations should observe decorum.

**Ma**: Don't be pompous. [*To **Juan**] : And you are such an old crony of mine. Why did you wait until you were announced?

**Juan**: This is the Prime Minister's mansion. How could I be so informal?

**Ma**: You are both too ceremonious. [*All sit down. Ma sings*] :

Now the world belongs to us.

7. Prime Minister Ma Shih-ying to Yang Wen-ts'ung
and Juan Ta-ch'eng: "You are both too ceremonious."

Under the blossoming trees,
We exchange confidences without reserve.
Bosom friends and close relations
Need never cool their heels outside my door.
Never doubt that you and I
Have sprung from the same root.
Wherever we are,
We rekindle our friendship with wine.
Why should we fuss about rank?
Let not my position as Prime Minister
Keep away my favourite guests.

[*Tea is served. Ma bows politely, saying*] : It is rather chilly.
Let us warm ourselves.

**Yang** and **Juan** [*bowing*] : Delighted, Your Excellency.

**Ma:** I have just returned from Court, yet I find it is past noon.
The days are getting too short and the nights too long.

**Juan** and **Yang** [*bowing*] : The seasons vary with regularity. It is a
good omen. [*Though they finish drinking, they hold their
cups until Ma puts his down.*]

**Ma** [*to Yang*] : I was expecting Masters Yueh and T'ien. What has
happened to them?

**Yang:** Master Yueh is suffering from piles and begs to be excused.
Master T'ien is leaving for his new post tomorrow. After
escorting his family to the boat, he will come round to say
goodbye.

**Ma:** That's a pity. We shall have to dine without them. [*Music is
played while they take their seats, each at a separate table.
Ma sings*] :

After paying homage to the Emperor,
My sleeves still smell of incense.
I have changed into light fur coat and crimson shoes.
The buds of the plum have burst into scarlet
    blossoms:
With such brilliant guests I can enjoy the scene
    at leisure,
Discussing poems and paintings through the night.
Alas, how few achieve such intimate delight.

**Juan:** May I inquire which guests have already had the honour of
being entertained in this mansion?

Ma: Only members of our circle, but none so accomplished as you. Steward, bring me a list of my previous guests.

> [*Steward presents the list. Juan examines it and reads several names aloud.*]

Yang: All these are renowned for their talents.

Ma: They are all men I have promoted to high office.

Juan [*bowing*]: Even those like me, who were deprived of their former posts, have been generously sustained by Your Excellency, our noble patron. That you should have collected such a galaxy of talent proves that you are as great a Prime Minister as the ancient Duke of Chou.[1]

Ma [*bowing*]: I am unworthy of the compliment. Both of you are so superior to the others that I shall make a point of recommending you for higher promotion tomorrow.

> [*Yang bows and Juan kneels before him.*]

Yang and Juan: We thank Your Excellency for all your kindness.

Juan [*sings*]:
Like a forgotten arrow flying to Heaven,
Like a buried sword unsheathed again for battle,
I am reinstated in official rank.
"Dog-skin among the fox fur," some will say;
Yet after banqueting in this great mansion,
I feel my face caressed by balmy breezes.
The favour now so graciously bestowed
Will prove incalculably beneficial.

Ma: Remove the dishes and bring more wine. Let us indulge in a heart-to-heart talk. [*They sit at the same table.*] Pray help yourselves and excuse me for not pouring. Let us all be quite informal.

Yang and Juan: We must not put you to trouble.

> [*Two servants enter to acknowledge the gratuities distributed by Yang and Juan.*]

---

1. Duke of Chou, died 1105 B.C.; his regency during the minority of the second emperor of the Chou dynasty is held by orthodox historians to have been ideal. In traditional belief, the whole administrative organization of the Chinese empire, which remained a pattern for thousands of years, was planned by this remarkable man.

**Ma** [*to Yang* and *Juan*] :  You shouldn't have done that. I merely asked you to enjoy the flowers with me. Besides, I haven't engaged a troupe of actors to entertain you. Why do you insist on being so punctilious?

**Juan:**  My private players are often idle. If Your Excellency would care to have them, they are entirely at your disposal.

**Ma:**  I had better employ them for other guests. You know them far too well. [*Sings*] :

Yours is a remarkable company,
The latest songs and dances at their command;
But as these are your own inventions,
They would hardly entertain you.

**Juan** [*sings*] :
The hills and water in your famous park
Provide you with the music of nature.
What need for tunes on string and bamboo?

**Yang:**  Famous flowers should be enjoyed with fair women. Now that the plum blossoms are out, theatricals are superfluous, but a lovely singing-girl would be a welcome addition. [*Sings*] :

The scarlet buds of the plum tree open;
The voice of a lovely girl would add perfection.

**Ma** [*laughing*] :  Dear brother-in-law, I see that you are amorously inclined. Do you want to be another Mayor of Soochow? [2] [*Sings*] :

The Mayor of Soochow's soul
Stirs with longing for a pretty mistress.

[*Speaks*] :  Well, that's easy to arrange. Steward! Send for some singing-girls as soon as possible.

**Steward:**  Does Your Excellency wish for those from the Old House or from the Pearl Bazaar?

**Ma** [*to Yang*] :  Which do you prefer, brother-in-law?

**Yang:**  I have seen most of them, but few have any real distinction. Only Fragrant Princess of the Old House has exceptional talent. She can even sing "The Peony Pavilion."

---

2. Liu Yü-hsi, a T'ang poet of pronounced amorous tendencies.

**Ma**: Steward, go and fetch her. [*Exit **Steward**.*]

**Juan** [*to **Yang***]: Is that the girl Master T'ien wished to take as a concubine for three hundred silver taels?

**Yang**: Quite so.

**Ma**: Why didn't she accept?

**Yang**: The wench is absurdly foolish. She wants to preserve her chastity for Hou Fang-yü. That is why she stubbornly refused T'ien's proposal. I went several times to persuade her, but she would not even come downstairs. It was most annoying.

**Ma** [*angrily*]: What impudence for such a slave! [*Sings*]:

Does she not fear the teeth and claws of rank
That can crush the humble like lice?
Laughable, the fate in store for her,
A moth to the candle-flame.

**Juan**: It is all because she was spoiled by Hou Fang-yü. Even I was once insulted by her.

**Ma** [*more angrily*]: This is preposterous. The new Director of Military Supplies cannot buy a harlot with three hundred taels of silver! [*Sings*]:

How could a whole basket of pearls
Fail to purchase a moth-browed hussy?

**Juan**: Moreover, Master T'ien is a fellow provincial of Your Excellency. This insult to him is a serious matter.

**Ma**: Precisely. When she arrives I shall give her what she deserves.

**Steward** [*returning*]: Your Excellency, I have been to the Old House to enquire for Fragrant Princess, but they told me she was sick and confined to her chamber.

**Ma**: Whether she is sick or not, you collect a few men, take some money and clothes to her, and force her to consent. [*Sings*]:

No need to call in the old matchmaker in the moon.
A little red silk,
A decorated litter,
And a gift or two will do the trick.

[*Speaks*]: Never mind the hussy's caprices. Just drag her to the litter and bundle her onto Master T'ien's boat this evening. [*Sings*]:

In his rapture he will fancy her
The River Goddess on the misty waves.

[*Exeunt Steward and servants.*]

**Juan:**  That's the best course, and a mighty good joke too!

**Yang:**  It is getting late, so I shall wish you goodnight.

**Ma:**  The fun has only started. Why leave so early?

**Juan:**  We should not keep Your Excellency up too late. [*Juan and Yang both bow.*]

**Ma:**  Let me show you to the door.

**Yang** and **Juan:**  We dare not put you to such inconvenience. [*They bow thrice. Exit Ma.*]

**Juan** [*to Yang*]:  Though the Prime Minister has so gallantly sponsored the cause of his fellow countryman, you should also lend a hand, good brother Yang.

**Yang:**  What do you mean?

**Juan:**  The Old House is a favourite haunt of yours. Why don't you go there yourself, drag the wench downstairs, and speed her on her way?

**Yang:**  We shouldn't deal too harshly with her.

**Juan:**  Too harshly! It seems to me far too lenient. When I consider her treatment of me, I would gladly put her to death. [*Sings*]:

To satisfy so deep a grudge,
Gladly I would despoil the flowers and willows.

[*Speaks*]:  Now all Hou's efforts to keep her will come to nought. [*Sings*]:

He will see her carry her lute to another man.

**Juan:**
When will her noble lord return?

**Yang:**
Close-curtained and alone she waits.

**Juan:**
But she will hear the storms of love,

**Yang:**
And feel their force before dawn breaks.

# The Rejected Suit

## 1644, TENTH MONTH

[*Steward and young servant enter holding lanterns inscribed "The Prime Minister." Others carry clothes, silver, and a litter.*]

**All** [*recite*]:
    The Old Matchmaker has not been sent down from the moon,
    But the Go-between Star has been seen here below.[1]

**Steward:** Fragrant Princess must be compelled to marry by order of the Prime Minister. Let us make haste.

**Young Servant:** I have heard that there are both a mother and daughter living in the Old House. How can we tell them apart?

**Yang** [*entering quickly*]: Wait a minute, you two. I shall accompany you.

**Steward** [*greeting him*]: If Your Excellency will be so kind, there will certainly be no mistake. [*They walk on.*]

**Steward** and **Yang** [*reciting*]:
    The moon beams on the azure river,
    The frost gleams on the wooden bridge.
    Here we are. Let us knock at the door. [*They knock.*]

**Maid** [*entering*]: As soon as I close the back door I have to open the front one, like the master of a posting-station. Who's there?

**Steward:** Open quickly.

**Maid:** Mercy on us! Lanterns, torches, a litter, horses, and attendants. Is Your Honour Yang holding a parade?

**Yang:** Fie, run and call your mistress.

**Maid** [*loudly*]: Madam, His Honour Yang is here.

---

1. The Old Man in the Moon ties together the feet of future marriage partners with an invisible red thread. The Go-between Star is a device of the fortune-tellers.

**Li Chen-li** [*entering*]: Where has your Honour been banqueting this evening?

**Yang**: I have come from the Prime Minister to bring you glad tidings.

**Li**: Please explain.

**Yang**: A very high official has asked to marry your daughter. [*Sings*]:

Behold the gorgeous litter,
See the garments glitter,
The servants how they pour
In brocade outside the door!
Behold the silver crowns
And the rich embroidered gowns!

**Li**: Who sent them here? Why weren't we told in advance?

**Yang** [*sings*]:
Don't you see the lanterns, pair by pair,
Bearing the insignia
Of the Prime Minister himself?

**Li**: Is it the Prime Minister who wants to marry her?

**Yang**: No. [*Sings*]:

Her lot will be to offer cups of jade
To Master Ts'ao, Director of Supplies,
The Prime Minister's close kinsman.

**Li**: We have already rejected this T'ien's proposal. Why should we be pestered again?

**Servant** [*arriving with silver, says to* **Mistress Li**]: Are you the Fragrant Princess? Please take this gift of money.

**Li**: I must run upstairs and talk things over.

**Steward** [*appears and says*]: This is the Prime Minister's command. There's no time for discussion. Take the money and come to the litter at once.

**Yang** [*to* **Steward**]: She will never dare refuse. You wait outside. I'll look after the money while she gets ready.

**Steward** and **Servant**: Let us find a couple of wenches and have some fun.

[*Exeunt.* **Mistress Li**, **Yang**, *and maid go upstairs with the clothes and the money.*]

守樓

8. Prime Minister's Steward:
"Here we are. Let us knock at the door."

**Yang** [*calling*] :  Fragrant Princess, are you asleep?

**Fragrant Princess:**  What is all the hubbub about?

**Li:**  Have you no idea?

**Fragrant Princess** [*to Yang*] :  Does Your Honour wish to hear me sing?

**Li:**  This is no occasion for music.  [*Sings*] :

> In a violent rush,
> They thrust nuptial gifts upon us,
> Resolved to ravish my daughter from me.
> How can we escape their grasp?
> Will no substitute suffice?

**Fragrant Princess:**  This is terrible. I'm frightened to death. What cursed fiend is threatening me now?

**Li:**  It is the same T'ien Yang, and the Prime Minister is backing his efforts. [*Sings*] :

> How hapless is the fate of a singing-girl!
> At any moment blown away
> Like a poor willow catkin.

[*To Yang*] :  Your Honour has been so kind to us in the past. Why are you so cruel now?

**Yang:**  I am blameless in this matter. On hearing that you had rejected T'ien Yang, the Prime Minister lost his temper and sent fierce retainers to enforce his will. I was afraid they might treat you roughly, so I came along to protect you.

**Li:**  Please continue to be kind and think of some way to save us.

**Yang:**  To my mind, three hundred silver *taels* are nothing to sneeze at. Nor does it seem beneath Fragrant Princess's dignity to marry the Director of Military Supplies. Besides, how can she resist two such powerful officials?

**Li:**  Perhaps Your Honour is right. In the circumstances, I don't see how we can persist in our refusal. Dear daughter, please be reasonable. It would be wiser to pack and go along with them.

**Fragrant Princess** [*angrily*] :  How can you even suggest such a thing, Mother? When I married my lord Hou, His Honour Yang was the matchmaker, and you presided over the nuptial ceremony. The token of my solemn vow is still in my keeping. [*She fetches the fan and says*]: My lord wrote this poem as a pledge. Your Honour has seen it. Have you forgotten? [*Sings*]:

Our vow is sacred;
I shall devote my whole life to my lord.
My heart will never change,
Fixed as the poem on this silken fan.
Had we been together only a single night,
Our love would last forever.

**Yang**: But Master Hou came to grief and had to fly. Now nobody knows where he is. If he does not return in three years' time, will you wait for him all your life?

**Fragrant Princess**: I'll wait for him three years, ten years, a hundred years. Never shall I marry this T'ien Yang.

**Yang**: Mercy, what a temper! You are behaving as you did when you refused the trousseau, scattering your hairpins, tearing your dress, and cursing old Juan.

**Fragrant Princess**: Both Juan and T'ien belonged to the eunuch Wei's clique. Having refused Juan's bribe, why should I embrace T'ien Yang?

**Voices from back stage**: It is getting late. Make haste and enter the litter. We have strict orders to carry you to the boat.

**Li**: Dear daughter, pray consider your future. Think of the security you will enjoy at T'ien's house.

**Fragrant Princess**: That means nothing whatever to me. I am determined to keep my chastity for my lord. [*Sings*]:

I would rather freeze and starve
Than leave this tower.

**Li**: As things are, I cannot let her have her way. Your Honour, please set the gifts down while we help her to get dressed. [*Mistress Li tries to dress Fragrant Princess's hair, and Yang attempts to help her on with a gown. Fragrant Princess struggles and beats them off with her fan.*]

**Yang**: How fierce. She uses her love-token as a murderous sword.

**Li**: Let us try to get her dressed and carry her downstairs. [*Yang attempts to carry her.*]

**Fragrant Princess** [*crying*]: Even if I die, I shall not leave this room. [*She falls to the ground wailing, and knocks her head against it till she faints.*]

**Li**: Alas, alas! Do rouse yourself, dear daughter. You have ruined your fair complexion. [*To Yang*]: Look, she has bled so much that she has stained her fan. [*She hands the fan to a maid, saying*]: We shall have to put her to bed. [*The maid carries Fragrant Princess out.*]

**Voices from backstage**: It is now the third watch of night. After grabbing the money, you will not come to the litter. We shall put you under arrest.

**Yang** [*calls downstairs*]: Wait a minute, steward. It is very distressing for a mother and daughter to part. Don't be too rough with them!

**Li**: Now that my daughter has fainted, with all this commotion outside I don't know where to turn or what to do.

**Yang**: Remember the power of the Prime Minister. If you provoke him further, resentment may drive him to extremes. Then your life as well as your daughter's will be in danger.

**Li**: I implore Your Honour to save us.

**Yang**: I can see no way out unless we attempt a makeshift.

**Li**: Please explain.

**Yang**: For a singing-girl to marry into an honourable family is generally considered a piece of good luck. T'ien's rank is superior, and his family is rich. Since Fragrant Princess will not have him, I think you should take her place.

**Li** [*shocked*]: But that is out of the question. Besides, how could I ever bear to leave my daughter?

**Yang**: If they come to arrest you, you will have to bear the wrench.

**Li** [*stupefied*]: So be it then. Let Fragrant Princess keep to her room, I shall have to go. But it isn't safe. I fear they will recognize me.

**Yang**: I shall maintain that you are Fragrant Princess. Nobody will dare contradict me.

**Li:** Then I shall have to dress myself up as a bride. [*She proceeds to do so, calling backstage*]: Dear daughter, I beg you to take care of yourself. I am going in your stead. Keep the three hundred silver *taels* for me. Don't squander them recklessly. [*Sings*]:

Red lanterns light the street below;
Out in the night, a bitter wind will blow.
Once swept away, the flower may not return.

**Steward** and **Young Servant** [*entering with litter and lanterns*]: Hurrah, at last the bride appears. Please step into the litter.

**Li** [*to Yang*]: Farewell, Your Honour.

**Yang:** Take care of yourself on the journey. We are bound to meet again.

**Li:** I hope Your Honour will spend the night here and look after my unhappy daughter.

**Yang:** I promise to do so.

**Li** [*entering the litter, sings*]:
Henceforth my friends early and late
May but glance at me from the road.
It is hard to step out of the gate,
Once inside an official's abode.
I go to my uncertain fate
Lacking all knowledge of my mate.          [*Exit.*]

**Yang** [*laughing*]: Now Mistress Li will be married into a respectable family, and Fragrant Princess will keep her chastity. Brother Juan is avenged, and the Prime Minister's prestige is saved. All's well that ends well, thanks to my brilliant plan! But the parting of mother and daughter was sad to witness. [*Sings*]:

A hurried switch of partners in the night,
A melancholy song as parting nears.
Now in the tower of swallows, sore distress,
And only the pillow's chill to soothe her fears.

# The Message on the Fan

1644, ELEVENTH MONTH

[*Fragrant Princess enters, looking pale and wan.*]

**Fragrant Princess** [*sings*]:
  The cold wind pierces my thin gown,
  I am too weary to burn incense.
  A streak of bright blood still glistens on my eyebrow.
  My languid soul floats over my lone shadow;
  My life is spring gossamer in this frosty moonlit tower.
  The night seems endless:
  When dawn appears, the same grief lingers on.

[*Speaks*]: In a moment of despair, I tore my flesh to defend
my virtue. Alone, I peek and pine in my empty room. I have
lost my sole companion. [*Sings*]:

  Long Bridge is wrapped in cloud and frozen snow,
  My tower is closed and visitors are few.
  Beyond the balustrade, a line of wild geese;
  Outside the curtain, icicles are dripping.
  The brazier is burnt out, all perfume faded —
  I shrink and shiver in the biting wind.

[*Speaks*]: Though I live in a pleasure resort, the flowers and
moon have ceased to bring me joy. I have done with worldly
vanities. [*Sings*]:

  My 'broidered window curtain is forlorn,
  Though the parrot's foolish voice cries "Serving tea,"
  And the white cat sleeps serenely on its cushion.
  So loose my skirt, it flaps about my waist;
  So tired my feet, their phoenix-patterned shoes
  Feel tossed upon the crests of boisterous waves.
  Excess of grief breeds sickness. Love and joy
  Have fled this chamber never to return.

[*Speaks*]: I never cease thinking of my beloved lord. Since
his flight I have had no news of him, but I shall preserve my
chastity for his sake. [*Sings*]:

In a twinkling, our song of rapture was interrupted;
At midnight the passionate lovers had to part.
Neither at Swallow Cliff nor Peach-leaf Wharf[1]
Shall my true love be seen.
Over the mazy clouds and windy mountains
The solitary swan has taken flight.
Each year the blossoms of the plum return,
Each year my love is ever more remote.
From my balcony, I gaze into the distance,
My falling tears like pools of autumn rain
which only the harsh wind will ever dry.

[*Speaks*]: The Prime Minister's sycophants would have forced me to marry, but how could I betray my lord? [*Sings*]:

They persecute me, feeble blossom afloat on the mist,
Helpless before the arrogance of these ministers.
But to preserve my purity, jade without flaw,
Gladly I wound the flower-like bloom of my cheeks.

[*Speaks*]: My poor mother is most to be pitied! Suddenly she left without a word, to take my place on that disastrous night. Her bed remains, but when will she return? [*Sings*]:

Like a peach petal adrift in a snowstorm,
Like a willow catkin wafted by the wind,
Hiding her face behind her sleeve, she left at dead
    of night.
Now I am left alone,
No one to brush the dust from my coverlet,
Desolate,
A flower that opens for none to view.

[*Speaks*]: When I think of all this, I am heartbroken. [*She weeps and sings*]:

A broken heart,
How many tears that fall!
And never a companion's cheery call,
Only the knocking of the curtain-hooks.

---

1. Famous beauty spots where lovers used to meet.

[*Speaks*]: I shall take out my precious fan again and read my beloved's poem. Ah me, it is stained with blood. What shall I do? [*Sings*]:

The bloodstains spread in bright confusion,
Some thick, some thin, some heavy and some light;
Not the cuckoo's tears of blood,
But raindrops reddened by the peachbloom of my cheeks
Spattering this silken fan.

[*Speaks*]: My lord, my lord! All this was for your sake!
[*Sings*]:

I tore my cloudy hair and bruised my limbs
Until I swooned into a world of darkness,
Like a long-buried queen beneath a hill-slope.
Dripping with blood, my body seemed to fall
As from the summit of the highest tower,
Unconscious of the voices calling me;
My melting soul past human invocation.
The red clouds darken in the setting sun:
I wake to find my pillow drenched with tears.
Sorrow is graven on my heart and brow,
Washing the rouge from my face,
Staining the silk of my robe.

[*Speaks*]: I'm so overwhelmed with weariness that I shall fall asleep at this table [*She dozes off, clutching her fan.*]

**Yang Wen-ts'ung** [*enters and recites*]:
The tower a slanting shadow throws
Over the stream, and nesting crows
Caw in the withered willow boughs.

**Su K'un-sheng** [*entering*]:
This chamber where sweet music used to flow,
Is now a hermit's cell where wild winds blow.

**Yang**: Oh Master Su, I'm so glad to see you again.

**Su**: Since Mistress Li's departure, Fragrant Princess has been living here alone. I felt anxious about her, so I came to pay her a visit.

**Yang**: The night of Mistress Li's departure, I kept vigil with Fragrant Princess till dawn. Since then I have been so occupied with official business that I have not been able to see her. [*They enter the house together.*]

**Su:** Fragrant Princess will never come downstairs. Let us go up and see her. [*Both walk upstairs to find **Fragrant Princess** asleep.*]

**Yang:** How ill and woebegone she looks in her sleep. We ought not to wake her.

**Su:** The fan lies open before her. But why is it splashed with red?

**Yang:** This was Brother Hou's gift of betrothal. She treasured it above everything in the world and was always reluctant to show it. Finding it stained with her blood, she must have intended to dry it. [*Examining it*]: The stains are still very bright. I'll paint a few leaves and twigs around them, so that it will resemble a picture of peach blossoms. Unfortunately, I lack green paint.

**Su:** If I squeeze some sap from the plant in yonder vase, perhaps you may use it instead.

**Yang:** What a clever idea. [*Su procures him some, and Yang proceeds to paint, reciting*]:

The leaves are green with the sap of a fragrant plant
To protect the blossoms dyed in a beauty's blood.

**Su:** This is the finest picture of peach blossoms I have seen.

**Yang:** It is a genuine peach blossom fan.

**Fragrant Princess** [*waking up*]: O gentlemen, forgive my lack of courtesy! Pray sit down.

**Yang:** The wound on your forehead looks almost healed. [*Laughing*]: I have brought you a little gift — on which I have painted some peach blossoms. [*Hands it to her.*]

**Fragrant Princess:** But this is my old fan. As it is covered with bloodstains, I would rather not look at it. [*Puts it in her sleeve.*]

**Su:** But there is an exquisite picture which you really ought to see.

**Fragrant Princess:** When was it painted?

**Yang:** Forgive me for not asking permission. I fear I might have spoiled it.

9. Yang Wen-ts'ung: "The stains on the fan
are still very bright. I'll paint a few leaves
and twigs around them. . . ."

**Fragrant Princess** [*opening and examining it*]: Alas, peach blossom is the most ill-fated of flowers, condemned to float forever on this fan. I thank Your Honour. You have almost painted a portrait of myself. [*Sings*]:

Each branch a swaying sorrow in the wind,
Each petal a lost soul swept by the rising tide.
Only a master's hand could render thus
A vivid line so natural, evoking
The lips of beauty and the lotus cheek.
A few bold strokes, and the tree springs to life,
Red petals and green leaves; but evil fate
Awaits the pictured flower and its possessor.

**Yang**: Now that you have this peach blossom fan, you need a partner to appreciate it with you. Why turn yourself into a widow? Do you want to be like the Moon Goddess who flew from the world?

**Fragrant Princess**: What is the use of discussing it? The famous Kuan P'an-p'an[2] was also a professional singing-girl, but she lived alone in her Swallow Tower until extreme old age.

**Su**: Supposing Master Hou returned tomorrow, would you promptly recover your spirits and come downstairs?

**Fragrant Princess**: Ah, then the whole world would be different. I should feel as if my future were spread out like a beautiful tapestry. Not only would I leave this tower, I would travel anywhere.

**Yang**: Such steadfast resolve is most unusual. Master Su, to prove your devoted relationship as teacher to pupil, would you try to find Brother Hou and bring them together again? I am sure it would be a blessing for all concerned.

**Su**: After repeated inquiries, I finally discovered that he spent half a year in Huai-an-fu with Minister Shih, whence he proceeded to Yang-chou by way of Nanking. He is at present with General Kao's army defending the Yellow River. I had intended to return to my home, so I may search for him on

---

2. Kuan P'an-p'an, brilliant dancer and singer who became the favourite of Chang Chien (died 651), a great-nephew of the founder of the T'ang dynasty. Chang held many important posts. When he died, P'an-p'an refused to marry and lived alone in the Swallow Tower for ten years.

the journey. But I should have a letter from Fragrant Princess to take with me.

**Fragrant Princess** [*to Yang*]: Though my thoughts and emotions are boundless, I have never been trained to express them in writing. Would Your Honour be so kind as to write the letter for me?

**Yang**: How could I express what lies in the depths of your heart?

**Fragrant Princess** [*pensively*]: All my fears and sorrows are associated with this fan. Perhaps it will suffice if you merely take it to him.

**Su**: What an original notion, to use a fan as a letter!

**Fragrant Princess**: I'll seal it now. [*She seals it, singing*]:

The poem he will recognize as the fruit of his
    flourishing brush,
The red blossoms he will see as a new picture.
So small a space holds the blood of a faithful heart,
Ten thousand longings bound with silken strands —
It is worth a volume of characters on paper.

**Su**: I promise to deliver it safely to his hands.

**Fragrant Princess**: When will you start on the journey, Master?

**Su**: Within the next few days.

**Fragrant Princess**: I hope you will set out as soon as possible.

**Yang**: It is time for our departure. Fragrant Princess, take care of yourself! The hardship you have suffered for purity's sake deserves the highest credit. When Brother Hou hears of it, he will certainly hasten to see you.

**Su**: I may not have time to say goodbye before I leave. Truly, a new message on the peach blossom fan.

**Yang**: An old constancy, locked in the Swallow Tower.

[*Exeunt Yang and Su.*]

**Fragrant Princess** [*weeping*]: My mother has left me, and now my dear teacher has gone. Alone in this room, my sorrows will seem eternal. [*Sings*]:

I have ceased to sing the ballads of north and south,
My lute is silent, nor do I touch the flute:

I have thrust aside my instruments, and left them to rot
  away.
If only my fan could reach him soon, and my teacher were
  on his way!
When my lord returns, upon that joyful day,
Hand in hand we shall leave the tower together.
I hope my message reaches him before the snow has melted,
Though hills and vales seem endless on the voyage.

---

SCENE 24

# The Revellers Upbraided

1645, FIRST MONTH

**Juan Ta-ch'eng** [*enters and sings*]:
  Days of ease return,
  The glamour of the Six Dynasties[1] revives,
  And mine is the charge
  Of arts and letters for all the court.
  Behold me now, resplendent
  In smart black cap, scarlet robe,
  And green-lined leather shoes.

[*Laughs and says*]: Thanks to the special friendship of the
Prime Minister, I have been invited to serve in the Inner
Court. Today I have entered my new office. What a triumph!
Luckily His Majesty has a passion for literature. Such distinguished writers as Wang To and Ch'ien Ch'ien-yi[2] have
both received high appointments, and I have also been admitted to the Emperor's literary circle. I have won His
Majesty's confidence to such an extent that there is nothing I
cannot say to him. The day before yesterday, I presented him
with four of my plays. His Majesty was so gratified that he
promptly issued a decree, ordering the Ministry of Ceremonies to select the most beautiful singers for his delecta-

---

1. On the Six Dynasties, see Scene 1, n. 7.
2. For Wang To, see Scene 4, n. 3. Ch'ien Ch'ien-yi, 1582-1664, was famous for his
library and for his anthology of Ming verse.

tion. These are to be trained to perform my *Swallow Letter*, which His Majesty regards as an expression of the new spirit pervading his reign. In my own opinion it is a difficult play to produce, owing to its extreme subtlety. If the rehearsals are entrusted to novices my reputation will suffer, so I told His Majesty that I would sooner engage experienced singing-girls. His Majesty was so appreciative of my advice that he issued a second decree, ordering a thorough search for musicians and singing-girls the length and breadth of the Ch'in-huai River. These were to be examined and allotted roles by the Ministry of Ceremonies. So far, the result has been disappointing. Not one has shown any notable talent. A conspicuous minority are old friends of Yang Wen-ts'ung, who made a special plea to have them exempted. Yesterday the Prime Minister remarked that His Majesty is very eager for the production of my play. Why should the best artists be exempted? Consequently, I have summoned them to appear in any case. As it is New Year's day, I have asked my friend Yang to join me in entertaining our patron the Prime Minister. The banquet will be served in the Pavilion of Heart's Delight, where wine will help us to enjoy the snowy landscape. I have also ordered the newly chosen singing-girls to appear. [*Recites*]:

Truly,
Pipes and singing under the willows bring back the
    glories of Sui,
Witty girls in skirts and pattens recall the beauties
    of Chin.        [*Exit.*]

>   [**Mistress Pien Yü-ching** *enters hurriedly, in the costume of a
>   Taoist nun and carrying a bundle.*]

**Pien** [*sings*]:

I was pure as a virgin in the palace of an Immortal
When an ill wind blew me among the misty flowers.
There I had to sing until my throat was hoarse,
And dance until the skirt hung loose about me.
All my life has been spent in the Cave of Witches'
    Mountain.[3]

---

3. Witches' Mountain, Wu-shan, above the Yangtze Gorges, was the site of an amorous encounter with a goddess in an early poem, and has ever since been used, as here, as a symbol for a place of sexual dalliance.

[*Speaks*]: I am dressed like this because the Imperial court is conducting a search for singing-girls. As a climax to my previous experience, it has been revealed to me that I must abandon this dusty world. Last night I took leave of my sisters. Disguised as a Taoist nun, I fled from the Old House. Now I shall seek a Taoist instructor. [*Sings*]:

East of the city, mountains fill my gaze;
The road to the world of Immortals seems endless.

[*Pien floats off the stage as in a trance. Enter the musicians
Ting Chi-chih, Shen Kung-hsien, and Chang Yen-chu.*]

**Ting** [*sings*]:

I was playing my flute on the shore of the river,
Enjoying the moon and the flowers,
Watching the shadows creep along my curtain,
When my name as a minstrel was called from the phoenix
    scroll:[4]
His Majesty's heart is thrilled with thoughts of spring.

[*Speaks*]: I have passed my sixtieth birthday, and it is years since I practised my profession. Recently I begged His Honour Yang as a personal favour to spare me from being called to the Inner Court. Why have I been summoned today?

**Shen** and **Chang**: We were also exempted, but since they have called us, what can we do but obey?

**Ting**: It is unusual for an Emperor to take much notice of musicians.

**Shen** and **Chang**: The same thought occurred to us.

**Ting**: As younger men, you may hope for a career at Court. I am too old and decrepit, and have little more to expect from this existence. All I want is to go into hiding. I trust you will keep my secret.

**Shen**: That seems sensible. To avoid coercion you will have to escape.

**Chang**: Yes — surely you will not be treated as a criminal.

**Ting**: I shall go now. Farewell. [*Walks off, singing*]:

---

4. I.e., the palace roster.

I shall return towards the far green hills,
Seeking a new path through the pine forest.

[*He stamps his foot and recites*]:

Until from this drear dusty world you flee,
From human bondage how can you be free?

[**Ting** *produces a Taoist cap and yellow sash, which he puts on. He calls to* **Chang** *and* **Shen**]: Behold, I have wakened from a Yangchow dream[5] in the guise of a Taoist priest. [*Exit, striding off in a leisurely fashion.*]

**Shen**: So he has turned Taoist. It takes a tough heart to reach such a decision.

**Chang**: Let us wait for the girls and go to the Ministry of Ceremonies together. [*They sit down. Enter the singing-girls* **K'ou Pai-men** *and* **Cheng T'o-niang**, *with attendants.*]

**Cheng**: A peach petal blown by the breeze will never bear fruit.

**K'ou**: A willow catkin swept by the tide will only meet with weeds.

[*Speaks*]: Look at old Shen and Chang gossiping over there. I wonder why they never greeted us. Let's slap them on the back.

[*They greet and joke with each other. An official* **messenger** *appears.*]

**Shen** [*to* **messenger**]: Now where are they sending us?

**Messenger**: To the Inner Court, of course, to train the actors.

**Shen**: But we were specifically exempted.

**Messenger**: The Prime Minister insisted on recruiting you, and your names are on this list. [*He reads the list aloud and asks*]: Where is old Ting?

**Shen**: He has retired to become a Taoist.

**Messenger**: Then I shall have to report him. Go to the ministry at once.

---

5. An allusion to the lines of Tu Mu (see Scene 6, n. 4):

I awake from a ten-year Yangchow dream
With the name of a rakehell of the pleasure quarter.

**Chang:**  Let's wait until all the girls are here.

**Messenger:**  Their Excellencies are banqueting beside the river, where the girls are to be examined.

**Chang** and **Shen:**  In that case, we had better be off.

> Truly,
> Flute in hand, song on lips,
> We steal our tunes from the palace.         [*Exeunt.*]

**Messenger** [*to K'ou*]:  Are you K'ou Pai-men?

**K'ou:**  Yes, I am.

**Messenger** [*to Cheng*]:  Are you Pien Yü-ching?

**Cheng:**  No, I'm T'o-niang.

**Messenger:**  Oh, Cheng T'o-niang. Where is Pien Yü-ching?

**Cheng:**  She has "left the world" to become a Taoist nun.

**Messenger:**  Even those who "leave the world" depart in couples. Who is that girl walking so slowly? How tiny her feet are! Is it Li Chen-li?

**K'ou:**  No, it cannot be, since she was married some time ago.

**Messenger:**  I dragged her from her tower myself, and she told me she was Li Chen-li. Who else could she be?

**Cheng:**  Perhaps it is Mistress Li's daughter, assuming her mother's name.

**Messenger:**  Never mind. As far as my business is concerned, I only have to count you girls by numbers. Ah, here she comes!

> [*Enter Fragrant Princess.*]

**Fragrant Princess** [*sings*]:
> I have left my tower for the depths of snowy winter;
> Unused to treading on ice, my feet torment me.
> The moth-browed are chosen by phoenix decree:
> Court messengers on prancing steeds
> Drive them on with silken whips,
> As fierce winds lash the flowers.

[*Speaks*]:  I was removed from my tower by force, and now they are taking me to the Inner Court. I may be helpless, but even if I die they cannot quell my spirit.

**Guard** [*shouting*]:  Make haste, make haste, you laggard!

[*Fragrant Princess walks faster to the front of the stage.*]

**K'ou:** So you have stepped down from your tower after all.

**Cheng:** You should consider it a great good fortune to come and serve His Majesty!

**Fragrant Princess:** I hope this great good fortune alights on you. [*They walk along together.*]

**Guard:** Here is the Pavilion of Heart's Delight. The Prime Minister and their Honours Juan and Yang will arrive at any moment. Mind you behave yourselves. [*Exeunt* **Cheng** *and* **K'ou** *with the guard.*]

**Fragrant Princess:** This will give me a chance of seeing the villains together and venting my pent-up rage. [*Sings*]:

The shameless flatterer will sit with the cruel tyrant,
His face a powdered mask of obsequious guile,
Fawning on the despot's whim in a thousand odious ways.
Soon the play called *Singing Phoenix*[6] will be acted
    in real life,
And I shall resemble Mi Heng when he cursed and beat
    the drum.[7]
It remains to be seen whether they will understand.

[*Enter Ma Shih-ying, Juan Ta-ch'eng, Yang Wen-ts'ung,
Steward, and young page. Fragrant Princess hides.*]

**Juan:** The lacquered towers with scarlet are bedight.

**Yang:** The green and golden hills are flecked with white.

**Ma:** What a gorgeous snowscape.

**Juan:** This Pavilion of Heart's Delight is an ideal place for enjoying the splendour of snow.

**Ma:** Is there any historical reason to explain this?

**Juan:** Emperor Chen-tsung of the Sung dynasty once presented his favorite minister with a painting of a snowy landscape by Chou Fang.[8] On presenting it, the Emperor said to him:

---

6. *Ming feng chi,* attributed to Wang Shih-chen of the sixteenth century. The play describes the protests by the Censor Yang Chi-sheng and others against the villainous Prime Minister Yen Sung (see below, n. 9).

7. See Scene 1, n. 12.

8. Chen-tsung, 968-1022, third emperor of the Sung dynasty, who was devoted to Taoist practices. Chou Fang painted between the years 780 and 810.

"When you reach Nanking, you should select a suitable spot to hang this painting, where the scenery harmonizes with the work of art." This pavilion was built in consequence.

Ma [*looking up at the wall*]: The picture on this wall must be the one you mentioned.

Yang: No, this was painted by a contemporary, a friend of mine named Lan Ying. He arrived here recently.

Ma: What artistry! Compare it with the snow outside, and it stands to reason that this should be called the Pavilion of Heart's Delight.

Yang [*to servants*]: Now lay the tables. Let us take our seats. [*All sit down.*]

Juan [*to Ma*]: Having only prepared a frugal repast, we feel deeply honoured by Your Excellency's presence.

Ma: No ceremony, please. I prefer simplicity: it is the true badge of culture.

Juan: Since Your Excellency holds so generous an opinion of us, we shall be our simple selves without play-acting.

Ma: Don't talk about acting, I beg. Actors can be dangerous fellows. When they impersonate a character successfully, he will live forever in the image of this caricature. If they paint his face white like a traitor's, he will remain so infamous that even his descendants will repudiate him as an ancestor.

Yang: Yes, actors can be dangerous, but I think they are usually fair. They provide a warning to evil-doers.

Ma: In my opinion, most of those who have gone down to posterity as villains allowed themselves to be intoxicated by flattery. Take the Prime Minister Yen Sung,[9] for instance. He was quite an accomplished statesman in his time, but since that play, "The Singing Phoenix," he has always appeared with a hideous white face. I imagine this is due to his patronage of the sycophant Chao Wen-hua.

Juan [*bowing*]: Yes, that is profoundly true. I know that Your

---

9. Yen Sung was the most notorious of the Six Wicked Ministers of the Ming dynasty. Finally, in 1562, he was dismissed and his property confiscated. It was commonly asserted that the Emperor Chia-ching sent him a silver bowl to collect alms, but no one would give him anything or even buy the bowl, so that he died of starvation.

Excellency abominates flatters. We admire you all the more
on that account.

**Yang**:  Let us toast Your Excellency. [*All do so.*]

**Juan** [*to Steward*]:  Have the singing-girls arrived?

**Steward**:  They await Your Honour's instructions.

[*Guard leads in Cheng, K'ou, and Fragrant Princess.*]

**Ma** [*scrutinizing them*]:  I don't think we need them just now.
Tell them to go to the Ministry of Ceremonies.

**Juan**:  But I summoned them on purpose to entertain Your Excellency.

**Ma**:  Well then, let us only keep the youngest. [*Exeunt all the girls
except Fragrant Princess.*] What is her name?

**Guard**:  The Virgin Beauty, Li Chen-li.

**Ma** [*laughing*]:  She seems a beauty, but I doubt if she's a virgin.
Let us hear her sing.

**Juan**:  Virgin Beauty, come here. Pour wine and give us a song.

[*Fragrant Princess shakes her head.*]

**Ma**:  Why do you shake your head?

**Fragrant Princess**:  I don't know how to sing.

**Ma**:  If you cannot sing, how did you come by your reputation as
a famous courtesan?

**Fragrant Princess**:  I'm nothing of the kind. [*Wipes her tears.*]

**Ma**:  What is ailing you? You may confide in us.

**Fragrant Princess** [*sings*]:
    The anguish in my heart grows wild as weeds;
    Save to the Emperor himself I could not reveal it.
    They have severed husband and wife by frightening their
      souls away,
    They have brutally torn a mother from her daughter.
    More savage than brigands, they play at deaf and dumb,
    Pretending ignorance of their gross guilt.

**Ma**:  You seem to have endured much hardship.

**Juan**:  Poor lass!

**Yang:** We are gathered here for enjoyment. Let us not listen to dismal stories.

**Fragrant Princess:** Your Honour knows whether my dismal stories are worth telling. [*Sings*] :

> The people look up to the great Prime Minister
> To recover that half of the country which is lost,
> But you merely promote your personal ambition,
> Pandering to the Emperor's lust for pleasure.
> Seeking to cram his Inner Court with flowers,
> You have dragged me to this place of ice and snow,
> A sorrowful maid to sing and pour your wine.

**Ma** [*angrily*] : Fie, what is all this nonsense? You deserve to be slapped on the mouth.

**Juan:** I've heard that this creature was a favourite of the Eastern Forest gang. They must have perverted her, since she has no manners. Certainly she deserves a thrashing.

**Yang:** But she looks too young for the person you refer to.

**Fragrant Princess:** What if I am she? [*Sings*] :

> The Eastern Forest patriots won universal esteem,
> But not the upstart foster sons of eunuchs.

**Juan:** What brazen insolence! Who can she be reviling? Stewards, seize her and cast her out into the snow.

[*A steward tries to grasp her, but **Fragrant Princess** struggles with him and pushes him onto the floor.*]

**Fragrant Princess** [*sings*] :

> My limbs are transparent as ice, and my heart is chaste
>   as snow,
> Outside in the snow I shall find sympathy.
> With my will of iron, I have no fear of freezing.

**Juan:** We cannot apologize sufficiently for the monstrous behaviour of this vixen. We are deeply ashamed of having called her. She must be severely punished.

[***Juan** leaves the table and begins to kick **Fragrant Princess**. **Yang** tries to stop him.*]

**Ma:** It would be easy to put her to death, but it is beneath my dignity to bother about such a trifle.

**Yang:** Precisely. A Prime Minister and a mere singing-girl are poles apart. Your Excellency had better forget it.

**Juan:** Let her be sent to the Inner Court to perform the most arduous roles. There she will reap her deserts.

**Ma:** I quite agree.

**Yang:** Remove her. [*Guards proceed to do so.*]

**Fragrant Princess:** Until I die, I shall never stanch the longings in my breast. [*Guards drag her out.*]

**Ma:** We should not allow so congenial a gathering to be spoiled by that little fool.

**Juan** and **Yang** [*both bowing repeatedly*]: Please pardon us for this unexpected affront. We shall make amends as soon as possible.

**Ma** [*standing up*]: After this unpleasant incident, I shall wend my way home through the snow.

**Juan:** For insulting our guest, the beauty should be beheaded. [*Exeunt Ma and Juan with attendants.*]

**Yang** [*aside*]: What a piece of irony that Fragrant Princess should run into her two worst enemies as soon as she leaves her tower. She would have been killed, had I not been there to shield her. She will have more to suffer, but since she is destined for the Inner Court I cannot be held responsible. During her absence, however, there will be nobody to look after the Tower of Enchanting Fragrance. Ah, I've an idea! My friend the painter Lan Ying is searching for lodgings. I shall ask him to move into it until Fragrant Princess is released. [*Sings*]:

As snow invests the scene at Heart's Delight,
And wine and braziers warm the revellers through,
Sad are the Ch'in-huai singing-girls tonight
To see Hsi-shih exiled alone to Wu.[10]

---

10. More allusions are made to Hsi-shih than to any other beauty in the history of China. Sent by the King of Yueh as a gift to the King of Wu, she brilliantly accomplished her mission of debauching her new master and ruining his state.

SCENE 25

# The Cast Selected

1645, FIRST MONTH

[*In the center of the stage is a tablet inscribed Hsun Feng Tien, "The Hall of Balmy Breezes," with aphoristic couplets on either side. On the first is written: "Among ten thousand alternatives, what is better than to hold the wine cup?" On the second: "In a hundred years, how often does one see the full moon overhead?" The inscription reads: "Respectfully submitted by the Senior Tutor Wang To."*] [1]

[*Enter the two musicians* Shen Kung-hsien *and* Chang Yen-chu, *and the two singing girls* K'ou Pai-men *and* Cheng T'o-niang.]

**Shen:** The Son of Heaven dotes on his darling Shen. [2]

**Chang:** I love to paint beauties' eyebrows, like the renowned Chang Ch'ang of old. [3]

**K'ou** [*punning on her own name*]: I'm like a willow before a fine white gate.

**Cheng:** I'm just Cheng T'o-niang, but I excel in the arts of love.

**Shen:** Two days have gone by since we were summoned to the Inner Court, but so far nothing has happened.

**Chang:** At least we are in the Hall of Balmy Breezes, where the palace music is performed. I hear that His Majesty will soon select players for the next rehearsal.

**Shen:** Why do they call this "The Hall of Balmy Breezes"?

**Chang:** It's an allusion to the words of the old zither song, "Perfumed by the breezes of the south."

---

1. See Scene 4, n. 3.
2. "Darling Shen" was the famous and favoured scholar Shen Yueh of the Liang dynasty in the sixth century.
3. Chang Ch'ang, died 48 B.C., distinguished scholar and official under the Emperor Yuan-ti of the Han dynasty. He made a practice of painting his wife's eyebrows, and when the Emperor teased him about this, he replied that this was a matter of the highest importance to women.

**Cheng:** You men have your "breezes from the south,"[4] so what use have you for girls like us?

**K'ou:** Ah, but when we become favourites, we shall be ladies of imperial rank, real queens.

**Cheng:** Perhaps the men will become queens too.

**Chang:** That is most insulting.

**Shen:** When we are put in charge of the company, she will be punished for it.

**Chang:** I'll not forgive her. Tomorrow when the rehearsal begins, that hussy will get a taste of my drumstick.

**Cheng:** I've tried it before, and it's nothing to be afraid of. [*General laughter. Enter Juan Ta-ch'eng.*]

**Juan** [*sings*]:
  The palace of Han is like a classic painting
  Where pearly curtains float in the spring morning.
  Beauties will come like butterflies, like orioles,
  To sing and dance to talent's high creations,
  Mingling bright sleeves with ministerial robes.

  [*To the actors*]: Are all of you present? Where's Virgin Beauty Li?

**K'ou:** She slipped in the snow and hurt herself. At present she is lying down.

**Juan:** His Majesty will soon be here to choose players for the rehearsal. She cannot absent herself as she pleases.

**All:** Of course not, of course not. We'll drag her along by force. [*Exeunt, except Juan.*]

**Juan** [*to himself*]: That she-slave has infuriated me. Today I shall make her act the role of a clown.


  [*Enter two court eunuchs with ceremonial dragon fans, then the Emperor, followed by two more eunuchs holding a casket and other vessels.*]

**Emperor** [*sings*]:
  In misty groves, dead dynasties lie buried

---

4. "Breezes from the south" is *nan-feng;* substituting the homonym *nan,* "male," gives the common term for sodomy.

Mid labyrinthine terraces and towers.
I'm sovereign of the spring in the sweet south,
I who have ever loved the Loyang flowers.

[*Sits down and speaks*]: It is almost a year since I succeeded to the Empire. Thanks to the valour of the four garrison generals, the bandits have been prevented from marching south. Certain rebels have plotted for the Prince of Lu to usurp the Throne, but these are all in jail. Since the restoration of peace, I have been searching for a worthy Empress. However, I am often bored by the pomps and ceremonies of my existence. It is sad that my dignity should prevent me from indulging in the pleasures of song and dance.

Juan [*kneeling*]: Your Majesty's servant and Imperial Counsellor Juan Ta-ch'eng pays homage.

Emperor: Please rise. [*Sings*]:

The melting snow and first spring buds I see
With knitted brow. This landscape wearies me.

Juan: When the world is at peace, it is time for entertainment. Why does Your Majesty feel weary?

Emperor: I am tormented by a secret worry which you may guess.

Juan: Is Your Majesty afraid of the bandits coming south?

Emperor: No. [*Sings*]:

They face the Yellow River in dismay —
They'll hardly fly here down the Milky Way!

Juan: Is Your Majesty perturbed by the insufficiency of military supplies and victualling of the army?

Emperor: No, it isn't that, either. [*Sings*]:

My stalwart warriors line the River Huai,
My ships bring grain in plentiful supply.

Juan: Perhaps Your Majesty is anxious to discover a virtuous Empress?

Emperor: No, that will soon be settled. The Minister of Ceremonies has been investigating on my behalf. Meanwhile, [*sings*]:

Nine maids of honour, and my consorts three,
Ably control palace affairs for me.

**Juan:** If none of these matters disturbs Your Majesty, perhaps you are worried by the rebellious ministers Chou and Lei, plotting to enthrone the Prince of Lu?

**Emperor:** You are farther than ever from the point. [*Sings*]:

Those lying traitors were foredoomed to fail;
Already they repent their deeds, in jail.

**Juan** [*lowering his head*]: What else could trouble Your Majesty? I confess that my imagination begins to fail me.

**Emperor:** As my most intimate servant in the Inner Court, how can you be so obtuse?

**Juan** [*kneeling*]: Your Majesty's wisdom is so lofty, and your thoughts are so profound, that his humble servant is too dense to understand. I beg Your Majesty to be so gracious as to enlighten me, and I'll try to relieve your anxiety.

**Emperor:** Let me explain, then. As Emperor I should be able to satisfy my every mood. Since I have recognized your *Swallow Letter* as representative of the spirit of my reign, it is important that it should be performed at the Lantern Festival[5] for the celebration of peace and prosperity. I'm afraid we shall not find suitable players in time for the rehearsal. [*Pointing to the couplets on the wall*]: "Among ten thousand alternatives, what is better than to hold the wine-cup?" "In a hundred years, how often does one see the full moon overhead?" There is only one Lantern Festival during the year. This thought has depressed me night and day, so that I have lost both sleep and appetite.

**Juan:** So it's all on account of that modest play of mine! That it should have caused Your Majesty worry is entirely my fault. [*Kowtowing*]: I am so utterly devoted to Your Majesty that I would gladly sacrifice my life to your slightest whim. [*Sings*]:

I dedicate myself to gallant verses,
Displaying all my wit to divert Your Majesty.
I am ready to wear powder and rouge and carry a lute,
Tripping in the role of a tender light-foot maiden,
To win a glance from Your Majesty at the feast,

---

5. The fifteenth day of the first lunar month, climaxing the New Year festivities on the evening of the first full moon.

Or the smallest token you deign to fling on the carpet.
It is the luck of three lives and ten thousand years of
    fame
To partake of Your Majesty's Imperial bounty.
I shall strive to fulfill my duty with highest merit . . .

[*Speaks*]: But I do not know which roles lack interpreters.

**Emperor:** A young hero and heroine and a little clown are required most urgently.

**Juan:** That should be easy. The Ministry of Ceremonies have sent
several musicians and singing-girls. They are waiting outside.

**Emperor:** Call them in.

**Juan:** I obey Your Majesty.

> [*Exit* **Juan**, *to re-enter with* **Shen, Chang, Fragrant Princess,
> Cheng,** *and* **K'ou**. *All kneel before the* **Emperor**.]

**Emperor** [*to* **Shen** *and* **Chang**]: Are you musicians?

**Shen** and **Chang:** May it please Your Majesty above, we humble
folk have some knowledge of musical drama.

**Emperor:** Are you familiar with all the latest plays?

**Chang** and **Shen:** Our recent productions include *The Peony Pavilion, The Swallow Letter*, and *The Western Tower*. [6]

**Emperor:** If you know *The Swallow Letter*, I shall appoint you to
direct it in the Inner Court. [**Shen** *and* **Chang** *kowtow*.] Are
the three singing-girls also familiar with *The Swallow Letter*?

**Cheng** and **K'ou:** We are, Your Majesty.

**Emperor:** That is good news. [*To* **Fragrant Princess**]: But you,
young woman, why don't you reply?

**Fragrant Princess:** I do not know the play.

**Juan** [*kneeling*]: May it please Your Majesty, these who know the
play may take the leading roles. This ignorant wench should
be made to act the clown.

**Emperor:** If that is the custom, do accordingly, [**K'ou, Cheng,**
*and* **Fragrant Princess** *kowtow*.] Rise now, and prepare for
the rehearsal.

---

6. *The Western Tower (Hsi-lou-chi)* was a play by one of the leading contemporary
dramatists, Yuan Yü-ling.

**Cheng:** Now I shall be the greatest leading lady in the world.

**Emperor** [*to Juan*]: Choose a scene from *The Swallow Letter* and
make them rehearse it in your presence. [*Chang, Shen, K'ou
and Cheng practise a few arias. Juan gives them directions.
The Emperor says contentedly*]: Most interesting. You all
seem well acquainted with the play. I need fret no further.
[*To servant*]: Pour the wine. I shall drink three cups to
congratulate you. [*Wine is served. The Emperor drinks, then
rises, saying*]: We, the Emperor and his loyal subjects, share
the subtlest enjoyments of life. Let us give a concert
together. I am a proficient drummer. Each of you choose
your favorite instrument. [*They play a piece called "Rain
and Snow." When it is finished the Emperor laughs aloud.*]
Nearly all my depression has left me. Serve wine. I'll drink
another three cups. [*Sings*]:

The old palace of Wu re-opens its gates to music,
The finest talents are trained for our performance.
The spring breeze thrills to the rhythmic Huai-yang drum,
To strings of K'un-shan and melodious Wu-hsi song.
The sleeves of the dancers whirl like coloured smoke,
The palace ladies sway like graceful willows.
Vermilion towers and green-tiled palaces
Provide the noblest setting to their art.
All contribute with laughter and with song
To the delight of a carefree Emperor.

[*Noticing Fragrant Princess*]: That girl is beautiful beyond
the common run. It is a pity that she should have to act the
clown. [*Addressing her*]: Young maid, though you do not
know *The Swallow Letter*, are you familiar with any other
play?

**Fragrant Princess:** I know parts of The Peony Pavilion.

**Emperor:** That will do. Will you sing for me? [*Fragrant Princess
hesitates.*] Your fair face flushes. Why are you so shy? She
should be given a palace fan painted with peach blossom to
match her spring complexion. [*A fan is thrown to her.*]

**Fragrant Princess** [*picking it up, sings*]:
"Why did the Immortal Beauty, Emerald Jade,
Seek to discover the Fountain of Peach Blossoms?
Because the running stream and whirling petals

Have rapt her fancy, and the Lord of Heaven
Seems niggardly with flowers, she mourns their plight.
Alas, the early spring has fled in vain."

**Emperor:** Wonderful! She has sung it to perfection. [*To servant*]: Bring wine. I'll drink three more cups. This girl is as fine a singer as she is a beauty. She deserves the heroine's role. [*Pointing to Cheng*]: That swarthy wench is indicated for the clown.

**Juan** [*crestfallen*]: I obey, Your Majesty.

**Cheng** [*punning on her own name*]: I'm supposed to be fit, but I'm not fit enough — it's enough to give one a fit!

**Emperor** [*to Juan*]: Take the hero and the clown to the rehearsal chamber. Tell the musicians to teach them under your personal supervision.

**Juan** [*kneeling*]: That is merely my duty, Your Majesty. [*Exit with Chang, Shen, K'ou, and Cheng.*]

**Emperor** [*to Fragrant Princess*]: You may remain in this Hall of Balmy Breezes. Three days should suffice you to memorize "The Swallow Letter," after which you may join in the general rehearsal.

**Fragrant Princess:** I shall obey Your Majesty. Unfortunately I have no copy of the play.

**Emperor** [*to servant*]: See that this girl is provided with a clear libretto. [*Servant hands it to her. She kneels to receive it. The Emperor recites*]:

Songs will fill with joy a thousand years,
And wine dispel the state's ten thousand cares.

[*Emperor exits with retinue.*]

**Fragrant Princess** [*weeping*]: Alas. Now that I am immured in the Inner Court, I shall never be free again. [*Sings*]:

The willows droop; the crows of evening gather.
Behind a thousand portals locked, I see
Only the somber pines outside the window,
And green-tiled roofs. A chill wind blows my sleeves,
And scattered blossoms flutter in my hair.
The lovers torn apart like mandarin ducks,
Their tortured souls by cloud-capped hills divided,

Yearn for each other bitterly. In vain
I sent the fan of peach blossoms, since now
Even the thinnest ray of hope is thwarted.
In vain I peer beyond the fragrant meadows.

[*Sighs and says*]: There is nothing I can do now but memorize this play, and hope that perhaps His Majesty will some
day release me from the palace so that I may dream of
finding my love again. [*Sings*]:

Sorrow enters my bones.
Like the lone Goddess of the chilly Moon,
I've grown so thin a hand could circle my waist.
The singers scatter when the song is done,
I stand alone to watch the setting sun.
A frail peach blossom in the palace waits,
But no spring breeze can enter these tall gates.

---

SCENE 26

# The General Tricked

## 1645, FIRST MONTH

**Hou Fang-yü** [*enters, singing*]:
By the river, walls and hilltops vanish in mist,
And dust overlays the blossom-bowered wineshop.
Beneath those distant clouds my old home lies,
But warlike duties press; I find no way
To cheer the parents who await me there.

[*Speaks*]: His Excellency Shih K'o-fa sent me as staff adviser
to General Kao, defending the river. So fierce is General
Kao's temper that he has abused his neighbour Commander
Hsu to his face. I'm afraid this will lead to disaster. I'll go to
the General's camp and try to conciliate them.

[**Hou** *proceeds to the camp. Enter* **General Kao Chieh.**]

**Kao:**
The river changes course as my orders roar;
My two hands clear a path through the smoke of war.

[*He sees* **Hou** *and greets him. Both sit down.*] Have you brought any news, Master Hou, or have you merely come to offer me advice?

**Hou:** I have followed Your Excellency a thousand miles to help you defend the river. Since we are here, . . . [*sings*]:

Everybody shudders at the sound of your name:
Whole families depart, without leaving a dog or a chicken;
Soldiers and civilians are at perpetual strife.
Terror prevails, and the sound of lamentation;
Inside the camp hostility increases.
Calamity will surely befall us.

**Kao:** Hsu Ting-kuo boasts of the strength of his hundred thousand troops, but at yesterday's review I found that most of them were senile or decrepit. He is enriching himself at government expense, and ought to be court-martialled. I was lenient enough to let him off with an admonition.

**Hou:** Your Excellency was mistaken. [*Sings*]:

Now half the mountains and rivers have changed colour.
A loyal general must ensure swift victory,
Restore the public confidence in his worth.
Try to win hearts, abstain from quarrelling;
The success of our arms depends on harmony.

**Kao:** However that may be, Hsu feigned illness to avoid coming to meet me; instead, he invited me to drink with him inside the city, which proves that he is apprehensive. I have noticed that the city is entirely surrounded by water. It is only connected with the mainland by a narrow bridge, so the position has strategic importance. Tomorrow I shall order Hsu to cede his camp to me. I want absolute control of the city. If he obeys, well and good; if not, I shall deprive him of his seal and appoint another Commander in his stead.

**Hou** [*waves his hands*]: This is the very last thing you should do. You provoked him sufficiently when you berated him in public. There's a proverb, "Even a mighty dragon should not attack a serpent in its lair." We are surrounded by his partisans. If he makes trouble for us, we cannot expect to defend ourselves efficiently.

**Kao:** That is merely a bookworm's view: it is quite absurd. I have never been afraid of any man. Even the three garrison generals had to bow before me. This Hsu is a nonentity. Why should I bother about him?

**Hou** [*standing up*]: So be it: if that is Your Excellency's opinion, I shall waste no more words. I beg to take leave and visit my old home, hoping that you will prosper in the meantime.

**Kao** [*bowing*]: Please follow your inclinations. [*Exit Hou, laughing ironically and flapping his sleeve. Kao rises and calls to his troops. Two officers enter, and Kao says to them*]: Bring a few guards. We'll ride into the city for some refreshment. See that discipline is maintained among the troops during my absence. [*Exeunt officers. They re-enter with four guards. Kao continues*]: Let us be off. [*Sings*]:

The Yellow River forms a safe frontier for the
   southern dynasty,
Plunging from cloudy heights towards the east.
When even birds find it too far to fly,
What use is the strongest bow a man could buy?

**All** together [*singing*]:
   Towards the deserted city,
   Over the ruined bridge:
   Light-hearted warriors,
   Slowly our steeds advance.        [*Exeunt.*]

[*An officer of General Hsu Ting-kuo's bodyguard enters,
accompanied by fellow officers and carrying a seal.*]

**Officer:**
   An execution requires no general's writ;
   Success may often depend on a woman's wit.

[*Speaks*]: I'm an officer of General Hsu's bodyguard. My commander was upbraided by Kao Chieh, and alarm has turned his stomach. But her ladyship, his spouse, is full of courage and resource. Last night she thought of a ruse. I am to surrender this seal to Kao and invite him to a banquet inside the city. During the feast, an explosion of firecrackers will be the signal. It is an ingenious plan, and pray Heaven it succeeds. Otherwise, the prospect ahead of us is grim. [*Peering backstage*]: Ha, Kao Chieh is on his way. I'll have to fall on my knees to meet him.

[*Kao enters with his retinue. Hsu's officer kneels
before him.*]

**Kao:** Where are you from?

**Officer:** I am a special envoy of General Hsu, and have come respectfully to welcome Your Excellency.

**Kao:** What prevented him from coming in person?

**Officer:** Commander Hsu is lying sick in bed. He delegated me to escort Your Excellency to a banquet in your honour. Here is the seal, which he surrenders to Your Excellency.

**Kao:** Where is the banquet to be held?

**Officer:** At Commander Hsu's headquarters.

**Kao** [*to his guards*]: Keep this seal for me. [*Laughing*]: So he has finally delivered it! Tomorrow I shall take full control of the city. Let us ride on. [*They advance accordingly.*]

**Officer** [*kneeling*]: This is Commander Hsu's headquarters. Allow me to show Your Excellency the way. [***All** dismount from their horses.*]

**Kao:** Let the soldiers wait outside. [*To his own two **officers***]: You two trusty friends shall keep me company at the banquet.

> [*They put away the seal, kowtow, and sit down with **Kao**. **Hsu's** officer pours wine for **Kao**, and **Kao's** officers are served by others. Servants hand round the dishes.*]

**Officer:** Please drink some wine, Your Excellency.

**Kao** [*angrily*]: This is wretched stuff. How can you expect me to swallow it? [*He throws his cup on the ground.*]

**Officer** [*changes the wine and says*]: Please eat some food, Your Excellency.

**Kao:** This is quite inedible. How can you expect my chopsticks to touch it? [*He throws his chopsticks on the floor, and other dishes are brought in. **Kao** continues*]: I understand I had been invited to inspect the arrangements for the Lantern Festival. Why are there no lanterns and musicians?

**Officer** [*kneeling*]: This is a poor city, Your Excellency; consequently such amenities are scarce. We can only illuminate our headquarters and provide some martial music.

> [*Official lanterns are hung, and martial music is played.*]

**Kao** [*to his own **officers***]: Let us drink. [*Sings*]:

My power is absolute, as guardian of the river's shore.
My encampment glitters among the willows, and my
    banners are as numerous as stars.
My seal and arrows of command gleam in the lamplight
    at the banquet-board.

[*Kao's officers stand up and toast him. Kao sings*]:

My officers and I prefer wine to strategy;
We play fist-games,[1] our fingers
Spread as in battle array.

**Kao's officers:** Their secret formations would puzzle the greatest
military genius. . . . We seem to have drunk enough. Will
Your Excellency review the troops inside the city?

**Kao:** Let us wait till tomorrow and drink a few more cups.
[*Wine is poured again. They drink. Firecrackers sound
behind the stage. A servant grabs Kao's wrist, and Hsu's
officer draws his sword to kill him. Kao struggles and
shakes himself free. Another servant kills one of Kao's
officers, and a third servant catches Kao's other officer,
who is also killed. The firecrackers continue, while all
rush in pursuit of Kao, who jumps onto a beam of the
roof.*]

**Officer** [*shouts*]: Kao has escaped. Bring torches and hunt him
everywhere. There is a hole in the ceiling; perhaps he has
climbed to the roof. [*A servant searches. Hsu's officer points
and says*]: Above that corner I see something like a human
figure. Shoot! [*His fellow officers shoot arrows in Kao's
direction. Kao jumps down, and the servants catch him. Hsu's
officer exclaims*]: Well, it's old Kao after all!

**Kao:** Shame on you! The Emperor appointed me Commander-
in-Chief to defend the river. How dare you lay hands on me?

**Officer:** We only recognise our own General Hsu. Who cares what
you are? Stretch out that neck of yours.

**Kao** [*stamping*]: So all is over. I have been basely betrayed. How
I regret that I did not heed Master Hou's advice! [*Stretches
out his neck*] I'll make you a present of my head.

**Officer:** Old Kao has guts, that cannot be denied. [*He cuts off
Kao's head and says*]: Comrades, let us recover the seal and

---

1. A reference to the Chinese *morra*, a game in which one player guesses the number
of fingers held up by another. It is played with great rapidity and noise.

report to General Hsu. Wait a minute! These three are dead, but their escorts are still outside.

**Second Officer:** No, sir, I took the precaution of having them slaughtered.

**Third Officer:** We must be careful. Kao's troops are outside the city. When they learn about this, they will come to avenge him. Let us be prepared.

**Officer:** Her Ladyship Madam Hsu has planned everything in advance. Tonight we leave the city and offer Kao's head to the northern leaders. They will lend us reinforcements to destroy Kao's troops, after which we may proceed to attack the south. [*Sings*]:

The steeds of the north sniff victory in the wind,
The Yellow River is their road to conquest.
Preoccupied with lanterns, the southern court
Offers up its General to our slaughter.

---

SCENE 27

# A Meeting of Boats

### 1645, SECOND MONTH

[*Su K'un-sheng enters with a bundle on his back, riding a donkey.*]

**Su** [*sings*]:
Mail-clad horses jostle;
The smoke and dust of war have darkened the world.
My soul is struck with dread and my heart quails
As I pass through village after shattered village.

**Donkey Driver** [*enters and shouts*]: Mr. Traveller, pray go slowly. Don't you see the retreating soldiers on the dyke of the Yellow River? Beware, lest they steal your donkey.

[*Su, not listening to him, quickens his pace. Three soldiers enter and accost him.*]

**Su** [*sings*]:
Armour abandoned, shields thrown away,

Nursing your heads, you flee like rats.
But who am I to mock you?
All of us alike
Suffer this defeat.

[*The soldiers push Su into the river and take his donkey.
Exeunt. The driver rushes after them. Su stands up in the
water with his bundle on top of his head, shouting for help. A
boat is rowed onto the stage. It contains Mistress Li Chen-li
dressed as a poor woman.*]

**Li** [*sings*]:
The river rolls angrily;
The wind whips the waves into whirlpools.
Let us seek shelter near the dyke,
Find a mooring under the willows.

[*The **boatman** does accordingly. **Li** says*]: Boatman, do you
hear somebody crying for help near the shore? Please row
towards him. His life may yet be saved, and we shall be
blessed for it.

**Boatman:** The current's so treacherous, madam, that it is courting
death to row further.

**Li:** Please perform this errand of mercy. Heaven will reward you
for it.

**Boatman:** Very well, I can but try. [*He rows laboriously, singing*]:

How strong the tempest blows, how swift the current!
I risk my life for another. His desperate cry
Sounds like a soul half lost.

[*Approaching **Su***]: Climb in, climb in! You were fated to
meet with benefactors, to be preserved from a sudden death.
[*The **boatman** extends his oar to **Su**, who grasps it and climbs
into the boat shivering.*]

**Su:** I'm freezing, freezing. [***Boatman** gives him dry clothes. **Mistress Li** turns her back while he changes. **Su** then kowtows to
the **boatman** and exclaims*]: Thank you, sir. Like a parent
you have given me another life.

**Boatman:** Don't thank me. It was this lady who begged me to
save you.

[*Su bows to Mistress Li and is amazed to recognize her.*]

**Su:** Good gracious! Mistress Li! What are you doing here?

**Li:** Oh, it's Master Su! Where have you come from?

**Su:** Ah, that is a long story.

**Li:** Pray sit down and tell me. [*Both sit down.*]

**Boatman** [*anchoring boat*]: I shall go ashore and fetch some wine to warm us.

**Su** [*sings*]:
> After you passed as a bride through the lacquered gates,
> The tower of song was locked,
> The dancers' skirts folded away.
> In the loneliness of a bitter winter,
> Fragrant Princess grieved endlessly.

**Li** [*weeping*]: How has she been since I left her?

**Su:** It is entirely for her sake that I undertook to search for Master Hou. [*Sings*]:

> Among the hosts and the cavalry troops,
> No word of Master Hou,
> Though I searched the farthest outposts.

**Li:** How did you fall into the river?

**Su:** When I was riding along the dyke, some fugitive soldiers stole my donkey and pushed me in. [*Sings*]:

> Thank you, dear friend, for rescuing me from the torrent.
> Old friends tonight are reunited.

**Li:** Oh, now I understand. How lucky that I happened to be near! You must have a long life in store for you.

**Su:** But how came you here, after marrying the wealthy T'ien?

**Li:** Before I tell you my story, I'll light a fire to dry your clothes.

> [*Mistress Li lights a fire. Another boat enters, containing Hou Fang-yü.*]

**Hou:** As soon as I leave the tigers and leopards, I fall among whales and sharks! Boatman, we must be near Lü-liang. Please hoist a sail so that we may gather speed. And tomorrow let us make sail early.

**Hou's Boatman:** I crave Your Honour's patience. The wind is against us. But this seems to be a good place to anchor and spend the night.

**Hou:** Do as you think fit. [*The boat is moored.*] We might as well take some rest, I feel so drowsy. [*He lies down, not far from the other boat, where **Su** dries his clothes while **Mistress Li** sits beside him, telling her story.*]

**Li:** Fate has been cruel to me. Eventually I had to escape from T'ien's mansion. [*Sings*]:

That night when I dressed as a bride,
I was carried away like lightning.
I won T'ien's affection,
As if I were caressed by Spring.
He fell deeply in love with me,
And forgot his concubines.

**Su:** That sounds satisfactory.

**Li:** But T'ien's wife turned into a terrible harpy. [*Sings*]:

Wild as a tigress,
Poisonous as a snake.

[*Speaks*]: She dragged me from my room and beat me till I nearly died.

**Su:** How dreadful! Didn't T'ien try to defend you?

**Li** [*sings*]:
He swallowed his resentment without a word.

[*Speaks*]: Finally he married me off to a soldier.

**Su:** Why are you on this boat?

**Li:** It belongs to the officer of military supplies. My old soldier went ashore to deliver an official message. [*Sings*]:

So here in the bow I sit,
Narrating my misfortunes to my old friend.

**Hou** [*listening*]: I hear two people talking in another boat. The man's voice reminds me of Su K'un-sheng; and the woman's sounds vaguely familiar. I'll call out and make sure. Su K'un-sheng!

**Su:** Who is calling me?

10. Hou Fang-yü: "The man's voice reminds me of
Su K'un-sheng, and the woman's sounds vaguely familiar."

**Hou** [*delighted*]: So it really is Su K'un-sheng! [*His boat approaches.*]

**Su:** Oh, Master Hou, I have been searching for you everywhere. I should never expect to find you in such a place. Heaven and earth be thanked for this fortunate encounter. Please come over and meet another old friend.

**Hou** [*stepping across*]: Who can it be? Ah, Mistress Li, so you are here too, but why? This is most extraordinary. Where is Fragrant Princess?

**Li:** Since the night you left, she has never stepped out of her tower. She was determined to remain faithful to you. [*Hou hides his tears behind a sleeve.*] Later Ma Shih-ying sent his fierce retainers to us with a large sum of money. They tried to force Fragrant Princess to marry T'ien Yang.

**Hou:** But she is my own Fragrant Princess. How could she ever accept another?

**Li:** She refused to submit. In a violent struggle she tried to beat her brains out on the floor.

**Hou** [*gives a loud wail*]: My Fragrant Princess. Is she dead?

**Li:** She did not die, but she injured herself till her face was streaming with blood. Ma's odious lackeys kept on shouting outside the door, so I took her place in despair and married T'ien Yang.

**Hou:** That was magnanimous. Words fail to express my relief. Now where are you going in this boat?

**Li:** It has become my home. I live in it.

**Hou:** Why?

[*Mistress Li remains silent.*]

**Su:** She was driven out of T'ien's house by his shrewish wife. Now she is married to an officer, whose boat this is.

**Hou:** How cruel that she should endure so many misfortunes. [*To Su*]: And why are you here?

**Su:** Fragrant Princess has been pining for you day after day. Finally she begged me to trace you. I have brought you a message from her.

**Hou:** Where is it, where is it?

**Su** [*opening his knapsack, sings*]:
> The message is not in the form of a letter;
> It is of silk folded between sticks of bamboo,
> A love poem written at her dressing table.

**Hou:** But this is the fan I gave her.

**Su** [*sings*]:
> Look at the side which is red with peach blossoms —
> A thousand emotions more eloquent than words.

**Hou:** Who painted these?

**Su:** Fragrant Princess wounded herself, and the fan was stained with her blood. Master Yang transfigured it by adding leaves and branches.

**Hou** [*examining it*]: Now I see they are bloodstains. Master Yang has shown great artistry in concealing them. Henceforth this fan will be my most treasured possession. Yet I fail to understand why you brought it.

**Su:** When I took leave of her, Fragrant Princess said that all her sorrows were linked to this fan. Therefore she sent it to you instead of a letter.

**Hou** [*weeping*]: Fragrant Princess, my true love. How shall I ever be able to reward you? [*To Su*]; And how did you happen to find Mistress Li?

**Su** [*sings*]:
> My donkey and I were toiling along the dyke
> When soldiers pushed me into the icy torrent.

**Hou:** How frightful! But I am amazed that the fan was not ruined. It is not even wet.

**Su** [*sings*]:
> The river rose up to my shoulders,
> But I held the fan over my head
> To save the precious message.

**Hou** [*bowing*]: You risked your life for it. How can I express my gratitude? What happened after that?

**Su:** Mistress Li braved the wind and waves to rescue me. [*Sings*]:
> To jump into a well to save a drowning man:
> Who else in the world would have done so?

**Hou:** Yes, only Mistress Li would have shown such courage.

**Li**: At first I had no idea who it was. Eventually I recognised Master Su.

**Hou**: This was all the will of Heaven.

**Su**: But I have not asked why you are here, Master Hou.

**Hou**: Since last autumn I have been with Kao Chieh, who was sent to defend the river. He proved so stubborn and deaf to my advice that he was tricked by Hsu Ting-kuo and killed at a banquet. I hired a boat and fled. Now you can see his soldiers running wild about the roads. I am too mortified to face my master, Minister Shih.

**Su**: Why not go to Nanking and find Fragrant Princess? You may then decide on your future course of action.

**Hou**: Yes, that is what I shall do. When I have taken farewell of Mistress Li, I'll continue my journey.

**Li**: I shall never forget when the four of us were together at the Old House. If only Fragrant Princess were with us now! I wonder if I shall ever see her again in this world! [*Sings*] :

A household scattered,
To meet again amid clouds and waters.
Speech has an end,
But not the sorrows of separation.
Daughter whom I cherished,
When shall we exchange our tales of suffering?

**Hou**: We may still be pursued by our enemies, Master Su. Please change your clothes and we'll say goodbye.

> [*Su changes; then he and *Hou* step into the latter's boat. Both shed tears.*]

**Su**: The homeward voyage is full of vicissitudes.

**Hou**: When old friends meet, their sorrows often swell.

> [*Hou's boatman rows them off the stage. *Mistress Li* remains.*]

**Li**: I had long grown tired of my profession, and had resigned myself to living with an old soldier. This meeting today was completely unexpected. My friends have reminded me of anguish best forgotten. How loud the waves are roaring! Tonight I shall get no sleep. [*Sings*] :

Old friends who meet and part like drifting duckweed;
Past sorrows, new regrets: how many words?
But say not this floating life holds nothing certain:
Even on the Yellow River men find a home.

---

SCENE 28

# The Painting Inscribed

1645, THIRD MONTH

[*Enter **Lan Ying** in the garb of a mountain hermit.*]

**Lan** [*recites*]:
Listless she sits, the incense cold, her embroidery
    neglected,
The peach-flowers open, but the garden gate is shut.
In the limitless mists and rain of the rising spring,
All that's left of the Southern courts are these painted
    hills.

[*Speaks*]: From early youth I have won fame as a painter. I
heard that my old friend Yang Wen-ts'ung has recently been
appointed to a post in the Ministry of War, and I bought a
boat and came to visit him. He has persuaded me to lodge in
this Tower of Enchanted Fragrance, which used to be the
home of the celebrated singing-girl Frangrant Princess. Since
her departure the house has been empty, but it is quiet
enough to suit me. I shall now return to my painting. [*He
washes his ink-stone and painting-brush, and mixes the pig-
ment.*] But where can I find pure water? Ah, I had almost
forgotten that the morning dew on leaves and flowers is the
purest for mixing colours. I'll gather some in the garden.
[*Exits with a cup.*]

**Hou** [*enters and sings*]:
I have roamed between earth below and Heaven above,
My heart ever bound by a thread of perfect love.
Now the lanes are full of willow catkins; lo,
They float while swallows flutter to and fro.

Seeing the familiar house, the crimson tower,
My tenderest feelings like green meadows flower,
Fresh longings rise and fall in a misty shower.

[*Speaks*]: After meeting Su K'un-sheng on the Yellow River,
I curbed my excitement and travelled with him to Nanking.
This morning I left him at an inn, and came alone to look for
Fragrant Princess. How wonderful to see the Old House
again! [*Sings*]:

So little trace of human habitation,
The birds are twittering in consternation.
The walls are crumbling among weeds in piles,
And green moss gathers on the lustrous tiles
Beside the blossoms which should harmonize
With her fair features. Now my spirit flies
To meet my love and gaze into her eyes.

[*Pushing the door, he says*]: Oh, the doors are not locked!
I'll walk in and see who is there. [*Sings*]:

My footsteps startle the birds and raise a squall,
While mud from nests drops down into the hall;
It seems this empty hall, where no man follows,
Provides the perfect mating-place for swallows.
I'll steal on tiptoe till I reach her room . . .

[*Speaks*]: Here is the Tower of Enchanted Fragrance — but
oh, how desolate! Though it is daytime, the curtains are
drawn. Perhaps she is still asleep. Instead of rousing her, I
shall creep up the Tower and stand beside her bed. When she
wakes up and recognizes me, what rapture we shall share!
[*Sings*]:

Clutching my gown, I part the drooping branches,
And climb the crumbling staircase step by step,
Among the dust and cobwebs. Out-of-doors
The spring is all-pervading.
Why does my love retire behind her curtains?

[*Seeing the bare table, he sings*]:

Since when has she banished her lute?
And all these pigments in boxes and jars:
Has she become a recluse who paints for a living?

[*Speaks*]: The tower of song and dance has been turned into a studio. How strange! I wonder why. . . . Perhaps to protect her virtue, she wished to forget the arts of her vocation. Perhaps she hoped to express her lonely thoughts with her brush. Here is her bedroom. I'll open the door gently. Why is it barred? It seems to have been so for ages. This is very strange. Is there no caretaker in the house? [*Sings*]:

The room is forlorn; my beauty's far away,
Where has she fled beyond the myriad hills,
Locking her door?  Maybe the birds can tell.
Light-heartedly they frolic in the air,
Heedless of my fond question.  In despair
I turn; by yonder hedge the twigs are stirring,
A curtain rustles:  do I hear her breathe?

[*Lan enters with a jar.  Seeing Hou, he starts with surprise.*]

**Lan:**  Who are you, sir? And why do you come to my tower?

**Hou:**  It belongs to my beloved Fragrant Princess. I was about to ask you the same question.

**Lan:**  I am an artist, and my name is Lan Ying. My friend Yang Wen-ts'ung invited me to stay here.

**Hou:**  So you are the eminent painter! I have long been your distant admirer. [*Lan asks his name, and Hou answers*]: I am also acquainted with Master Yang, and my name is Hou Fang-yü.

**Lan:**  Your literary fame has even reached my ears. What good fortune has brought us together? Pray sit down.

**Hou:**  First of all, please tell me where is my Fragrant Princess?

**Lan:**  I have heard that she has been removed to the Inner Palace.

**Hou** [*in amazement*]:  But how and when did that happen?

**Lan:**  I'm afraid I do not know.

**Hou** [*wiping away tears, sings*]:
     After searching everywhere,
     I stand alone in the east wind.
     It is clear noon,
     But she is not to be seen.

[*Looking round*]:

The window-paper and the curtain-gauze are torn.

No relic of her remains;
Neither an old scarf or hairpin,
Nor the familiar flute.
Her mandarin-duck quilts are put away;
The mirrors are turned face down.
There is no beauty left for the flowers to compete with.

[*Speaks*]: The peach trees were in full blossom on our
marriage day. This tower had been newly decorated; now, no
sooner has she left than it looks desolate again. I return to
find the peach trees again in flower. How can I check my
tears at the sight of them? [*Sings*]:

Their petals flutter in the light spring breeze.
Gossamer fills the air like snowflakes,
Petals fall and scatter.

[*Speaks*]: I'll look at the peach blossoms on my fan.
[*Sings*]:

Painted in blood,
Brighter petals are here than on the trees.

[*Speaks*]: And I was responsible for them. [*Sings*]:

Opening this fan,
Here in the desolation of her boudoir,
I realize it was this very peach bloom
That joined her fate with mine, to live or die.

**Lan:** Who painted this fan of yours?

**Hou:** Your distinguished patron, Master Yang.

**Lan:** But why does it make you weep?

**Hou:** This fan is the tangible token of our vow. [*Sings*]:

Full of tenderness she held the ink-stone;
In the candlelight she asked me for a poem.
Thus line by line, I wrote a vow of love.

[*Speaks*]: But within less than a month, I had to escape my
foes. Fragrant Princess segregated herself for my sake, and by
doing so she offended the ruling powers. They sent blood-
hounds after her and drove her from her tower, so that in
despair she tried to destroy her beauty. Still clutching this
fan, she stained it with her blood.

**Lan:** Your story has moved me deeply.

**Hou:** Our friend Yang painted in a few leaves and converted it into a peach blossom fan. It is my only keepsake of my beloved.

**Lan:** The brushwork is so skillful that one cannot detect the bloodstains. How did you recover it?

**Hou:** Fragrant Princess sent her teacher to search for me, taking it instead of a letter. Immediately upon receiving it, I made this journey, never dreaming that she would have been removed to the Imperial Palace. [*Weeps.*]

[*Enter **Yang Wen-ts'ung**, with attendants to clear the way for him.*]

**Yang:** The Beauty is long gone from her tower, but in her place is installed a famous painter.

**Servant** [*comes in and announces*]: His Honour Yang has come to visit Master Lan.

[***Yang** steps out of his sedan-chair. **Lan** advances to meet him and escorts him upstairs.*]

**Yang** [*seeing **Hou***]: When did you arrive, Brother Hou?

**Hou:** This very day, so I have not yet had time to visit you.

**Yang:** I heard that you were on the staff of His Excellency Shih, and also that you accompanied Kao Chieh to the Yellow River. This morning I read an official report that Kao was murdered last month by Hsu Ting-kuo. Where were you in the meantime?

**Hou:** At home in my native village. On hearing of that disaster, I had to escape with my father into the hills, and there we stayed a month. Then I was warned that Hsu might send soldiers in pursuit of me, so I hired a boat and came south. On the way I chanced to meet Su K'un-sheng, who was searching for me. So I hurried to Nanking to find Fragrant Princess, or rather to find her gone. Where is she now?[1]

**Yang:** She was taken to the palace on the eighth of the first month.

**Hou:** When will she be able to leave it?

**Yang:** I cannot tell.

---

1. Though aware of the facts, Hou evidently requires verbal confirmation from Yang, who conduct has been ambiguous.

**Hou:** Then I shall have to wait here until she is set free.

**Yang:** There is no sense in that. You should find some other beauty to replace her.

**Hou:** How could I break my vow? You do not understand. If I could only obtain a message from her I would have a grain of comfort. [*Sings*]:

Her dwelling, close at hand,
Seems as remote as the sky.
How can I find a fairy maiden
To smuggle a letter to her?
She has left the blossom-shaded tower,
The wine pavilions, shrouded in mist and rain,
And languishes unwilling in the palace;
While I, her husband, wait at the far horizon
Where each day seems a year.

**Yang:** Don't distress yourself unduly, Brother Hou. Let us watch Brother Lan at his painting. [*Yang and Hou sit beside Lan as he paints. Yang asks*]: Is this a picture of the Peach Blossom Fountain?[2]

**Lan:** You are right.

**Yang:** For whom are you painting it?

**Lan:** For Chang Wei, the Commanding Officer of the Imperial Guard. The picture is to be mounted on a screen for the Pine Wind Pavilion he has recently finished building.

**Hou:** I congratulate you on its fine qualities. Both the color and the composition are extremely original, quite different from the traditional school of Nanking.

**Lan:** Thank you for taking so much notice of it. Would you kindly grace it with an inscription? That would increase its value considerably.

**Hou:** If you are not afraid of my spoiling such a work of art, I shall practice my lame calligraphy upon it. [*He composes a quatrain for the inscription*]:

"I dwelt in the hidden cave by Peach Blossom Fountain,
But on my way back I could not find the road.
For the fisherman had misled me over the mountain,
To keep this sanctuary for his own abode."

---

2. See Scene 1, n. 10.

[*He signs his name to it.*]

**Yang:** There are several recondite allusions in your poem. You appear to blame me somewhat.

**Hou:** No, there you are mistaken. [*Points to the painting and sings*]:

How lovely the rippling brook,
Where thousands of crimson petals fall,
And streaks of cloud drift over
Dense woods and far blue hills!
The place remains the same,
But no love is there to welcome me.
The cave at Peach Blossom Spring is desolate;
I turn back my boat as the sun sets.

[***Hou** rises.*]

**Yang:** It is useless to repine, brother. Now Ma and Juan are in power, and you know how vindictive they are. Though intimate with both of them, I dare not appeal on behalf of either of you, especially since the New Year's banquet when Fragrant Princess was asked to sing. Instead of singing, she pointed at Ma and Juan and denounced them to their faces.

**Hou:** Alas! I fear she must have been tortured in consequence.

**Yang:** Luckily I was present. I tried my best to calm their indignation, so she was only cast out into the snow. No doubt she was distressed, but as long as she is in the Inner Court her life will be protected. But your connection with her is too well known, and you had better not remain here.

**Hou:** Thank you for the warning. [*Sings*]:

Though my enemies use all their power against me,
I'll clasp the peach blossom fan to my heart.

[*He turns abruptly to leave.*]

**Yang:** Let us bid Brother Lan farewell and leave together.

**Hou:** Forgive me; I had forgotten to say goodbye.

[*Farewells are exchanged. Exit **Lan** first, closing the door. **Hou** and **Yang** walk off together, singing*]:

**Hou:**
Bewildered by this return to the crimson tower,

**Yang:**
    Idly we watched the painter at his task.

**Hou:**
    The beauty and her lover are cast asunder,

**Yang:**
    But peach flowers are as fine this year as last.

---

SCENE 29

# The Club Suppressed

1645, THIRD MONTH

[*Enter Ts'ai Yi-so, the bookseller.*]

**Ts'ai** [*sings*]:
    In my shop, like the famous caves of Yu-shan,
    A myriad precious volumes are assembled;
    My labours as a collector have won for me
    Both learned reputation and hard cash.
    A scholar-merchant, I, who only hope
    To avoid any book-burning First Emperor of Ch'in!

[*Speaks*]: Nanking ranks first among cities for the wealth of
its books, and most of these are in Three Mountain Street,
where I keep the largest bookshop. [*Points*]: Here are the
Thirteen Canons, the twenty-one Dynastic Histories,[1] all the
tomes of the nine schools of philosophy, of the three reli-
gions and the hundred thinkers, besides collections of eight-
legged essays[2] and fashionable modern novels. They cram the
shelves and innumerable boxes and rooms. I have travelled
north and south to gather this collection, minutely examining
old editions to make fine reprints with scholarly annotations.
As well as earning a handsome profit by these transactions, I
have helped to preserve and circulate the noblest thoughts of

---

1. See Scene 1, n. 11 for the Six Canons. Later subdivisions and additions led to a
corpus of thirteen works which remain canonical to this day. The dynastic histories have
by now reached a total of twenty-four.

2. The examination essay of Ming and Ch'ing times was christened "eight-legged"
because it developed a prescribed form in eight sections.

mankind. Even the doctors and masters of literature greet me
with deference. I have reason to be satisfied with my reputation. [*He laughs*]: This year the general civil service examination will be held again, and the finest literary talents will
receive due honour. The government has endorsed a proposal
by the Minister of Ceremonies, Ch'ien Ch'ien-i, advocating a
new style of writing to express the spirit of the new reign.
Consequently I have invited several leading critics to compile
anthologies as models for composition. They will start work
today. I'll hang up my latest advertisement. [*He hangs a
couplet on each side of the door, which he reads*]:

"The style in vogue was created by men of renown,
Imitation of these models will please the chief examiner."
    [*Exit.*]

    [*Enter Hou Fang-yü and Su K'un-sheng, with baggage.*]

**Hou** [*sings*]:
The moonlit tower of those bygone years
Is far off as a dream;
And the sound of pipes is stilled,
Remote from each other as the star-lovers
Across the Milky Way,
Will no one bear a message,
No one aid us in our distress?

[*Speaks*]: Master Su, we have travelled hundreds of miles to
answer the summons of my Fragrant Princess, but we arrived
too late. She is now immured in the palace, and it is impossible even to reach her with a message. Last night I was
warned to leave my lodgings. I don't know where we can stay
in safety until we get news of her. [*Sings*]:

If needs be,
I shall wait for her till my hair turns white.
But perhaps that happy day
Is reserved for another lifetime.

**Su:** It is clear that the political situation is going from bad to
worse. Public opinion has also changed considerably. Those
in authority are launching an offensive against the virtuous to
settle old scores. It would be wiser to keep out of their way
and practise patience.

**Hou:** You may be right; I have hardly any friends left in this neighbourhood. My old comrades Ch'en and Wu have retired to their native provinces. Perhaps I should follow them. [*Sings*]:

My friends are seagulls by the shore.
Prouder than kings,
They turn aside from the dusty world,
And frown at the muddled chess-game in the capital.
Why not sail to the south
And seek them among the hills?

**Su:** We are near the book market in Three Mountain Street, where there is always a large crowd. We had better avoid it. [*He quickens his pace, singing*]:

Keep away from the leopards and wolves,
The apes who wear the robes of government.
On Three Mountain Street the mob is like a torrent.

**Hou** [*stopping*]: Here is Ts'ai Yi-so's bookshop, where my old comrades used to stay. Let us inquire whether they are still here. [*Looking up*]: I see two new advertisements posted on these pillars. [*Reads*]: "The Revival Club reopened." And there's a small notice beside it: "New selections of model examination essays by Messrs. Ch'en Chen-hui and Wu Ying-chi. Do you think they are here now?

**Su:** I'll ask. [*Calls*]: Is the worthy proprietor at home?

**Ts'ai** [*entering*]: Welcome. Are you gentlemen looking for books?

**Hou:** No, sir. I come for some information. Have you seen Messrs. Ch'en and Wu?

**Ts'ai:** They are inside at the moment. I'll go and call them. [*Exit.*]

**Ch'en** and **Wu** [*entering*]: Oh, it's Brother Hou and Master Su as well. What a delightful surprise! [*Mutual bows.*]

**Ch'en:** Where have you come from?

**Hou:** I have been in my native village.

**Wu:** When did you arrive in the capital?

**Hou:** Only yesterday. [*Sings*]:

The smoke of war has covered half the land.

I have been with the army north and south,
One camp after another, three wasted years.
Now I return; who pities this wasted body?
I have lingered by the Ch'in-huai River,
Among the peach blossoms of my former haunt,
But the shore no longer extends its former welcome.

[*Speaks*]: So I see that you, brothers, are creating a new literary style.

**Ch'en** and **Wu:**  You mock us.  [*Sing*]:

Here in Chin-ling,[3] seat of ancient learning,
We labour side by side on compilations
To hold up T'ang and Sung as worthy models
And discourage the decadent Six Dynasties styles.
Studying our selections from the Eastern Forest,
All will acknowledge our classic purity.

**Ts'ai** [*from backstage*]:  Please join me for a cup of tea.

**Ch'en** and **Wu:**  Thank you, we are coming.

> [*They accompany **Hou** and **Su** to a room at the back. A
> servant of Juan Ta-ch'eng enters with a bundle of large
> visiting cards.*]

**Servant:**  My master, His Excellency Juan, has just been promoted to Vice-Minister of War, and has received a new python robe and jade belt as tokens of Imperial favour. He will be sent to direct the defence of the river, so he is paying a round of farewell visits to his friends.

> [***Juan** enters in python robe and jade belt, sitting
> proudly in his sedan chair, followed by retainers with
> fans and official umbrellas.*]

**Juan** [*sings*]:
See my attendants, rank on rank,
Fans waving, parasols held high.
And who is this, in lofty state?
The man you scorned in years gone by.

**Servant:**  Let Your Excellency's chair be halted. We are near the

---

3. Chin-ling is one of the ancient names for Nanking.

residence of His Excellency Yueh. [*Leaves a card at the latter's gate.*]

**Juan:** You need not clear the street. Allow the public to gather round and admire me. [*Waving his fan, brags*]: Having received this high appointment from His Majesty, I'm paying a series of ceremonious visits. My foes of the Eastern Forest Party will be arrested by Imperial decree. They seem to have fled, for I see no sign of them. [*Sings*]:

Now I'll show them power and glory!
At last the wrinkles on my brow will vanish.

[*Noting the sign on the bookshop*]: What's this advertisement? Revival Club? Tear it down and show it to me. [*Servant does so. Juan reads*]: "Reopening of the Revival Club. Ch'en Chen-hui and Wu Ying-chi are editing new selections." How now! That Club is an offshoot of the Eastern Forest Party which has been in close collaboration with the rebels Chou and Lei. Now that a warrant is out for their arrest, who dares invite them to make anthologies? This book dealer is a rash fellow. Stop my chair! [*Steps out of the sedan, sits before the bookshop, and says*]: Summon the local official in charge of the book trade. [*The **official** is summoned.*]

**Official** [*kneeling before **Juan***]: What is Your Excellency's wish?

**Juan** [*sings*]:
This bookseller defies the law
By conspiring with the Revival Club.
My duty is to suppress these rebels,
Yours, to expose them root and branch.

**Official:** Don't worry, Your Excellency. I'm an expert at making arrests. [*Exits and re-enters with **Ts'ai Yi-So**.*] The criminal Ts'ai Yi-so is here, Your Excellency.

**Ts'ai** [*kneeling*]: As a loyal subject of His Majesty, I protest that I have not violated any law.

**Juan:** You have commissioned members of the Revival Club to work for you.

**Ts'ai:** New selections of model essays are made every year before the civil service examination.

**Juan:** Fie! Are you ignorant of the Imperial decree, whereby all rebels are to be arrested? The law knows no mercy. You have harboured these rebels in your shop, yet you refuse to admit your guilt. You had better plead guilty at once.

**Ts'ai:** I did not give them shelter. The gentlemen came of their own accord, because they are interested in the new anthologies.

**Juan:** So you admit that they are inside your shop. [*To his attendants*]: Make sure that none of them slip out.

> [*Exeunt attendants*]

**Juan** [*whispers to the official*]: Send an immediate message to the City Marshal, who has the exclusive duty to deal with rebels. He must send his guards to arrest them. [*Sings*]:

The Scarlet Guard will see the prisons filled,
As these new rebels are in turn suppressed.

**Official:** Yes, Your Excellency. [*Exit hurriedly. Juan re-enters his sedan.*]

**Hou, Ch'en,** and **Wu** [ *enter, shouting*]: What crime have we committed that we should be kept in custody? Whoever you are, you have no regard for justice.

**Juan** [*smiling*]: I have given you no offence. Why are you all so indignant? What are your names? [*They announce them.*] Aha, so it's you three gentlemen. Don't you recognize this humble official? [*Sings*]:

How imposing now my dignity must appear,
How overwhelming my majestic frame!

[*To Wu*]: Do you remember how you prevented me from joining the sacrifice at the Temple of Confucius? [*To Ch'en*]: Do you remember borrowing my troupe of actors? Why did you call me ugly names while enjoying my "Swallow Letter"? [*To Hou*]: When I bought you a valuable wardrobe, you threw it away.

**Hou:** So it is Bearded Juan gloating on his revenge!

**Ch'en** and **Wu:** Indeed. Let us drag him to the palace and tell what sort of man he is.

**Juan** [*laughing*]: No need to hurry: you will have ample opportunity to tell. [*Pointing*]: See who is coming to fetch you! [*Exit in sedan.*]

**Four Guards** [*enter, shouting*]: Which is Ts'ai Yi-so?

11. The bookseller Ts'ai Yi-so:
"What is behind all this?"

Ts'ai: I am. What is the matter?

Guard: We have come from the Marshal's headquarters to make certain arrests.

Ts'ai: Who are you arresting?

Guard: The three graduates Ch'en, Wu, and Hou.

Hou: We are all present. On what grounds do you arrest us?

Guard: Come at once to headquarters. There you will discover. [*He leads them out in chains.*]

Ts'ai: What is behind all this? [*Calls*]: Brother Su, come quickly.

Su [*entering*]: What has happened?

Ts'ai: It is terrible, terrible! The two scholars who were making selections for me have been arrested, and Master Hou as well.

Su: So it has really come to this! [*Sings*]:

Hawks swoop down on innocent citizens;
The Revival Club is an unprotected babe.
Ma and Juan are now omnipotent.
Woe to the world
When the savage Prime Minister of a foolish Emperor
Gives public pretexts for private revenge!

[*Speaks*]: Let us find out what is happening. We may yet be able to save them.

Ts'ai: We must. I'll inquire where they are being kept, so that I can take them some food. [*They sing*]:

Ts'ai:
Court officers are furthering private feuds.

Su:
Like the man of Ch'i, we fear the sky will fall.

Ts'ai:
Who can prevent this new Burning of Books?[4]

Su:
On the Commander-in-Chief, Earl Tso, we call.

---

4. The most opprobrious burning of books in Chinese history was the work of the First Emperor, Ch'in Shih-huang-ti, 259-209 B.C., the unifier of the country whose name became a byword for ferocious despotism.

# The Return to the Hills

## 1645, THIRD MONTH

[*Chang Wei enters; he wears a long white beard.*]

**Chang** [*sings*] :
Aged retainer of the Imperial court,
I look back in vain towards my northern home.
Mist and rain shroud the city of Nanking.
Alas, the hopeful notes of restoration
Have changed into the wail of a new tyranny,
And the old court robes cannot hide the new decline.

[*Speaks*] : Formerly a Commander of the Imperial Guard in
Peking, I came south after the downfall of the old capital.
Here the new Emperor rewarded me with the same rank I
held before, but evil counsels sway the government. The
condition of the country deteriorates. As for me, I have built
myself a house in the southern suburbs, with a pavilion called
Pine Wind Hall, where I hope to retire and and enjoy a calm
old age. Unfortunately I have charge of two state prisoners,
the so-called rebels Chou and Lei. These are sworn adversaries
of Ma and Juan, who are determined to have them convicted.
I am aware that this is grossly unjust, but I have not been
able to find a way to save them. This harasses me day and
night, so that I cannot decide to retire. [*Sings*] :

The court is all intrigue and party strife:
All honest men retire from such a life.
Wherefore should I uphold the butcher's knife
For malefactors? Quickly would I flee
To my thatched Pine Pavilion and be free,
Singing aloud to every passing cloud.
But a terrible injustice haunts my breast,
Until I stave it off I cannot rest.

**Servant** [*entering*] : Your Excellency, the City Marshal has captured three rebels, who await your immediate judgment.

[*Four guards carrying instruments of torture enter and stand on*

*either side of the stage. **Chang** ascends the tribune of justice.*
*A **Guard** leads in **Hou**, **Wu**, and **Ch'en**, and kneels before*
***Chang** to hand him the written warrant. **Chang** examines it.*]

**Chang:** According to a report from the local official in charge of the book trade, you are accused of organizing a secret society and plotting to purchase the freedom of Chou and Lei with bribes. Therefore you have been arrested. What have you to say in self-defense?

**Ch'en and Wu** [*sing*]:
We plead not guilty.
Scholars of the Revival Club,
Our friends are none but literary men.
Only the tyranny of Ch'in Shih-huang[1]
Would convict such innocent people as ourselves.

**Hou** [*sings*]:
Do not torture us.
I came to Nanking to visit old friends,
And have no part in any clandestine meeting.
Why should we be destroyed
Like fish in a pond or swallows on a beam?

**Chang:** You allege that you have been arrested without cause. It is impossible that the City Marshal should have committed such a blunder. [*Pounding on the table with a wooden block*]: Bring out the whips. Make them confess the truth.

**Ch'en** [*kneeling*]: Please do not take umbrage, Your Honour. I am Ch'en Chen-hui from I-hsing. My only crime is to have selected literary models at Ts'ai Yi-so's bookshop. I can think of no other offence.

**Wu** [*kneeling*]: I am Wu Ying-chi from Juei-ch'ih, and a colleague of Ch'en Chen-hui. I was engaged in the same work, apart from which I did nothing.

**Chang** [*to **Guard** *]: If these men are accused of organizing a secret society and plotting at Ts'ai's bookshop, Ts'ai himself should know the truth. Why was he not arrested? [*Throwing a warrant to the **Guard***]: Make haste and fetch Ts'ai Yi-so. [*Exit **Guard.***]

**Hou** [*kneeling*]: I am Hou Fang-yü from Kuei-te in Honan, and I travelled to Nanking with the sole purpose of visiting friends.

---

1. See Scene 29, n. 4.

When I heard that these old schoolmates of mine were in the bookshop, I called to visit them and was promptly arrested.

**Chang** [*pondering*]: Recently the artist Lan Ying brought me a picture of the Peach Blossom Fountain for my Pine Wind Pavilion. It contained an inscription signed Hou Fang-yü of Kuei-te. Are you the same individual?

**Hou**: It is I, the accused, Your Honour.

**Chang** [*with a faint bow*]: This is most regrettable. I was greatly impressed by your calligraphy, and your verse is full of subtle import. I am sure you had nothing to do with this business. Please stand by.

**Hou**: I thank Your Honour for your kind expression of sympathy. [*He is offered a chair and sits down.*]

**Guard** [*re-entering with warrant*]: Your Honour, Ts'ai Yi-so has bolted his shop and fled.

**Chang**: How can this case be judged without any proof of the organization or of the alleged bribery?

**Guard** [*entering with a letter*]: Here is a letter from Their Excellencies Wang and Ch'ien for Your Honour's perusal.

**Chang**: So it comes from two highly respected Ministers of State. [*After reading it*]: They are absolutely right. I did not realize that Ch'en and Wu were leaders of the Revival Club. [*sings*]:

One is an essayist of renown;
The other has won fame as a poet.
What harm have they done to deserve arrest,
And why should I serve as the agent of vile intrigues?
As a judge, I hold independent authority;
I should bring the light of the sun to the darkest hell.
Let not the righteous be persecuted,
Or art and literature decay in consequence.

[*Politely, to **Ch'en** and **Wu***]: Gentlemen, excuse my lack of courtesy. Are Their Excellencies Wang Chueh-ssu and Ch'ien Mu-chai old friends of yours?

**Ch'en** and **Wu**: We have never had the pleasure of knowing them personally.

**Chang**: Even so, they have written to me about your lofty characters and literary attainments.

**Ch'en** and **Wu**: Perhaps it was due to Their Excellencies' sense of justice.

**Chang:** Precisely. Though a member of the military profession, I am also devoted to literature and learning. How can I sacrifice worthy men just to please the powers that be? I understand how deeply you have been wronged. Please stand by and wait until I pronounce the verdict. You will then be released. [*Ch'en and Wu are given seats while he writes the verdict. A guard arrives with a court bulletin.*]

**Guard** [*to Chang*]: Today's bulletin contains an important new decree. Please read it, Your Honour.

**Chang** [*reading it aloud*]: "In accordance with Prime Minister Ma's memorial concerning the swift execution of rebels to pacify the country, Chou Piao and Lei Yin-tso, who plotted with the Prince of Lu and have been conclusively proved traitors, should promptly be executed to vindicate justice. A decree is hereby issued to that effect. Furthermore, a memorial has been presented by Vice-Minister of War Juan which runs as follows: 'Concerning the extermination of secret societies and the pacification of the country: it has been discovered that the former members of the Eastern Forest Party are still as numerous as locusts darkening the sun, and the young upstarts of the Revival Club are breeding like their larvae. The locusts have already become a plague and must be wiped out. Their larvae are the calamity of the future and should be exterminated as a precaution. I, Your Majesty's servant Juan Ta-ch'eng, possess a black list of these locusts and larvae. Mass arrests will be effected with the guidance of the aforesaid list.' The decree is hereby issued that those enumerated on the list aforesaid are to be searched for and arrested. The urgent attention of authorities concerned is called with regard to these matters." [*Chang, deeply shocked*]: Ma and Juan are growing more and more vindictive. I'm afraid no good man will survive. [*Sings*]:

While I try to serve justice and mitigate penalties,
They impose iniquitous laws and persecutions.
A foul torrent has invaded our clean rivers,
Every action of theirs is a monument of infamy.
Soon they will catch everyone of worth in their evil snare;
Few dare resist their authority.
The members of the Revival Club and Eastern Forest Party
Will be hunted down as victims of the new tyranny.

[*To Hou, Ch'en, and Wu*]: Sympathising with the wrongs

you have suffered, I was about to release you, but the latest decrees prevent me. Not only are Masters Chou and Lei to be executed but all members of the Eastern Forest Party and Revival Club are proscribed.

**Hou, Ch'en** and **Wu** [*kneeling*]: We implore your Honour to save us.

**Chang**: If I released you, you might be caught by others. Then you would certainly be doomed. I advise you to be patient. [*Reading aloud as he writes*]: "After cross-examination, no evidence of secret organizations or bribery could be discovered. The accused should be kept in temporary custody. When Ts'ai Yi-so becomes available as a witness, the verdict will be given." [*To Hou, Ch'en, and Wu*]: Although he is mainly concerned with self-advancement, the City Marshal is not devoid of conscience. I shall send him a personal letter. [*Reading aloud as he writes*]: "Having served for many years in the Imperial Guard, I have seen more than most people of victims sacrificed to intrigue. I have reached the conclusion that the good and the evil are in perpetual conflict: they rise and fall alternately. Every situation changes after a crisis. We who are responsible for preserving justice and the law should beware of favouritism. It is not our business to wield the butcher's knife for those in temporary power. There is a heaven above, and public opinion never dies. Let us avoid mistakes we shall never cease to regret." [*He bows to Hou, Ch'en, and Wu*]: Please wait patiently in confinement for the day when these wrongs will be righted. [*The prisoners are led off, and Chang continues*]: I served the late Emperor throughout his reign, but now that the country is ruined and my home destroyed, I have given up all hope of a future career. Why should I continue in the service of tyrants? There is an old proverb, "When you make a decision, don't wait till the day is over." I can hesitate no longer. [*Calls*]: Groom, bring my horse. I shall ride to my Pine Wind Pavilion. [*Groom leads in horse. Chang mounts it, singing*]:

In the Spring, evening petals fill the sky,
Green undulating mountains soothe the eye.
South of the city, I waken from a dream
As a tired traveller finds a gushing stream.

[*Speaks*]: Here I am back in my Pine Wind Pavilion. It seems as far from the world as the Peach Blossom Spring. I'll go and enjoy the view. [*Sings as he goes upstairs*]:

Few people approach this stream among the rocks.
The wind in the pines recalls the murmur of waves.

[*Calls*]: Tell the gardener to open the windows and sweep the porch.

**Gardener** [*entering, sweeps and recites*]:

Catkins have flown where the swallow settles,
Cobwebs have caught the flying petals.

[*Speaks*]: The porch is swept clean, Your Honour. [*Exit.*]

**Chang** [*gazing out from the porch*]: How the shadows of the pines caress the window. My heart feels calm and rested. This would be a suitable place to put my couch. [*Wanders across to the balcony*]: Spring water fills the pond and casts a green reflection on my beard. Here I ought to set up a tea-stove. [*Laughing*]: What a hurry I was in! I am still wearing my official uniform, most unbecoming to this hermitage. I must look ridiculous. [*To servant*]: Open my bamboo chest. I shall change into my loose robe, straw sandals, and bamboo hat. [*Changes and sings*]:

This is my compensation for old age.
Once my three houses are roofed with plain bamboo
I'll pack my uniform.

[*Enter **guard** with **Ts'ai Yi-so**.*]

**Guard:** Among pines he must still preside over the law, and among the bamboos over documents pore. I have just captured Ts'ai Yi-so. Though His Honour Chang has left his office, I must report that his order has been executed. [*Calls*]: Is anybody there?

**Servant:** What urgent business has brought you so far from the city?

**Guard:** Please report that Ts'ai Yi-so is at His Honour's disposal.

**Servant** [*goes upstairs and announces*]: The guard has caught Ts'ai Yi-so, and he is waiting for Your Honour's instructions.

**Chang:** Now that this has happened, what can I do about the others? Tell the guard to wait downstairs and listen to me.

12. Chang the Taoist, former Commander
of the Imperial Guard: "Few people approach
this stream among the rocks."

[*To* **guard** *from the porch*]: This is a very serious case and it must be kept secret. Ts'ai Yi-so is one of the chief witnesses; he will have to remain here. I shall question him presently.

**Guard**: Yes, Your Honour. [*Guard fastens* **Ts'ai** *to a tree, and is about to leave when he is recalled.*]

**Chang**: Come back. You may take my horse to the city as well as my official cap, belt, robe, and boots. I wish to meditate in peace. Remember not to disturb me here again. [*Exit* **Guard** *with horse, etc.* **Chang** *stamps his foot.*] What an outrage, that a guard should trespass in my private garden and tie a witness to my favourite pine-tree! What sort of a hermitage is this? I shall have to see the prisoner. [*Seeing* **Ts'ai**]: So it is you, Ts'ai Yi-so.

**Ts'ai**: Perhaps Your Honour may remember meeting me before?

**Chang**: Of course I do, but that has nothing to do with the case. You have been accused of violating the new decree by harbouring rebels of the Revival Club.

**Ts'ai** [*trying to kowtow*]: Yes, Your Honour.

**Chang**: The latest books in your shop have some connection with the members of that club. They will be held as evidence against you.

**Ts'ai** [*again trying to kowtow*]: Please be merciful, Your Honour!

**Chang**: Your life can only be saved if you are willing to sacrifice your fortune.

**Ts'ai**: I'm willing to give up everything.

**Chang** [*delighted*]: Then everything will turn out well. [*To servant*]: Unbind him quickly. [*Ts'ai is released.* **Chang** *says to him*]: If you are willing to give up your property, why not follow me to the hills?

**Ts'ai**: My life depends on Your Honour.

**Chang** [*pointing*]: Look towards the northeast. How white the clouds are and how blue the hills. [*To servant*]: Take good care of the house. Master Ts'ai and I are going to view the scenery. We shall soon return.

[*Exit servant.* **Chang** *and* **Ts'ai** *walk along together.*]

**Chang** [*points*]: We shall spend tonight in the green forest.

**Ts'ai:** If Your Honour wants to enjoy mountain scenery, you should send a servant to prepare lodgings in advance. Otherwise where can you stay except in some secluded temple?

**Chang:** You are still in the dark. Once I have surrendered my official cap, I shall become a poor Taoist priest. Any mountain cave will serve me for a dwelling.

**Ts'ai:** What does Your Honour mean?

**Chang:** Come, hesitate no longer. Ask no questions. Follow me. [*Sings*]:

My eyes are fixed upon the floating clouds,
Regardless of the rocky distances.
Slowly the pine woods darken, peace descends.
Deep in the forest men are very few;
A lonely path will wind between the peaks.
Over the hills I'll walk with open heart,
Visiting all the temples and forgetting
Whatever dynasty may rule the land.
In the realm of Immortals, far from the world's dust,
A few wild peaches will be my nourishment.
Now I know how easy it is to escape the turmoil.
At dawn we shall leave our hut among the clouds;
When we reach the summit the sun will still be high.

---

SCENE 31

# The Impeachment Drafted

1645, THIRD MONTH

**Su K'un-sheng** [*enters and recites*]:

The Wan-li Emperor reigned in my youth;
The Ch'ung-chen era saw me old and grey.
Every court favourite I've seen come and go
From T'ien-ch'i to the present day.[1]

[*Speaks*]: For half a century I have seen the country ruled by four Emperors in succession; and under the fourth, by

---

1. He has lived through the following reigns: Wan-li, 1573-1620; T'ai-ch'ang, 1620-1621; T'ien-ch'i, 1621-1628; Ch'ung-chen, 1628-1644.

two execrable monsters. Oblivious of Heaven and the sun above, these are resolved to exterminate righteous men. My friend Master Hou is one of their first victims. Since he and I are fellow countrymen, I have come all the way to the lake district to solicit the help of Earl Tso, the Commander-in-Chief. I have been here three days, but his headquarters is so closely guarded that I cannot approach him. Today there is to be a grand review of the armies defending the river. Wherever the Commander passes, it is so quiet that neither a dog nor a chicken dare make a sound. I must think of some way to attract his attention. [*He calls the **Innkeeper**.*]

**Innkeeper** [*enters and recites*]:

Few visitors come to the Yellow Crane Pavilion,
Though many wineshops grace our White Cloud City.

[*Speaks*]: What is your wish, sir?

**Su:** Please tell me how soon His Excellency the Commander will be returning to headquarters.

**Innkeeper:** Not for a long time yet. There are three hundred thousand troops to be reviewed. Usually their maneuvers continue till nightfall. Today His Excellency has asked Governor Yuan and Inspector-General Huang to join him. There will be a banquet after the review, so they are bound to be late.

**Su:** In that case you had better bring some wine. I'll drink while I wait.

**Innkeeper** [*bringing wine*]: Why wait? Why don't you drink your wine and go to bed?

**Su:** Don't worry. Just close your door. I'm not spying on anybody. [*Exit **Innkeeper**.*] Now that the full moon has risen above the Eastern Hills, one should enjoy the beauty of night along the river. The pity of it is that one cannot feel in a happy mood. While drinking I might as well sing to banish gloom. [*Sings*]:

Amid a boundless Heaven glows
A spotless moon; aloft it rose,
Filling twelve balconies with light.
A breeze through pearly curtain blows,
And silver screen; I seem to sit
On the Queen of Heaven's parapet,

Pouring wine into cups of jade.
How seldom does an earthly sight
So dazzling to man's eyes appear!
What rapture thus to live each night,
The moon and I so clear!

[*Drinks and says*]: Old Juan Ta-ch'eng was very partial to
this song, but I would stop singing it rather than oblige him. I
hope the Commander-in-Chief will soon return. I'll sing again.
If he hears me, he may ask questions; then my chance will
come. [*Sings*]:

Your lonely shadow is a bough,
Swaying on the twilit air.
Dimly I see the magpies, now
Suddenly startled and aware . . .

**Innkeeper** [*entering*]: Will you please go to sleep! If your singing
annoys the Commander-in-Chief, I shall get into trouble.

**Su** [*sings*]:
Where can I find the myriad hills
And build a hut among bamboos . . .

**Innkeeper** [*pulling him*]: Please go to sleep.

**Su**: Don't worry. I'm a fellow countryman of the Commander's,
and I want him to hear me.

**Innkeeper**: Very well, sing on. But don't say that I didn't warn
you.

**Su** [*sings*]:
Where Ch'ang O[2] forlornly dwells,
Who will pluck a laurel branch?
People dear are seldom near —
Heart is torn from heart's delight.
Oh, the bliss to live each night,
The moon and I so clear!

[*Several armed soldiers with bows and arrows pass by. Su
says*]: I hear horses' hoofs; perhaps they are returning to
headquarters. I'll sing again:

"How bright the moon!

---

2. Ch'ang O, Goddess of the Moon who fled to that sphere after stealing the elixir of
immortality from her husband, the prodigious archer Hou Yi. Her husband became God
of the Sun, and the two are said to meet once a month at the time of the new moon.

I'll play a tune
Until my flute of jade will crack,
Then ride upon a phoenix' back,
Flying faster than the wind,
The city of my dreams to find."

[*Enter four guards with banners.*] The guards are coming nearer. I'll sing a bit louder. . . . [*Sings*]:

"Her pendants tinkle. Has she flown
From her palace all alone?"

> [*Enter Tso Liang-yü, Yuan Chi-hsien, and Huang Shu, all on horseback.*]

**Tso** [*recites*]:
The Court is engrossed in training singers and dancers;
Here on the river our drums beat to more serious purpose.

**Yuan**: Indeed? Maybe singers and dancers are also being trained near Your Excellency's headquarters.

**Tso**: Who would dare? Military discipline is strictly enforced here.

**Huang**: I am sure I hear somebody singing.

> [*Tso stands still and listens. Su sings even louder.*]

**Su** [*singing*]:
An aura round her cloudy hair,
And down her arms a lustrous light:
Only with one can she compare,
The Goddess of the Moon so bright.
Oh the bliss to live each night,
The Moon and I so clear!

**Tso** [*angrily*]: Who dares to break martial law by singing in the middle of the night? Arrest the culprit!

> [*Guards arrest Su and lead him before Tso.*]

**Tso**: Have you been singing?

**Su**: I can't deny it.

**Tso**: Are you not aware of the severity of martial law? What makes you so audacious?

**Su**: Because I am desperate. I had to sing, even at the risk of my life. I hope Your Excellency will pardon me.

**Yuan**: He talks as if he were drunk.

**Huang**: But his voice was admirable.

**Tso**: The fellow looks decidedly suspicious. Take him along to headquarters. [*Exit Tso, followed by the others.*]

**Tso** [*sings*]:
> After the review we enter Wuchang gate.
> Night has fallen, every sound is hushed,
> Not a dog barks; the city is a desert.
> At the third watch, suddenly we hear a minstrel.
> There must be a motive behind his mournful song.

> [*They arrive at headquarters. Tso says to Yuan and Huang*]: Please spend the night at my humble headquarters. There are further important matters to be discussed.

**Huang** and **Yuan**: We would rather not put you to such inconvenience. [*All enter and sit down.*]

**Yuan**: The minstrel should be cross-examined. Perhaps we may than release him.

**Tso**: You are right. [*To guard*]: Bring the singer here. [*Su is led in and kneels before Tso, who says to him*]: Why did you violate martial law? State nothing but the truth.

**Su**: I came all the way from Nanking to see Your Excellency. Since your headquarters was so closely guarded that I could not gain admission, I broke the law on purpose.

**Tso**: You will have to be punished. This cannot be true.

**Huang**: Please curb your indignation. Let us hear his reasons for wishing to see Your Excellency.

**Su** [*sings*]:
> A sinister fog envelops the capital,
> Each new dawn sees new arrests.
> Now Master Hou is locked away:
> For old-time friendship's sake
> I beg you to root out this new-risen spite.

**Tso**: I was indeed a friend of Master Hou's father. If he wants my assistance, you must have brought a letter from him. Let me see it.

**Su** [*kowtowing*]: Juan Ta-ch'eng gave orders that he was to be arrested on the spot. He had no chance to write a letter.

Tso: How can I believe this? [*Pondering*]: An old friend of Master Hou happens to be staying with me. I'll see if he can recognize you. [*To servant*]: Ask Master Liu to join us.

[*Exit servant. Enter Liu Ching-t'ing.*]

Liu: Good man, bad man, friend or foe, just ask old Liu and he'll tell you so! Let me take a look at him. . . . Ah, this is my sworn brother Su K'un-sheng! [*Su and Liu both wipe tears from their eyes.*]

Tso: So the man is no impostor.

Liu: No, it's Su K'un-sheng, the best minstrel in the world. Everybody ought to know of him.

Tso: I had no idea that I was listening to such a celebrity.

[*Tso helps Su to rise. They bow to each other and sit down.*]

Liu: Tell me, why has Master Hou been imprisoned?

Su [*sings*]:
    Associate of the Eastern Forest Party,
    Active member of the Revival Club,
    Master Hou offended the eunuch's henchman.
    Now bearded Juan is thirsting for revenge,
    Pig-headed Ma has lost all sense of justice.
    Fierce cavalry galloped to Three Mountain Street,
    Swooped upon their prey.

[*Speaks*]: I have heard no news of him since he was taken to jail, so I risked my life to come here and appeal for aid. How fortunate I was to meet you, Brother Liu! [*He bows to Liu.*] I hope you will persuade the Commander-in-Chief to do something to save him as soon as possible.

Tso [*angrily*]: Brothers Yuan and Huang, how can we tolerate such corruption at court? It makes my blood boil.

Yuan: I have also heard that Lady T'ung, the new Emperor's first consort, made an arduous journey to join him. Ma and Juan prevented her from seeing him because they want to create another Empress and thereby claim an Imperial connection. They deserve to be executed.

Huang: Besides, the genuine Heir Apparent has been discovered. Many veteran statesmen have testified to his identity. Now

the villains are about to imprison him too. Everybody is so
outraged that they would gladly hack Juan and Ma to pieces
and offer them at his late Majesty's sacrificial altar.

Tso: While we risk our lives in battle for the Emperor, who could
imagine that such villains would usurp the power? They
massacre the virtuous, sell titles and offices, and disport
themselves in a period of national crisis. The new Emperor
seems to be precipitating the ruin of the country. Shih K'o-fa
appears to be the only loyal minister, but he has been
thwarted by Ma and Juan, and has therefore accomplished
nothing. How can I hope to recover the central plain single-
handed? There is no alternative but an emergency measure to
coerce the new Emperor. [*Bowing to Yuan*]: Brother Yuan,
please draft an impeachment.

Yuan: What shall I say?

Tso: Set down all the crimes of Ma and Juan in the strongest
language.

Yuan: Very well, I shall proceed. [*Sings as he writes*]:

"Evil counsels are rampant at court.
They suppress the Emperor's Consort,
Imprison the true Heir Apparent.
They persecute the righteous,
From motives of private vengeance:
Justice is destroyed, the just have taken to flight.
Searching for harlots, they wallow in every vice;
Titles and offices are openly sold;
Words cannot circumscribe their crimes.

Tso: We shall also require a public declaration. [*Bowing to
Huang*]: Please draft it, Brother Huang.

Huang: In what terms?

Tso: Announce that I am mobilizing my armies to chastise the
villains, who will certainly be annihilated.

Liu: That is exactly what should be done.

Tso: You came here originally to dissuade me from marching east.
Now you urge me to the contrary. Why?

Liu: The situation has changed since the new Emperor mounted
the Throne.

Tso: Aye, so it has! I was a General under the late Emperor,
whose legitimate heir is my true sovereign. When Ma and

Juan raised Prince Fu to the Throne, I was far away on the frontier and never received the decree.

**Huang**: I shall now prepare the draft. [*Liu hands him paper and brush. He writes, singing*]:

"To cleanse the court, we make this declaration:
Borne by gallant warriors, our banners of justice
Will rise above the dusty road.
In a trice we shall enter Nanking,
March to the palace through the Phoenix Gate,
And worship at the Imperial Tombs.
We shall sweep out the cabinet,
And put our sharp swords to the proof."

**Tso**: Let us sign our names.

**Yuan**: This is a solemn undertaking. We should ask the new Governor Ho T'eng-chiao to join us.

**Tso**: He is an awkward fellow; just add his name without telling him. [*All sign their names.*] This will be issued early tomorrow morning, then I'll mobilize my armies.

**Yuan**: It may not be safe to deliver it by post.

**Tso**: Why?

**Yuan**: Many letters of protest have been pouring into the capital. Ma and Juan have been censoring them and having them burned.

**Tso**: Then we shall have to send a messenger to distribute them.

**Yuan**: That will also be hazardous. Ma and Juan have already taken precautions against us. They have secretly ordered General Tu to build forts along the river. As soon as the declaration appears in the capital, they will hunt out the messenger, who will surely be killed.

**Tso**: What are we to do?

**Liu**: Let me be your messenger.

**Yuan** and **Huang**: Old Master Liu, you are indomitable. If you go, we fear we must dress in mourning to see you off.

**Liu**: I have lived too long to set much value on this old carcass of mine. It is more material to help the Commander accomplish his task.

**Tso**: I should prostrate myself in homage before such a hero. [*Calls*]: Bring wine. [*Servant brings it. Tso kneels and offers* *it to **Liu**, saying*] : Please accept this wine. [***Liu*** *kneels and drinks it. All kowtow to **Liu**, who returns the courtesy.*]

**Liu** [*sings*] :

Holding this beaker of wine, I am moved to tears.
The ancient hero Ching K'o
Sobbed when he sang before his historic mission.[3]
Now at midnight we grasp each other's hand,
Souls united in chivalrous sorrow.
Ask me not when I shall return!
The moon has waned, the wind blows sharp and chill.

[*To **Su***] : Dear younger brother, please keep the Commander company. I shall pack and go east at once.

**Su:** I wish you complete success and a safe return. [*All say goodbye to **Liu**. Exit.*]

**Tso:** A great hero, a great hero!

**Huang** and **Yuan:** And a perfect gentleman! [*They sing*] :

Misty waves recede in the pall of night;
The wine-cup emptied, the watchers' spirits faint.
Another hero leaves, nor hopes to return,
And the great river rolls on without restraint.

---

SCENE 32

# The Imperial Mourning

1645, THIRD MONTH

[*Enter the old **Master of Ceremonies** with a long white beard.*]

**Master of Ceremonies** [*sings*] :

Evil days for our dynasty:
Half its house already fallen in ruins,

---

3. Ching K'o made a heroic though abortive attempt to assassinate the tyrannical First Emperor of Ch'in (see Scene 29, n. 4). He is the subject of one of the most dramatic of the biographies in Ssu-ma Ch'ien's *Records of the Historian* (see Scene 1, n. 6).

And the new scion plays his childish games
While enemies go unpunished
And traitors rob the storehouse.

[*Speaks*]: I am an Imperial announcer of ceremonies. My
duty is to attend to the rites at the ancestral tombs and
temples of the Emperors. In the midst of general upheaval, a
new Emperor mounted the Throne. Nanking seems to have
entered a period of false prosperity. This is the first year
when the new reign-title is to be established, and the event is
to be celebrated in every household. After swallowing three
cups of wine, I could not help airing my views about present
conditions. Some well-meaning listeners reminded me that
every man should be content to sweep the snow from his
own doorstep, without concern for the frost on his neighbour's roof. My retort was, "Even when a noble tree is felled
by a storm, people inevitably point out a moral." [*Calls*]:
Children, what day is today?

**Voices from backstage:** The nineteenth day of the third month.

**Master of Ceremonies:** Bless me! Then it is the anniversary of the
late Emperor's death. A decree has been issued that the
sacrificial altar is to be raised outside the Gate of Peace. I had
almost forgotten my duties. I shall have to make haste.
[*Walks and says*]: One mound after another; dense clumps of
pine and bamboo. Here we come to the altar. Thank good-
ness none of the officials have yet arrived. I'll have to arrange
the ceremonial vessels. [*Proceeds to arrange them.*]

> [*Enter Ma and Yang with retinue, all dressed in their robes
> of state.*]

**Ma** and **Yang** [*sing*]:
The hills and rivers are old, the scene is new.
In the haze of spring, men's spirits are exalted.
The fields are covered with hemp and mulberry trees.
Who grieves for the late Emperor in his heart?
All hope to gain a fine Spring holiday.

> [*Enter Shih K'o-fa in ceremonial robe.*]

**Shih** [*sings*]:
I shall mourn in the fields by the river, and pour
sacrificial wine.

Tears of blood gush ceaseless from my eyes.
Tell me, O Heaven, on this anniversary:
Why should our country suffer such a fate?

[*Ma, Yang, and Shih greet each other.*]

**Ma:** In faithful memory of the late Emperor's death, let us inaugurate the ceremony.

**Shih:** Are all the officials present?

**Master of Ceremonies:** Aye, all are present.

**Ma:** Then let the ceremonies proceed.

[*Attendants bring in vessels and paper money. The* **Master of Ceremonies** *calls out for the late Emperor's Spirit to be evoked and worshipped. All kowtow four times, then rise and stand at attention, while paper money is offered at the altar. **Ma**, holding an ivory tablet, mounts before the sacred tablet, then kneels to offer the money and kowtows. After this, all kneel while the* **Master of Ceremonies** *reads the following elegy.*]

**Master of Ceremonies** [*reading*]: "On the nineteenth day of the third month in the year Yi-yu, the late Emperor's young cousin and successor, the reigning Emperor Yu-sung, respectfully makes this announcement to the Spirit of the Emperor Ssu-tsung.[1] Accomplished and virtuous wert Thou, most fitting to govern the land and uphold the Imperial dynasty for seventeen years. But an evil fate overwhelmed the country. The great canopy collapsed. Your Majesty was martyred for the nation, and the Empress and Heir Apparent departed with thee. I, thine unworthy young cousin, have shamelessly survived thee. Complying with the earnest petitions of all the people and ministers, I have ascended the Throne to tend the ancestral temples and fulfill the wishes of gods and mortals. Thy departure I shall never cease to mourn. I shall guide my officials, and uphold the Imperial dignity. Daily I tremble with alarm and anxiety. Swallowing my tears, I have taken a spear for my pillow: I have sworn an oath to recover the central plain. Today, on the anniversary of thine ascension to Heaven, I have reverently raised this altar to thee and have sent an official to sacrifice in my stead. Please examine the sincerity of my heart and deign to receive the sacrifice."

---

1. *Yi-yu* is the year 1645. Yu-sung was the personal name of the Emperor whose reign-title was Hung-kuang. Ssu-tsung was the dynastic title of his predecessor, the Emperor whose reign-title was Ch'ung-chen.

[*The Master of Ceremonies chants a lament. The officials cry
out three times. There are further prostrations. Ma offers wine
at the altar, kneeling and kowtowing. Further sacrifices are offered;
then the ritual vessels are removed, and the Spirit is escorted with
four more prostrations. The written elegy and paper money are burnt,
and the ceremony is over. Shih K'o-fa continues to weep.*]

**Shih** [*sings*] :
A yellow wind blows far above the earth,
Scattering the desert sand. Where will his Soul appear?
Sparse wildflowers bloom on the bare hills,
And a few crows roost at dusk . . .
Gazing towards the sunset, I see my home.
Your orphaned minister wails to the horizon,
An old man in the twilight of his life.

**Master of Ceremonies:** None of the other officials is weeping,
Your Excellency. As for me, in spite of my age, I am crying
my heart out. [*Exit, still weeping.*]

**Juan Ta-ch'eng** [*enters, crying aloud*] : My late Emperor, my late
Emperor! On this anniversary of your ascension to Heaven,
your former servant Juan has come to mourn. [*Wipes croco-
dile tears.*] What? Is the ceremony over already?

**Ma:** Yes, finished.

**Juan** [*goes to the altar, kowtows four times and cries*] : My late
Emperor, my late Emperor! The country is torn asunder.
Your martyrdom was caused by the villains of the Eastern
Forest Party. Now these traitors are dispersed. Only a few
loyal ministers like ourselves have come to offer you sacrifice
today. Can you hear from the other world? [*Bursts out
crying again.*]

**Ma** [*with a restraining gesture*] : I beg you not to make yourself ill
with grieving. [*Juan wipes his eyes and greets the others.*]

**Shih** [*aside*] : How ludicrous! [*Bids the company farewell,
reciting*] :

Smoke and dust obscure the road;
Imps and goblins prowl abroad.          [*Exit.*]

**Ma:** Let us all return to the city. Grooms, get the horses ready!
[*Ma changes into riding clothes and mounts; the others
follow suit.*]

**All** [*singing*] :
As libations poured and voices wailed,

None could tell true grief from false.
Now, homeward bound, this bright spring day
Gaily we exchange state gossip.
Soft breezes refresh our jaded spirits:
Who cares to ask how the fighting goes?
The rule of the southern dynasty should be gay,
For the beauty of spring is peerless.

**Ma:** Here we are at Cock and Goose Lane, not far from my humble abode. Why not step into my garden and see my peonies?

**Yang:** I regret I have a previous engagement. Farewell. [*Exit.*]

**Juan** [*to* **Ma**]: I shall be delighted to enjoy the peonies with you. [*Both dismount.*]

**Ma:** Pray come in.

**Juan:** After Your Excellency. [*They enter the garden.*] Your flowers are dazzling.

**Ma** [*to servant*]: See that a feast is prepared while we look at the garden. [*Servant arranges a table.* **Ma** *and* **Juan** *change clothes, sit down and drink.* **Ma** *laughs boisterously.*] Today we have brought Ch'ung-chen's reign to a formal conclusion. Tomorrow we shall ask the Emperor to mount the Throne. The past will be forgotten. We are installed as new Ministers to a new Emperor.

**Juan:** As I have been absent on a mission these last few days, I'm ignorant of recent developments at Court.

**Ma:** We have captured the former Heir Apparent and are deliberating how to deal with him. I'd like to have your opinion.

**Juan:** That's easy enough. Everything is in Your Excellency's power, which is based on your wholehearted support of the new Emperor. [*Sings*]:

If you recognize the Heir Apparent,
Where will you put the Emperor you have dethroned?

**Ma:** The best solution would be to clap the Pretender in prison and keep him out of the public eye. But there is also the Lady T'ung, His Majesty's First Consort. She has been making demonstrations outside the palace gate; and she insists on becoming Empress. What am I to do about that?

**Juan:** You should be firm with her. [*Sings*]:

Since time out of mind
All emperors have been partial to young women.
The beauties chosen should be led to the palace,
Ribbons tied to their arms;
Whereupon an Imperial match
May be settled to our advantage.

**Ma:** As a matter of fact, I have already made my selection. Lady T'ung must be excluded from the palace. You knew, of course, about the arrest of Eastern Forest and Revival Club members. How should I deal with these?

**Juan:** They are our inveterate enemies. No leniency should be shown. [*Sings*] :

Do not merely cut the grass and leave the roots.
Every last one of them must be executed.

**Ma** [*laughing*] : I see, I see. You are a man of deep experience. Every sentence you have uttered is enlightened. Let us each quaff three large beakers of wine.

[*A flustered **messenger** rushes in with a document.*]

**Messenger:** The Earl of Ning-nan, Tso Liang-yü, has sent a memorial to the Throne. A copy of it has been delivered to the chancellery. Here is a summary of the contents, which has been forwarded from the cabinet.

**Ma** [*taking it*] : Let us see what brilliant suggestion he has to offer. [*Examines it and explodes*] : What ho! this is an impeachment against us. It enumerates seven major crimes we are alleged to have committed, and requests His Majesty to take immediate action. How monstrous!

[*A second messenger rushes in with another document.*]

**Second messenger:** This document has just arrived for Your Excellency's perusal.

**Ma** [*reading it*] : This is a public declaration. It is an atrocious libel. Tso says he will mobilize his armies to chastise us. What shall we do?

**Juan** [*rises trembling*] : This is terrible, terrible! I have an answer to everything but this.

**Ma:** Are we then to stretch our necks and wait for our heads to be chopped off?

**Juan:** Let me think! Our only solution is to send the three garrison generals to stop him.

**Ma:** But who will remain to fight the northerners if they suddenly cross the river?

**Juan** [*whispering*]: Once the northerners come so far, will fighting be necessary?

**Ma:** What else can we do but fight?

**Juan:** There are two alternatives: either run [*he lifts his skirts*] or surrender [*he kneels*].

**Ma:** I am sure you are right. People like us have our dignity to consider. I would rather yield to the northerners than be butchered by the southern rebels, so that's that! Orders must be sent to the three garrison generals to oppose Tso Liang-yü. But wait! We must find a good pretext for moving these generals southwest.

**Juan:** It will be enough to state that Tso's troops are coming east, that he wants to enthrone the Prince of Lu and appoint himself Regent. The three garrison generals are bound to rush to our rescue.

**Ma:** Yes, yes. Perhaps you had better go in person to persuade them. [*Sings*]:

A lightning messenger will leave with this urgent order:
"In the same boat, we must steer in the same direction,
And thus save our bodies and souls.
We are not prone to panic,
But Tso's hundred thousand crack troops
Will soon descend on the capital.
We rely upon you as an iron chain to guard the Yangtze.
May your strong bows put up a heroic defence!"

**Juan:** I'll take leave of Your Excellency and start at once.

**Ma:** Wait a minute. I have a secret for your ear. [*Whispers*]: The two ministers Kao Hung-t'u and Chiang Jih-kuang have been dismissed for sympathy with the rebels. Since Chou and Lei are still alive, I fear they may work mischief. Should I have them executed at once?

**Juan:** Without a doubt.

**Ma** [*bowing*]: Excuse me for not escorting you.

[*Exit Ma. Juan leaves the house. A* **guard** *approaches him.*]

**Guard:** The messenger who was caught distributing the declaration is now under arrest. What are Your Excellency's instructions concerning him?

**Juan:** Send him to the Ministry of Justice to await execution by decree. [*Mounts his horse, but turns round as he is about to leave.*] I mustn't be reckless. It is just possible that the garrison generals may not succeed in repelling Tso Liang-yü. If I kill his messenger, he will be more vindictive. [*Calls*]: Guard, hurry to the City Marshal and tell him to keep this man under observation pending further orders. [*Exit* **guard.** *Juan exclaims*]: I nearly made an unfortunate mistake. [*He mounts horse and gallops off, singing*]:

North and south of the Yangtze,
Affairs are tangled as a skein of hemp.
Among three chess-players there is no hope of a draw:
The southwestern pawn must be played with the utmost
    caution.

---

SCENE 33

# Reunion in Jail

1645, THIRD MONTH

[*Enter* **Hou Fang-yü** *in shabby clothes.*]

**Hou** [*sings*]:
The old sophora tree has seen many changes,
As it droops in mist above the ruined wall,
At last the spring breeze reaches this gloomy yard.
We three, close comrades, pace with our shadows,
And tell each other of our tribulations.
Where shall we borrow money for our wine?

[*Speaks*]: Already I have been in durance half a month, awaiting trial when the chief witness becomes available. I am fortunate in the company of friends who prevent me from feeling too lonely. Now there is moonlight on the wall; the sophora tree casts a shadow across it, so I'll take a stroll in the courtyard. [*Sings*]:

Moonlight suffuses the azure sky,
But piercing lamentations rend the air,
As if the ghosts of the newly dead
Crept out of the wall to vent their grief.
We three comrades, together wronged in life,
Will share the same vengeance in death.
In our somber cell at midnight we glare our rage.

[*Speaks*]: Suddenly I feel my hair stand on end in fright. I'll rouse Brothers Ch'en and Wu. A little conversation would be a solace. . . . Brother Chen-hui, please wake up. Brother Ying-chi, are you asleep? [*Both come out, rubbing their eyes.*]

**Ch'en** [*sings*]:
Now the moon rides high and the stars are glittering.
Why does he walk alone in the empty yard?

**Wu** [*sings*]:
Forget misfortune for a while.
Though we use ten thousand words,
What sympathy can we hope for?

[*Speaks*]: Brother Hou, why don't you go to bed?

**Hou:** Since we cannot enjoy the spring in this dark prison, I thought of the moon as our sole companion and could not bear to leave it.

**Ch'en:** I can well understand. Let us wander in the moonlight.

**Hou** [*sings*]:
Cries of anguish fill the prison,
The clanging of fetters shakes the night.
Yet at least we three can stroll under the moon.
Light-bodied as sylphs in perfect freedom,
Let us cling to our prestige as scholars:
Many a hero has undergone such ordeals in the past.
Scorning the thorns of the prisoner's life,
We discuss each other's poems.

**Liu Ching-t'ing** [*entering in shackles, recites*]:
How to avoid the mail-clad steeds?
Half the heroes of our age are here confined.

[*Speaks*]: This is my first night in prison, and I'm already bored to death. I was about to fall asleep when I felt an urgent summons to relieve nature. What a nuisance to have to loosen my belt with these shackled hands! [*Crouches and listens.*] I hear a voice that sounds like Master Hou. I must investigate. [*Rising to look*]: I seem to be right. [*Calls*]: Are you Master Hou?

**Hou** [*recognising him*]: Oh, it's our old friend Ching-t'ing!

**Ch'en** and **Wu**: What are you doing here?

**Liu**: I was about to ask you gentlemen the same question. Almighty Buddha! This meeting must be by the grace of God.

**Hou**: It is certainly an unusual occasion. Let us sit on the ground and converse. [*Sings*]:

Old friends may meet in a foreign land
More easily than behind these walls
Which divide us from the world like a range of mountains.
Forgetting our weariness, we gaze at the moon together.
Let us imagine that this is the Peach Blossom Cave,
And talk of our escape from the Ch'in tyrant.[1]

[*Speaks*]: What crime has brought you here in chains to suffer such duress?

**Liu**: No crime whatever. After you were imprisoned, Su K'un-sheng made a long journey to appeal to Earl Tso on your behalf. His Excellency was so indignant that he sat up all night drafting an impeachment and a public declaration against Ma and Juan. I conveyed these documents to the capital, and General Tso's army is about to follow. It is hoped that Ma and Juan will be so alarmed that they will set you free. [*Sings*]:

The armies of Ning-nan were ready,
But no one stepped forth to deliver the declaration.
I alone braved water and fire
For the worthy scholars who have been so deeply wronged.
My spirit grows bolder as my hair turns white;
Under stress and strain my fortitude is strengthened.

---

1. See Scene 1, n. 10.

To exterminate the villains and avenge the virtuous,
I care nought for these shackles.

**Hou**: I never dreamed you would endure all this for me, or that Su K'un-sheng would go so far to save my life. No words could express my gratitude.

**Ch'en**: Although I am sorry to say so, I fear that since General Tso has mobilized his army, our lives will be further endangered.

**Wu**: The Earl of Ning-nan is too guileless to succeed. With the noblest of intentions he cannot save us.

> [*Enter the chief warder, followed by four guards with ropes and lanterns.*]

**Warder** [*recites*]:
From the four walls resound demonic wails,
At the third watch the prisoner's courage fails.

[*Speaks*]: The Ministry of Justice has sent word that the prisoners are to be executed tomorrow morning. Bind them quickly with ropes.

**Guard**: Which prisoners, sir?

**Warder**: Their names are on this written verdict. The two rebels Chou Piao and Lei Yen-tso.

**Guards** [*holding lanterns over Hou, Ch'en, Wu, and Liu*]: These are not the fellows we are looking for.

**Warder** [*shouting*]: You have nothing to do with this. Clear out!
[*Exeunt warder and guards hastily.*]

**Ch'en** [*whispering*]: Who is to be executed?

**Wu**: I heard the names of Chou Piao and Lei Yen-tso.

**Hou**: How iniquitous!

**Liu**: Let us wait and see.

> [*The chief warder re-enters, followed by guards with two prisoners stripped and bound. Exeunt hurriedly. Hou gazes at them stupefied.*]

**Ch'en**: So they have sentenced these virtuous gentlemen to death!

**Wu**: They will be made examples to us.

**Hou** [*sings*] :

    The downfall of the righteous is foretold in the almanac;
    The world is topsy-turvy.
    For this ruthless slaughter, Heaven should collapse.
    Because of a secret scrap of paper,
    They are taken in the dead of night to be beheaded.
    My heart fails me; I am trembling to the marrow.
    Heaven and earth turn black; we shall share the same doom.

    [*Says to Liu*] : What other news did you glean while you were free?

**Liu**: I arrived in too great a hurry to hear much news. I could only see that mass arrests were being made.

**Wu** and **Ch'en**: Whom were they going to arrest?

**Liu**: Inspector General Huang Shu, Governor Yuan Chi-hsien, the Commander of the Imperial Guard Chang Wei, and many other officials and scholars.

**Hou**: Please try to remember their names.

**Liu**: There were so many that I can only recall a few. [*He proceeds to mention several.*]

**Ch'en**: Indeed an astounding galaxy!

**Wu**: We shall be able to hold a conference here of all the most eminent men of letters.

**Hou**: That should be memorable. [*Sings*] :

    Our jail will become an oasis for men of letters.
    There should be a portrait to commemorate the event:
    A group of fallen Immortals,
    Enjoying the spring moon, listening to the cuckoo,
    Singing with the cicada in the autumn wind.

**Wu**: Restricted to such close quarters, we may converse at any time we please.

**Hou**: But while we three are able to move, poor Ching-t'ing is shackled like a dangerous criminal.

**Liu**: I should congratulate myself for not being clamped into a prisoner's cage. [*Sings*] :

    I can still join my hands in greeting
    And observe the rules of courtesy.
    I can even use my arms as a pillow.

Tonight I shall only miss a lady with slender fingers,
To rub my back before I fall asleep.

**Liu**:
We have met like four Immortals on an island.

**Ch'en**:
Across a vast expanse of boisterous waves.

**Wu**:
Here we may sing quite freely in seclusion.

**Hou**:
Though the sky be empty, the moon may still be full.

---

SCENE 34

# The River Fortress
1645, FOURTH MONTH

[*Enter Su K'un-sheng.*]

**Su** [*recites*]:
The country is carved into three separate spheres of
   influence.
Over rivers and lakes, two armies are locked in battle.

[*Speaks*]: In order to save Master Hou's life, I urged General
Tso to mobilize his troops and fight his way eastward. Inspector General Huang Shu and Governor Ho T'eng-chiao are
accompanying him. Today they entered Kiukiang, and they
have invited Governor Yuan Chi-hsien to join them at Hu-
k'ou to discuss plans for entering the capital. Ma and Juan
have already sent General Huang Te-kung to stop their
advance. The smoke of war is rising in all directions, and the
future is unpredictable. General Tso's son Meng-keng has
been sent to oppose Huang Te-kung. I am following the camp
as an intelligence officer. Truly the heavens reel, as dragon
and tiger strive. [*Exit.*]

   [*A fortress with cannon is set up on the stage, and iron chains are
   stretched across to block the river. **General Huang Te-kung** enters,
   with a pair of whips, and is followed by soldiers.*]

**Huang** [*sings*] :
> I fight without a pause,
> Against foes from north and south.
> Now my cannons point west towards Chiang-chou,
> To drive the enemy back in disarray.

[*Speaks*]: I am determined to devote all my loyalty and sacrifice my reputation to the service of my Emperor Hung-kuang. My ambition is to recover all the lost territories. Unfortunately, my colleagues are of scant assistance, and Tso Liang-yü is fomenting internal dissension. I have just received orders from Minister Juan, who is in command of the Yangtze river defences. Accordingly, I have moved to this area to stop the advance of Tso's rebellious army. This is no laughing matter. [*Calls*]: Where is my brave adjutant T'ien Hsiung?

**T'ien** [*entering in uniform*] :   Here, Your Excellency.

**Huang**:  Muster all the men to hear my new command.

> [*Soldiers enter with a war-whoop and stand in two rows.*]

**Huang** [*sings*] :
> Rebels attempt to force his Majesty's hand;
> Bandit hordes would overturn the empire.
> The Son of Heaven is weak and feckless,
> His ministers devoted to private gain:
> I stand alone to guard the public order.
> On watch against the northern cavalry,
> I learned of a great fleet sailing down the Yangtze.
> Under flying banners, I marched my brave troops here,
> Where our fortress hinders the foe from sailing downstream.

> [*Huang and his soldiers climb the ramparts. Enter Tso's army with white banners and white uniforms. They utter war cries as they row downstream. Huang's soldiers shoot at them and pursue them from the shore. General Tso Liang-yü in white uniform enters in a boat.*]

**Tso** [*sings*] :
> The worthless ruler allows his vile ministers
> To wreck their vengeance at will:
> Sycophants encourage him in every extravagance;
> Self-seeking renegades have joined the enemy in the north;
> Opportunists are ready to fawn on the nearest master.

I have risked being branded in history as a rebel,
But all my loyalty belongs to the late Emperor:
Let them pluck out my heart and show it to the people.
My aim is to rescue the wronged Heir Apparent;
I have nothing to be ashamed of.
Nothing can stop my boat as it sails eastward.

[*Speaks*] : But I am worried about my unruly son Meng-keng,
who has been attacking cities at random along the route. I
have often warned him, but I fear he is easily influenced by
rash companions. We must concentrate all our efforts to
storm this fortress ahead of us. I cannot punish him until we
succeed.

**Soldier** [*rushing in*] : Your Excellency the Commander-in-Chief, I
bring bad news. Huang Te-kung has blocked the road at
Pan-chi. Our vanguard has been repulsed.

**Tso**: I'm aghast. Huang Te-kung was a man I though I could trust.
How could he have been seduced by Ma and Juan? To think
that he should support their puppet emperor without con-
sidering the Heir Apparent! This is abominable.
[*Calls*] : Invite Their Excellencies Huang Shu and Governor
Ho to join me for an urgent conference.

**Huang Shu** [*entering, recites*] :
Our banner of justice
Waves towards the sky.

[*Speaks*] : I appear at the Commander-in-Chief's invitation.

**Tso**: So Your Excellency has come alone. Where is Governor Ho?

**Huang Shu**: He had to turn back halfway.

**Tso**: Why?

**Huang Shu**: Because he's a fellow-provincial of Ma Shih-ying.[1]

**Tso**: Let him do as his conscience dictates. I won't blame him for
that. Now Huang Te-kung has blocked us at Pan-chi. Our
armies cannot advance. What shall we do?

**Huang Shu**: This looks serious. Let us hear what His Excellency
Yuan has to say about the matter.

**Yuan Chi-hsien** [*entering with attendants, recites*] :

---

1. There was a sort of freemasonry between men from the same province.

Heaven frowns on the injuries of the orphaned Heir
   Apparent,
But the sun shines on the banners of the loyal.

[*Speaks*]: Here is General Tso's boat. [*To* **attendants**]: Announce my arrival. [**Guard** *does so.*]

Tso:  Please ask His Excellency to join me without delay.

Yuan [*entering boat*]:  I have just been mobilizing my troops, and
am now at Your Excellency's disposal.

Huang:  Our advance has been halted.

Yuan:  How's that?

Tso:  Huang Te-kung has barred the way. Our vanguard has been
repulsed.

Yuan:  At this point we cannot retreat. We must send an envoy to
negotiate with him.

Tso:  Liu Ching-t'ing has left. There is no one I can send.

Su:  I happen to know Huang Te-kung personally. Perhaps I may
succeed in winning him over. At any rate, I can try.

Huang Shu:  Master Su's wit and integrity are equal to Liu Ching-
t'ing's. He's the best man we could send.

Tso [*to Su*]:  What will you say to him?

Su:  I shall say [*sings*]:

When heron and oyster are locked in mortal combat,
The fisherman standing by is the one to profit.
A hero should look backward as well as forward.
Though you enjoyed the late Emperor's favour,
You forget his injured son and poor Lady T'ung.
Bloody hands will be your only reward.
Why fight against your natural allies?

Yuan:  Well spoken.

Tso:  You must also enlighten him about my aims. He should
know that the Heir Apparent must be rescued and that the
country must be purged of corrupt officials. When these tasks
are accomplished, I shall not disturb a speck of dust at Court
nor touch a hair of the people. You should appeal to his
sense of justice in this time of emergency.

Huang Shu:  Precisely. He has always been a military man. If he

understands the meaning of loyalty, he must admit that such
as we could never be rebels. Tell him to ponder this carefully.

**Su**: You may depend on me to make everything clear to him.

**Messenger** [*rushing in*]: Your Excellency the Commander-in-
Chief! A conflagration has broken out in Kiukiang. His Excellency Yuan's troops are ravaging the city.

**Yuan**: Why should my own troops have started this trouble?

**Messenger**: They are pillaging and looting.

**Tso** [*angrily*]: There's no doubt that my son Meng-keng is at the
bottom of this. He has made me appear a worthless renegade.
I am too discredited to persevere. [*He draws his sword as if
to cut his throat. **Huang Shu** intercepts him. **Tso** clutches
**Yuan's** hand and gazes at him*]: My dear friend, my dear
friend! I have brought this misfortune upon you. [*He vomits
blood and collapses on a chair.*]

**Su** [*imploringly*]: Your Excellency, please rouse yourself. Your
Excellency!

**Yuan**: He does not answer. What are we to do?

**Huang Shu**: Perhaps he has only fainted. Let us give him a cordial.

**Su** [*after trying to make him drink*]: His teeth are tightly
clenched. It is too late. [*All wail and sing together.*]

**All** [*sing*]:
    The star of a great warrior has fallen;
    The mast of our ship is broken.
    How valiantly he fought a hundred battles!
    How splendidly his coat of armour glittered!
    Under this window now he lies:
    The mortal fame is still intact,
    But the Soul has flown to the summit of Coal Hill[2]
    To tell its woes to the Emperor's weeping Spirit.

**Yuan**: Now the Chief is dead, and all my troops are scattered. Tso

---

2. Coal Hill, north of the Forbidden City in Peking, was an artificial hill, constructed
with the earth taken from the moats, which was intended to guard the Imperial palaces
against evil influences from the north. The Ming Emperor Ch'ung-chen is said to have
hanged himself from an ancient sophora tree on this hill, when Peking was captured by
Li Tzu-ch'eng's rebels in 1644. Though the truth of this account has been challenged, the
stone tablet which was erected in 1930 reads: "In respectful memory of the Emperor of
the Ming who, remembering his ancestors, chose suicide on this spot rather than to fall
into the hands of his enemies."

Meng-keng has siezed Kiukiang. Forward or backward, I don't know where to turn. What shall we do if Huang Te-kung attacks us?

**Huang Shu**: We have lost our cities, and orders have been issued for our arrest. If we are captured, our doom is sealed. We had better return to Wuchang and join forces with Governor Ho.

**Yuan**: We have no alternative. [*Exeunt **Yuan** and **Huang Shu**.*]

**Su** [*stupefied*]: They have all departed. Only I am left to guard the Commander-in-Chief's remains. What a pitiable sight. I'll light candles and incense and lament his death. [*He lights a candle and mourns beside the corpse, then sings*]:

The hero is dead of indignation, his people all dispersed.
There is only an empty boat to serve as his coffin.
I invoke his spirit by the river,
But where can I find wine for the sacrifice?

[*Speaks*]: I shall have to wait for his son to return before performing the burial service. I cannot abandon him here. [*Sings*]:

The hero failed to pass the river fortress.
His spirit hovers o'er the waves as dreary night draws on.
Green hills are all around, but he has no burial place,
While wind and rain beat on his empty boat.

---

SCENE 35

# Call to Battle

1645, FOURTH MONTH

[*Enter **Shih K'o-fa** in ordinary clothes and wearing a white felt cap.*]

**Shih** [*sings*]:
Two years the horns called men to battle,
Armed riders daily clashed and reared.
Now all have fled, not one old comrade
Notes the swift greying of my beard.

[*Speaks*]: All my efforts to recover the lost lands of the North failed to develop a single effective plan. Huang

Te-kung and the other generals lost a thousand *li* of the
Yellow River plains when they moved south at the dictates of
Ma Shih-ying and Juan Ta-ch'eng. Now comes a report that
northern troops advanced into the Huai region on the
twenty-first of this month. With less than three thousand
under my banner, how am I to stop their progress? Once the
Huai region falls there can be no defence of the capital, and
the Ming dynasty is doomed. In my distress, I pace the
ramparts to observe and to reflect. [*Enter servant with lantern
to guide him. Shih sings*]:

In private guise, I walk the city wall
In the late watches when the world's asleep.
Birds whistle from their roost;
The watchman strikes his wooden block;
And here behind the screening wall, I listen.

[*He stops to listen, and hears a complaining voice from
offstage.*]

Voice: The northern troops have entered the Huai region, without
a living soul to oppose their presence; and those of us still
here, just a handful of men, are left with the impossible task
of defending Yangchow. Our general must be a real
simpleton!

Shih [*nodding his head, and speaking to himself*]: You don't
understand. [*Sings*]:

This loyal little band of ours
Will prove a new Great Wall of stout defence.

[*He listens again.*]

Second Voice: This is the end! The general cares nothing about
us, he's already given in to the northern troops. Why don't
we get out while we can? Why hang on here waiting to die?

Shih: Ha! Surrender, that is what's in their minds! How to deal
with that? [*Sings*]:

If the word "surrender"
Blocks the word "defender,"
Then Yangchow has few moments left.

[*He listens again.*]

**Third Voice**: Surrendering is only a last resort. We can kill and plunder and then get out. The only question is, how long can we hold on?

**Shih**: Ai-ya, I had no idea it had reached this pass. [*Sings*]:

I start with alarm,
My fiery heart suddenly clamped in ice.
I must go back at once,
Not wait for dawn,
But muster my men this night.

[*He hastens off. Signal guns fire offstage. Enter four soldiers.*]

**Soldiers**: This is the twenty-fourth day of the fourth month, and there'll be no drill today. Why are they firing the signal cannon on Plum Blossom Ridge? Come on, let's find out. [*They hurry off. Enter **Adjutant** with lantern and arrow of command.*]

**Adjutant** [*recites*]:
Clouds mass above the river,
Urgent orders fly by night.

[*Shouts*]: Field Marshal's orders: All troops to muster on Plum Blossom Ridge for instructions.

[*Troops form up. **Shih K'o-fa**, in armour and flanked by banners, mounts platform.*]

**Shih** [*recites*]:
Horns sound the rally, as the moon
Soars to its zenith, and stars begin to fade.

[*Speaks*]: Adjutant! Reports from the north are critical. Huai city has fallen. We in Yangchow guard the gateway to the Yangtze region — if anything goes wrong here, the capital will be in peril. Pass the word at once to all units, to guard their posts with every man, day and night. Death penalty for all malcontents!

**Adjutant**: Sir! [*He relays the orders to listeners offstage. There is no response.*]

**Shih**: Why this silence? Adjutant, repeat the orders and tell them to acknowledge.

[***Adjutant** does so, but there is still no response.*]

**Shih**: Still no response: sound the drum roll and repeat the orders.

> [*Adjutant does so; still no response.*]

**Shih**: We are faced with mutiny and desertion. [*Stamps his foot.*] How can Heaven permit this! [*Weeps and sings*]:

I call on Heaven; Heaven is silent still.
How can I meet this final threat
Against the shattering of my army's will?

[*Speaks*]: Most wretched Shih K'o-fa! [*Sings*]:

Shorn of comrade or companion,
My sole reliance these three thousand men,
And each intent on making his escape!
Have I no choice now but to make a banquet
Of this land I hold, and summon the invader?

[*He beats his breast and says*]: Ah, Shih K'o-fa! To what avail is your lifelong loyalty now, what use the industry of all your years? [*Sings*]:

I weep for my ancestors,
I weep for my countrymen.

[*He cries aloud.*]

**Adjutant**: Take care for yourself, sir, your tears will not save the country now. See — the skirts of your armour are drenched with tears. [*Alarmed*]: Ha, here is blood! Bring a lantern! Sir, you are soaked in blood! How is this?

**Shih**: The blood is from my eyes. [*Sings*]:

I have wept until my tears are all of blood.

**Adjutant** [*shouts*]: You generals, come up and look — you will see that our Field Marshal has shed tears of blood!

**Three Generals**: It is true! Tears of blood! [*They kneel.*]

**First General**: The saying goes: "A thousand pay-days for an hour of action." We are no better than beasts if we fail to serve our Emperor now.

**Second General**: If our cowardice has caused such suffering to our Commander, let us not look to Heaven for support.

**Third General**: Death comes to all soon or late: the important

13. Three generals: "It is true! Tears of blood!"

thing is to die well. So be it: today this worthless life of mine goes to the defence of Yangchow for Marshal Shih!

**Adjutant**: Well said! And death by slow execution awaits all who waver!

**Shih** [*gives a great laugh*]: For this I bow in gratitude! [*He prostrates himself, but they raise him to his feet.*]

**Generals**: We are unworthy of this!

**Shih**: Hear my command: one thousand men to advance against the enemy, one thousand to guard the city, one thousand to patrol outside.

**Generals**: Sir!

**Shih**: If the advance against the enemy fails, withdraw to the city wall.

**Generals**: Sir!

**Shih**: If the defence of the city wall fails, fight street by street.

**Generals**: Sir!

**Shih**: If street fighting fails, hand-to-hand combat.

**Generals**: Sir!

**Shih**: If close combat fails – death.

**Generals**: Sir!

**Shih**: You well know that one who surrenders can never again rise from his knees; one who deserts can never again look behind him. Let there be no further craven thought or word, if you are true companions of Shih K'o-fa.

**Generals**: Sir!

**Shih**: Your response makes further orders unnecessary. Now shout our war-cry thrice, then to your posts. [*All raise three shouts and exit. **Shih** claps his hands and laughs*]: Wonderful! If we succeed in guarding Yangchow, we lock the north gate of the capital! [*Sings*]:

Dust of battle everywhere,
But here's a city will not yield.
Midnight tears from blurred old eyes
Against a host will hold the field.

# Flight from Disaster

## 1645, FIFTH MONTH

[*Enter two* **Eunuchs** *and two* **Palace Maidens** *with lanterns, escorting the* **Emperor Hung-kuang,** *who is in ordinary clothes and on horseback.*]

**Emperor** [*sings*]:
Water-clocks tell me the hour is late.
Through the winds of night I ride,
Where candles gutter by palace gate.

[*Speaks*]: Since I came to the Dragon Throne, I have been harried from one refuge to another, and now the northern armies have crossed the Huai River and are invading Yang-chow. Messages from Shih K'o-fa tell of a critical situation and panic among his forces. My ministers Ma Shih-ying and Juan Ta-ch'eng have gone into hiding, and the prospects for sustaining this revival of the Ming Empire seem very faint indeed. "Of all possible stratagems, the best is escape." I have left the palace behind, and issued orders to open the city gate. If I can only slip out of Nanking, I shall find security somewhere. [*Sings*]:

Streets of the capital silent now;
As I pass below the Phoenix Terrace,
The fate of my consorts grips my heart.

[*Calls*]: Order my consorts to make haste, or they will be trapped! [*Sings*]:

A melancholy flight for them,
Lutes cradled in their arms,
And tears like falling pearls!

[**Emperor** *hurries offstage. Enter, equally swiftly,* **Ma Shih-ying,** *also on horseback.*]

**Ma** [*sings*]:
The defences of the Yangtze are broken,
The capital faces disaster;
High offices go cheap, but there's none to buy!

[*Speaks*]: On presenting myself for the dawn audience, I discovered that His Majesty had fled. What else but flight remains for his Minister? [*Sings*]:

Quickly now don rustic guise;
Skulking out of Chicken Street,
Let me meet no hostile eyes!

[*Pointing behind him, Ma says*]: This bevy of beauties and these ten cartloads of treasure represent my modest possessions. I hope to save them from seizure by my enemies. Hurry along there!

[*Enter two **concubines** on horseback, followed by **coolies** pushing carts.*]

**Concubines** and **Coolies** [*calling back*]: Coming!

**Ma** [*sings*]:
Stay close to me, beloved consorts,
And dearest household goods!

[*As the convoy circles the stage a crowd of **rioters** enter, brandishing sticks and shouting.*]

**Rioters**: Ha, here's the traitor Ma Shih-ying who has filched the last penny from our pockets! Where are you off to with your women and your riches? You've taken them far enough!

[*The **rioters** knock **Ma Shih-ying** to the ground, strip him of his gown, and run off with the women and the treasure. **Juan Ta-ch'eng** enters on horseback.*]

**Juan** [*sings*]:
The defence of the Yangtze was a lucrative post,
But who desires it once the killing starts?
I fling my warrant down into the river!

[*Speaks*]: I'm on my way; but I wonder whether Ma Shih-ying has fled too, or whether he is planning to surrender? [*His horse stumbles over the prostrate **Ma***] Oh, here you are! What are you doing down there?

**Ma**: I wasn't fast enough. I was trapped by rioters who robbed me of all I had and left me lying here.

**Juan**: So that's what happened. My own baggage is somewhere behind me. I hope that doesn't get stolen. [*Sings*]:

Just to amass a handful of goods,
A pretty girl or two,
Costs a high price in public obloquy!

[*Speaks*] :  I must see what has become of it.

>[*Enter more **rioters**, armed with sticks. They carry bundles
>and are hustling a group of girls along with them.*]

**Rioters**: These are the ill-gotten gains of Juan Ta-ch'eng. Come on, let's share them.

**Juan**:  You scoundrels, how dare you lay hands on my property?

**Rioters**:  You are Juan Ta-ch'eng? Good, you came just at the right moment. [*They knock **Juan** down and strip him of his robe.*] Let him keep his miserable life, but on we go to Breeches' Bottom in Chicken Street. We'll burn his house down for him. [*Exeunt.*]

**Ma**:  Oh, my back's broken, I can't get up.

**Juan**:  I'll keep you company, they've broken my arms.

**Ma** and **Juan** [*sing*] :
What a mess! What a mess!
Victims of their vulgar fists
Here we languish in distress!

>[*Enter **Yang Wen-ts'ung** on horseback, wearing his official
>robes and followed by porters bearing his baggage.*]

**Yang**:  Today is the tenth of the fifth month, an auspicious day for me to begin the journey to my new post as Governor of Soochow. I have left my paintings and calligraphy scrolls in the Plum Fragrance Tower, with instructions for Lan Ying to bring them to me at his convenience, so that I shall not be overburdened with baggage.

**Porters**:  Please hurry, Your Honour.

**Yang**:  What's the matter?

**Porters**:  There are rumours that the northern forces are near at hand, and the Emperor and his ministers fled the capital tonight.

**Yang**:  Amazing! Let us get away from the city at once! [*He urges on his horse, but it rears and refuses to move.*] What's this, why does my horse rear and jib? You men, what's this?

**Porters**:  There are two corpses in the way.

**Ma** and **Juan** [*moaning*] : Oh! Oh! Help! Help!

**Yang**: They're not dead yet. Who are they?

**Porters**: It looks like Their Honours Ma and Juan.

**Yang**: Ridiculous, how could that be? Oh, oh, it really is! [*He dismounts.*] Heavens, how could this have come about?

**Ma**: I was stripped of all I possess by rioters, all they left me was my life.

**Juan**: I came to his rescue and met with the same fate.

**Yang**: Where are your retainers?

**Ma**: I suspect they made off with their share of the loot.

**Yang**: Help them up at once, you men, and find some clothes for them. [*The **porters** help **Ma** and **Juan** to dress.*] Fortunately I have a spare mount; why don't you share it and we'll leave the city this instant?

**Ma** and **Juan** [*now mounted, clinging to each other, recite*] : Two friends, one horse, knees together, lacking clothes, will freeze together! [*Exeunt.*]

**Porters**: You shouldn't travel in their company, Your Honour. If we fall in with their foes, we'll suffer too.

**Yang**: Very true. I spy another rabble of rioters. We had better make ourselves scarce.

> [*Yang and his porters hide at the side of the street. Enter K'ou Pai-men and Cheng T'o-niang, dishevelled.*]

**K'ou** and **Cheng** together [*singing*] :
The terrace filled with song,
The dancers' skirts a-swaying;
Deep in the night the gaiety goes on.

[*They greet **Yang***] : Your Honour Yang, what are you doing here?

**Yang**: Ah, it's K'ou Pai-men and Cheng T'o-niang. Why are you both out in the streets?

**K'ou**: We were performing in the palace when suddenly the drinking stopped, the lamps were dimmed, and eunuchs and palace ladies began rushing about in confusion. We didn't wait to be dismissed.

**Yang**: Where is Fragrant Princess?

**Cheng**: She left with us, but with feet so tiny she couldn't keep up with us, so she hired a palanquin and went off in that.

**Yang**: Has the Emperor left the city then?

**K'ou**: Shen Kung-hsien and Chang Yen-chu are behind us, they will know what is happening.

> [*Enter Shen, in tatters and clutching his drum, and Chang, dishevelled and cap in hand.*]

**Shen** and **Chang** together [*singing*] :
> On the Imperial revels at their height,
> The snorting war-steeds of the North descend.
> Are we to hold them off with pipe and drum?

[*They greet Yang*] : Your Honour Yang! It's a long time since we met.

**Yang**: Why are you in such dire distress?

**Shen**: You haven't heard? The northern troops have crossed the Yangtze, and tonight the Emperor fled the capital.

**Yang**: Where are you heading for?

**Chang**: To our homes, to await developments and see if we can't keep our heads.

**Cheng**: My sister and I need not worry; we're off to our house to make ready for our new clients.

**Yang**: Clients, at a time like this!

**Cheng**: You should realize, sir, there's a lot of money to be made from an army camp. [*Sings*] :

> One camp fares badly, one does well,
> But we have always a song to sell.

> [*Exit singing-girls and musicians.*]

**Yang**: This is a dismal prospect. They saw the Emperor's flight with their own eyes. I must hasten to collect my belongings from the Tower of Plum Fragrance and hurry home to my native village at once. [*He mimes the act of journeying, and sings*] :

> Streets full of fleeing rabble,
> Prince and ministers wandering apart,
> Where can we find an issue from these troubles?

[*He mimes arrival and says*]: Here is Mistress Li's abode. [*Dismounts and hammers on the gate*]: Open up! Open up!

**Lan Ying** [*rushing in*]: Who is it this time? [*Opens the gate.*] What brings you here, Your Honour?

**Yang**: There's desperate news of the northern troops, His Majesty and the Court have scattered in all directions, and there's no more governorship of Soochow for me! [*Sings*]:

Now to bundle books and zither,
Change these clothes for plain apparel,
Take a sampan up the river!

**Lan**: So that's how it is. Fragrant Princess just came back with the news that the Court had fled. Fragrant Princess!

[*Fragrant Princess enters and greets Yang.*]

**Yang**: So many weeks since I saw you, and now there is time only for a hurried word before I go far away.

**Fragrant Princess**: Where will you go?

**Yang**: Back to Kweiyang, my native place.

**Fragrant Princess** [*sleeve raised to conceal her tears*]: Hou Fang-yü is still imprisoned, and now you are leaving for home. I shall be left with no one to care for me.

**Yang**: Even father and son cannot care for each other in turbulent times like these. [*Sings*]:

When troubles press so close,
Each must follow his nose,
Not burden his back with others.

**Su K'un-sheng** [*rushing in, recites*]:
Generals give their lives,
But leave their lords deserted.

[*Speaks*]: Here is the place – in I go. Ah, His Honour Yang – and Fragrant Princess here also! But where is Master Hou?

**Yang**: Our friend Hou Fang-yü is still in jail.

**Fragrant Princess**: Honoured teacher, which way did you come here?

**Su**: Hoping to rescue Master Hou, I travelled as far as Wuchang, but found everything in an uproar. I returned directly to the

capital, and learning of the disorders there went straight to
the jail, whose gates stood open. [*Sings*]:

The prisoners all were fled,
The prison gates burst open,
But who has harmed our young scholar?

**Fragrant Princess** [*weeps*]: Teacher, please find him for me as
quickly as you can.

**Yang** [*points offstage and sings*]:
A pall of dust and smoke,
Wives and babes asunder,
When can they expect reunion?

[*Says to Fragrant Princess*]: Well, so be it. Now that you
have the company of your teacher, I can leave the capital.
[*Calls*]: Lan Ying, make your baggage ready and travel with
me.

**Lan**: My home is in Hangchow, how can I go with you?

**Yang**: In that case, when I have changed into travelling attire we
will take leave of each other. [*Recites*]:

A thousand miles like a soul's migration,
A three-year's journey in a dream.

[*Yang mimes the act of mounting his horse and exits, followed
by porters with baggage.*]

**Fragrant Princess** [*weeps*]: Now His Honour Yang has gone, and
you are my sole comforter. These past days you went to such
pains, crossing a thousand hills and streams, searching for
Master Hou on my behalf. But who could have imagined that
we should be so kept apart, myself in the palace and Master
Hou in prison. Now I have left the palace and he his prison,
but still we cannot meet. Take pity on me, sir, once again,
and let us search for him together wherever we can.

**Su**: Since Master Hou has not come here to your house, he must
have left the city. Where are we to search for him?

**Fragrant Princess**: Wherever he may be. [*Sings*]:

To the rim of the sky and the shore of the sea,
In every corner of the land,
In whatever world there be,
Till boots of steel are worn through!

[*Speaks*]: I cannot rest until we find Master Hou.

**Su**: Battles rage all over the northwest; he could not have crossed the river. If we are to find him, we must search the hills of the southeast.

**Fragrant Princess**: Then that is our direction. [*Sings*]:

> Over the rugged tracks of barren hills,
> To the land of the Immortals if need be.
> Our union, predestined, must prevail.

**Su**: Since your heart is set on seeking Master Hou, and since I too wish to flee these troubles, I shall endeavour to escort you. But where to start?

**Lan Ying** [*pointing*]: Yonder in the Clouds' Roost Hills east of the city, where few ever penetrate, is the retreat of Chang Wei, who relinquished his command of the Imperial Guard to practise the Tao in seclusion. I have long wished to submit myself as his disciple. Let us journey there together and see what fortune has in store for us.

**Su**: Excellent, excellent. Let us take up our loads and leave the city together. [*They do so.*]

**Fragrant Princess** [*sings*]:
> Farewell to the camp of mists and flowers.
> When shall it be dissolved,
> This deep devotion?

**Su**: Before us is the city gate. I fear we shall be questioned.

**Lan**: Let us slip through this instant.

**Fragrant Princess**: My feet hurt me so, I'm not sure I can keep up.

       [*They sing together*]:

**Fragrant Princess**:
> Cheeks wet with tears at the hardship of the road.

**Su**:
> Like broken stalks we are swept beyond the gate.

**Lan**:
> No strife disturbes the realm of Peach Blossom Cave.

**Fragrant Princess**:
> Pray that it shall be there I find my fate.

# Theft of the Jewel

## 1645, FIFTH MONTH

[*Enter General* **Huang Te-kung** *in full armour, followed by his adjutant* **T'ien Hsiung.**]

**Huang** [*sings*] :
Like the Long River, far as eye can see,
Flows the swift torrent of the warrior's woes.
When shall we hand our bows to waiting boys
And gather for joyous drinking bout?

[*Speaks*] : Here I come, Huang Te-kung, fresh from my
victory at Pan-chi, where my rival Tso Liang-yü died of
fright. But he has left a son, Tso Meng-keng, who maintains
his base at Kiukiang. Until these crows are dispersed, I must
hold Wu-hu against attacks from the north.

**Messenger** [*entering*] : Beg to report: The northern forces crossed
the Huai River overnight and are besieging Hangchow. Nanking's in a panic, its citizens have taken to flight.

**Huang**: Why was there no resistance from the garrisons north of
the river, at Feng-yang and Huai-an?

**Messenger**: There are reports that both generals Liu have turned
upriver to block the movements of Tso's troops, leaving
Feng-yang and Huai-an without a man to guard them.

**Huang** [*startled*] : What now! T'ien Hsiung, you are my most
trusted aide. Take troops and cavalry and hasten to the
defence of Nanking. [*Sings*] :

Juan Ta-ch'eng, War Minister of mighty powers,
Issues commands by night,
To defend this place and that.
But like a beggar whose tattered gown,
Tug as he may, cannot conceal his body,
He leaves Feng-yang and Huai-an
Bereft of all protection.
How can the boats of lotus-gatherers
Suffice to hold the river?

Dust of battle darkens the Nanking skies:
Let us devote all efforts to relieve it.

[*Exeunt. Enter, on horseback, the* **Emperor Hung-kuang**,
*attended by the* **Grand Eunuch**.]

**Emperor** [*sings*] :
Alas for a forsaken ruler
Who mourns alone beside the river,
Begging for nourishment from village huts.

[*Speaks*] : On my headlong flight from Nanking, I have been
abandoned by one after another of my eunuchs and consorts.
Now only the Grand Eunuch Han Tsan-chou remains by my
side. [*Sings*] :

My scrawny nag plods on
Through the heat of the day.
Where can cool shade be found?

[*Speaks*] : Yesterday I sought out the residence of Hsü
Hung-chi, Duke of Wei, but he pretended not to recognise me
and drove me forth. Now we are approaching Wu-hu, and the
garrison of General Huang Te-kung lies ahead. Will he agree
to take us under his protection? [*Sings*] :

In our distress
We roam the corridors of mansions
Pleading for hospitality.

[*Dismounts and says*] : Here is General Huang's headquarters. Grand Eunuch Han, inform the General of our presence.

**Grand Eunuch**:  Is anyone there?

**Soldier**:  Where are you from?

**Grand Eunuch**: From Nanking. [*He draws the man aside and
whispers*] : It's the Emperor − tell your General to hurry to
his welcome!

**Soldier**:  Ha! How could it be the Emperor turning up here? Don't
try to frighten me.

**Emperor**:  Call General Huang, and you will soon know the truth.
[*Sings*] :

Here is a General who once before
Received our royal procession by the river.

**Soldier** [*gnawing his thumb in doubt*]: Doesn't look like the Emperor, but he sounds like somebody important. Better announce him and find out. [*He hurries in to report.*]

**Huang** [*hastening onstage*]: How could this be? Let us promptly investigate.

**Emperor**: How have you been, General Huang?

**Huang** [*falls to his knees*]: Long live Your Majesty! Pray ascend this temporary throne and receive my homage. [*The Grand Eunuch seats the Emperor, whereupon Huang prostrates himself, then sings*]:

Here in full armour I salute my lord,
Raising my eyes to the Imperial visage.
But how comes Your Majesty here,
Riding the dusty road alone,
Dragon displaced from river home,
Buffeted by the storm?

[*Speaks*]: All of us share the guilt for this! [*Sings*]:

Each single minister
Each single general
Who has betrayed his lord.

**Emperor**: Now that events have reached this pass, it is too late for regrets. I only demand your protection.

**Huang** [*pounds the floor and weeps*]: When Your Majesty was secure in the recesses of his palace, I ventured my utmost in obedience to the Imperial command. Now that Your Majesty is in flight and powerless, I have no means either to advance to battle or to fall back in defence, I am left without the wherewithal to serve.

**Emperor**: Don't upset yourself so. My sole concern at present is for my personal safety. I have no desire to continue as Emperor.

**Huang**: Ai-ya! This empire is the empire of your forefathers. How can Your Majesty cast it aside?

**Emperor**: Whether the empire is cast aside depends on you, General.

**Huang**: Feeble as I may be, my powers are dedicated to Your Majesty's service, to the death.

**Emperor** [*wiping away tears*]: So you are loyal to the Throne after all.

**Huang** [*kneeling*]: Will Your Majesty deign to retire and rest after the hardships of the journey? Tomorrow I shall await Your Majesty's instructions concerning our problems of state. [*Grand Eunuch conducts the Emperor within. Huang muses*]: What a pass we have reached! The Ming dominion of three hundred years now hangs on this moment, the Imperial control of fifteen provinces centers on this spot. It is a heavy responsibility for me to bear. [*He shouts instructions*]: Orders for all troops: No horse to go unbridled, no man to remove his armour, strict watches to be kept with bells and rattles.

**Troops**: Aye, aye, General.

**Huang**: T'ien Hsiung, you and I must act as His Majesty's body-guards. We will keep our post here outside his lodging-place. [*Huang takes a whip in either hand and lies down with his head pillowed on T'ien's knees. Bells and rattles sound the watch.*]

**T'ien** [*whispers*]: General, this Emperor strikes me as one who has little good fortune to look forward to. The northern forces have already crossed the river, and everyone is declaring allegiance to them. You should be trimming your sails to the wind.

**Huang**: What sort of talk is this? "Filial service demands every effort; loyalty to the prince demands life itself." How can a servant of the Throne divide his loyalties? [*Drum rolls off-stage. Huang says, startled*]: What are these drums? [*Huang and T'ien sit up as Messenger enters.*]

**Messenger**: Beg to report: A troop of riders has arrived from the northeast. They say it is the two garrison commanders Liu, arriving to confer with Generalissimo Huang.

**Huang** [*rises*]: Excellent! With our three garrisons united, we can guard His Majesty from all harm. Let me see them.

> [*Enter on horseback General Liu Liang-tso and Liu Tse-ch'ing with their troops.*]

**Liu Liang-tso** and **Liu Tse-ch'ing**: Where is Brother Huang?

**Huang**: Ah, it's really you. I've been hoping so long for your arrival. [*The two Liu dismount.*]

**Liu Liang-tso**: You found yourself a jewel and were keeping it from your brothers!

**Huang**: What jewel?

**Liu Tse-ch'ing**: Hung-kuang!

**Huang**: Not so loud. His Majesty is resting.

**Liu Liang-tso** [*whispers*]: What are you waiting for? This is the time to make your gift.

**Huang**: What gift?

**Liu Tse-ch'ing**: Offer Hung-kuang to the northern Court, and we'll all be made mighty princes. This is the gift we mean.

**Huang**: Scoundrels! Don't ask me to put up with this dastardly trick! [***Huang** beats the **two Liu** with his whips. They call for help.*] Rebel scum! [*Sings*]:

Bowing to the prevailing wind,
Lusting for profit like Persian pedlars.
Appointed to serve the Throne,
You would betray this precious hostage,
Turning your blade against your Prince
To win reward for vilest treachery.
Miserable turncoats! Rebel curs!

**Liu Liang-tso**: No need for such abuse, we're all brothers here.

**Huang**: Ha! Curs like you who have lost sight of your own true Prince. You are no brothers of mine. [*Attacks them again.*]

**T'ien** [*dodging behind the **two Liu***]: There's a stubborn ox, who still doesn't see how the land lies. [*He draws his bow*]. I'll raise the siege for you!

[*His arrow pierces **Huang**'s leg. **Huang** falls, the **two Liu** laugh, and **T'ien** runs offstage, to reappear at once with the **Emperor** on his shoulders.*]

**Emperor**: Grand Eunuch Han! Quickly! [*There is no response.*] Ah, he has deserted me, the wretch. [*He beats his fists on **T'ien Hsiung**'s head.*] Where are you taking me?

**T'ien**: To Peking! [*The **Emperor** bites him in the shoulder.*] Ow! He's biting me! [***T'ien** flings the **Emperor** to the ground, then bows to the **two Liu**.*] One Emperor, at your disposal.

**Liu Liang-tso** and **Liu Tse-ch'ing** [*bowing in return*]: Many thanks. [*They tug at the* **Emperor's** *gown to drag him off.* **Huang** *clings to the* **Emperor's** *legs.*]

**Huang**:  T'ien Hsiung! Help me save the Emperor!

> [*T'ien pretends to add his weight to* **Huang's**, *but lets go, and the* **two Liu** *drag the* **Emperor** *offstage.* **Huang** *tries to rise but fails.*]

**Huang**:  Why can't I get to my feet?

**T'ien**:  You've been hit by an arrow, sir.

**Huang**:  Who shot at me?

**T'ien**:  We were shooting at the rebels and hit you by mistake, sir.

**Huang**:  Cross-eyed fool! And answer me this: What were you doing, bringing out the Emperor on your shoulders?

**T'ien**:  I was trying to help His Majesty escape. I never dreamt they would kidnap him like that.

**Huang**:  Follow them instantly!

**T'ien** [*laughing*]:  I don't need your orders for that, sir! Here's one escort, all ready and willing, baggage packed, off to see the Emperor safe — to Peking! [*He takes up baggage and umbrella and hastens off.*]

**Huang**:  Bah! Bunch of evil turncoats — I should have killed every one. Ah Heaven, Heaven, that ever the empire of the Ming was placed in the hands of Huang Te-kung! [*Sings*]:

None could match my martial pride —
Yet I gave up my Emperor!
The story of this tug-of-war
Will make old gaffers split their sides.

[*Speaks*]:  So be it. My life is all I have left to offer my country. [*Draws his sword and calls*]:  You men! Come and behold a headless general! [*With a single slash he cuts his throat.*]

# Lost in the River

## 1645, FIFTH MONTH

[*Enter **Shih K'o-fa** wearing bamboo rain-hat and felt cloak.
He looks behind him as he hastens onstage.*]

**Shih** [*sings*] :

Beacon fires blaze,
And the reek of blood rises;
Clamour fills the air of Yangchow;
Slaughter of the populace like rolling up a mat.
And my foolhardiness to blame for all of this!
Men and officers alike
Have reached the limits of their strength,
And all we have achieved is a pile of corpses.

[*Speaks*] : I, Shih K'o-fa, undertook the defence of Yangchow with three thousand loyal subjects, but our strength
failed, our rations were exhausted, and still no reinforcements arrived. Tonight the Northern troops breached the
north wall, and I determined to take my own life. But I
realize that three centuries of Ming rule rest on my shoulders
alone for their perpetuation. What is the value, then, in a
useless death which leaves my Prince deserted? So I scaled
the south wall by rope and made for Yichen, where I was
able to cross the river in a passing patrol-boat. [*He points
offstage*] : There, hazy in the distance, are the walls of
Nanking. But these old legs ache so that they will carry me
no further. But ha! From heaven knows where, a white mule
appears! I will ride it along the river bank. [*He mounts the
mule, plucking a willow branch for a switch, and sings*] :

Astride a white mule,
Down a wild track by the deserted river,
I fill the empty fields with bitter wailing.
"The sun itself is nearer than the capital."
But ply the whip,
And soon we'll see the palace in the clouds.

[*Enter, in haste, the old **Master of Ceremonies**, with his belongings
strapped on his back.*]

**Master of Ceremonies** [*recites*] :
> Old as I am, I seek to flee these troubles;
> as the sun goes down, I think of my old home.

> [***Shih's*** *mule bumps against him and knocks him down.*]
> Hey, hey! I nearly went into the river! You should look
> where you're going, General!

**Shih** [*dismounting to help him to his feet*] :  I beg your pardon.
But tell me, where have you come from?

**Master of Ceremonies**:  From Nanking.

**Shih**:  How is it in Nanking?

**Master of Ceremonies**:  You haven't heard? The Emperor fled two
or three days ago. Now the Northern forces have crossed the
river, and the city is in an uproar with all its gates locked.

**Shih**:  Ha! Then it's useless to try to go there. [*He gives a great
wail.*] O Heaven, O Earth, O ancestors! Not even this corner
of the empire can we hold!

**Master of Ceremonies**:  This sounds like the voice of General Shih
K'o-fa. Is that who you are?

**Shih**:  That is who I am. How did you guess?

**Master of Ceremonies**:  I was a Master of Ceremonies in the
Imperial Temple, and in the past I attended you by the Gate
of Peace.

**Shih**:  Of course! When you bewailed the late Emperor so bitterly.

**Master of Ceremonies**:  I confess it. But what has brought you to
such straits, sir?

**Shih**:  Tonight Yangchow fell, and I had to scale the wall to make
my escape.

**Master of Ceremonies**:  Where will you bend your steps?

**Shih**:  I was aiming for Nanking to help protect the Emperor. I
didn't realize he had fled. [*Stamps his foot, wails, and sings*] :

> Cast adrift, a sail-less skiff,
> Abandoned cur without a home,
> A thousand times I call on Heaven and Earth;
> But there is no way forward,
> No road back. [*He climbs a hillock.*]

The snow-capped waves roll on
In endless grief for Ch'ü Yuan and his wrongs[1].

[*Speaks*]: That's the way. There is my burial place. [*Sings*]:

Less cramping than the yellow clay
Is the flowing river,
And a resting-place in the bellies of myriad fish.

[*He looks down at himself and says*]: But it is not fitting
that robes of office should adorn the body of Shih K'o-fa,
culpable for the loss of an empire. [*Sings*]:

I strip myself of robe, hat, and boots.

**Master of Ceremonies**: You have the look, sir, of one preparing to
meet his death. [*He tugs at* **Shih**]: Think again, sir, don't
think only of the present moment!

**Shih**: And where in the wide world do you suppose there will be a
place for Shih K'o-fa? [*Sings*]:

A hero faces death:
When hills and rivers pass to other hands,
There is nothing to detain me.

[**Shih** *mimes leaping into the river, and exits in a series of rolls.*
**Master of Ceremonies** *gazes after him, clutching the robe, hat, and
boots. Long pause.*]

**Master of Ceremonies**: Ah, Lord Shih, Lord Shih! To the end a
loyal servant of the Throne. And if I had not chanced along,
who would ever have known of your self-immolation? [*He
wails aloud.*]

[*Enter* **Liu Ching-t'ing** *leading* **Hou Fang-yü** *by the hand.*]

**Liu** [*recites*]:
Escaping the clutches of prison guards,
We flee as fugitives.

[*They are followed by* **Ch'en Chen-hui** *and* **Wu Ying-chi.**]

---

1. See Scene 8, n. 1.

**Ch'en** and **Wu**: Daily we seek a patron; where shall we lodge tonight?

**Hou**: Hurry, gentlemen, twilight is gathering.

**Ch'en** and **Wu**: We are with you.

**Liu**: Since we escaped from prison we have wandered from one place to another, but no lodging can we find. Yonder is the Dragon's Pool. Let us resolve to separate and each fend for himself.

**Ch'en**: Very well. [*Sees Master of Ceremonies*.] What are you doing, weeping here, old man?

**Master of Ceremonies**: I am a refugee like you, and I have just seen the President of the Board of War Shih K'o-fa take his life here. It's more than I can do to restrain my tears.

**Hou**: How did President Shih chance to be here?

**Master of Ceremonies**: Last night Yangchow fell. President Shih made his way this far before he learned that the Emperor had fled. He stamped his foot in dismay and threw himself into the river.

**Hou**: How could such a thing come to pass?

**Master of Ceremonies**: See, here are the boots, hat, and robe he stripped from his person.

**Liu**: Look, inside there, the vermilion seal.

**Hou**: Let me see. [*Reads aloud*]: "Seal of the President of the Board of War and Grand Officer Entrusted with the Defence of the Region North of the River." [*He weeps.*] Alas for Shih K'o-fa!

**Ch'en**: Let us set up the robe and hat and make our obeisances to his Spirit. [*They do so, wailing.*]

**All** [*sing*]:
Wandering by the river,
To whom could he express his deep remorse?
The tears grew chill on his cheeks,
But though he strained his eyes,
No help could come from the abandoned city.
When battle drained the last drop of blood,
He burst through the besieging foe.
His whole intention was to guard the Throne,
Not dreaming that the song was ended,

The banquet hall left bare.
A thousand miles of river reach
From ancient Wu to the broad lands of Ch'u,
And all, alas, fallen to the hands of others.
Rainclouds shift and change,
The cold tide coils on eastwards
And all dissolves in empty mist.
Let your Spirit, great Lord Shih
Tower above the realm from sea to sky.

[*Hou strokes the robe and wails aloud.*]

**Liu**: By this heroic act, President Shih has proclaimed his match-less loyalty. Restrain your grief, sir, and let us now take leave of each other.

**Hou**: Where shall I turn in all this vast expanse?

**Ch'en**: Wu Ying-chi and I came as far as this only to see you across the river. Now that the northern route is barred, why not accompany us to the south?

**Hou**: I should not burden you in times of such calamity. Let each make his own way.

**Wu**: What is your plan?

**Hou**: Liu Ching-t'ing and I propose to take refuge in some ancient temple deep in the hills until we can find some way to return to the north.

**Master of Ceremonies**: I was going to Cloud's Roost Mountain, a secluded spot unlikely to be touched by the fighting. Why not join me?

**Hou**: An excellent proposal.

**Ch'en** and **Wu**: Since you have found a shelter, we shall bid you farewell. [*They bow and recite*]: Now is the time for griev-ing, but when will be the day of our reunion? [*Exeunt, in tears.*]

**Hou**: What is your business at Cloud's Roost Mountain?

**Master of Ceremonies**: I'll tell you my purpose, sir. I was a Master of Ceremonies at the Imperial Temple. At the memorial service for the former Emperor by the Gate of Peace, I was disgusted by the hypocrisy of the officials present, and I started a collection among some of the old folks to celebrate a mass for the Ch'ung-chen Emperor on the fifteenth day of the seventh month. The troubles in Nanking have forced me to change my plans, but I have the money with me, and I shall ask the monks at Cloud's Roost to help me accomplish my design.

**Liu**: What a noble plan.

**Hou**: Please let us accompany you.

**Master of Ceremonies**: I must gather up these garments of President Shih's.

**Liu**: What will you do with them?

**Master of Ceremonies**: It was at Plum Blossom Ridge outside Yangchow that President Shih mustered his troops. When the enemy withdraws, I shall bury these relics there in a tomb dedicated to him.

**Hou**: This is an even more memorable deed!

[*The **Master of Ceremonies** takes the robe, hat, and boots on his back and resumes his journey, followed by **Hou** and **Liu**.*]

**All** [*sing*]:
    Over river and hill
    Clouds swirl and shift.
    The loyal spirit vanishes,
    And who will find his tomb
    When the Feast of the Dead draws nigh?

**Master of Ceremonies**:
    This tale of the Southern Court will resound forever,

**Liu**:
    And tears of blood will swell the streams with woe.

**Hou**:
    We raise to Heaven our "Summons to the Soul"

**Master of Ceremonies**:
    As mist obscures the mighty river's flow.

# Temples of Refuge
## 1645, SIXTH MONTH

[*Enter Fragrant Princess and Su K'un-sheng.*]

**Fragrant Princess** [*sings*]:
  A thread of secret longing binds my heart —
  That we shall meet, however far the journey.
  I cling to this one love that I have known,
  Until our spirits can be joined forever.
  Here where green pines
  Are shrouded in a thousand layers of cloud
  Will be my "refuge of High Heaven's Terrace."

[*Speaks*]: Master Su, it was fortunate that Uncle Lan Ying led us here to Cloud's Roost Mountain. How surprising, yes truly a predestined meeting, to find when we knocked for admittance that the Abbess of Foster Purity Temple was none other than our friend Pien Yü-ching! The sole obstacle to my content is the absence of Master Hou. Please do all you can to discover his whereabouts.

**Su:** Try to curb your impatience. Where in this troubled world am I to seek him? Meanwhile, let us discuss with the Abbess our plans for a prolonged sojourn here.

[*Enter the ex-singing girl Pien Yü-ching, now in the costume of a Taoist Abbess.*]

**Pien** [*sings*]:
  Pipes play in the Realm of Jasper,
  Jade pendants tinkle as I wander
  Free as a cloud-borne crane.
  My former life of flowers and moon is over,
  But here I find another's passion blooming!

[*Speaks*]: You are welcome to this modest abode.

**Fragrant Princess:** We are truly grateful for this reception.

**Su:** We must throw ourselves on your mercy. We cannot proceed north of the river because of the fighting raging there; and

[279]

among these hills, my lays find no employment. We are
ashamed to give you so much trouble day after day.

**Pien**: Do not speak of it. [*Sings*]:
Old friends have found their way to Fairyland.
I still recall the rapture of other days,
And we shall hold ethereal intercourse.

**Su**: But I intend to earn my living. [*He puts on boots and rain-hat
and takes up axe and rope.*] While this fine weather holds, I'll
gather firewood along the ranges and gullies, to supply the
temple's needs. This will be better than "sitting and eating
the mountain away."

**Pien**: I could not let you do this.

**Su**: It would be wrong for me to idle. [*Shoulders axe and
recites*]:
Beneath my feet the cloud-wrapped hills are cold,
But on my back the pine-logs will smell sweet.

[*He exits,* **Pien** *closing the gate behind him.*]

**Fragrant Princess**: Rather than sit with nothing to do, perhaps I
may trouble you for some old clothes to mend this summer
day.

**Pien**: There *is* something I should like to ask you. On the fifteenth day of the seventh month, the villagers have vowed to
install a prayer-banner in memory of our Empress Chou. It
would be an act of great piety if you would devote your skill
to making the banner for us.

**Fragrant Princess**: I should be delighted to contribute to so noble
a project. [**Pien** *fetches the materials*]. Let me burn incense
and wash my hands before I begin. [*She does so, then sings
while sewing*]:

In former days, my sins were heavy,
My fingers knew nought but the music of pipes and strings,
Ignorant of the use of needle and thread.

**Pien**: But so nimble are your fingers, and so quick your mind, as
soon as you ply the needle you prove your artistry.

**Fragrant Princess**: I lack experience, but my devotion to the task
is complete. [*Sings*]:

Though my fingers swell with the effort,

I embroider the sacred banner
More delicately than any trousseau.

[*As they sew together,* **Hou Fang-yü** *enters in the company of the* **Master of Ceremonies** *and* **Liu Ching-t'ing**. *All are laden with baggage.*]

**Hou** [*sings*]:
The clash of arms gives place
To the sound of running brooks amid the pines.
The peaks of Cloud's Roost locked in mist,
Even in midsummer a cool breeze blows.

**Master of Ceremonies**: Here is Cloud's Roost Mountain. Let us find a temple for our resting-place.

**Hou**: Why not inquire at this Foster Purity Temple? [*Sings*]:

Neath walls of stone and gate with creepers hung,
We seek the alchemist who dwells within.
Along the mossy trail,
We call the hermit's serving-boy.
What do recluses know of the floating life's ordeals?

[**Master of Ceremonies** *knocks at the gate.*]

**Pien**: Who is knocking?

**Master of Ceremonies**: Refugees from Nanking, who would lay down their burdens for a while.

**Pien**: This is a Taoist convent, we do not entertain travellers. [*Sings*]:

Do you not see the lofty walls,
The gate tight shut the whole day long?
Here Taoists nuns seek purity
And shrink from contact with the throng.

**Liu**: We are no roaming Taoist priests; what harm would there be to let us rest a while?

**Pien** [*sings*]:
Reciting our sacred texts,
Observing the rules of our order,
We dwell as cloistered maidens in seclusion.

**Hou**: There is reason in what she says. This is no house of pleasure to enter at our will.

14.  Master of Ceremonies: "Here is Cloud's Roost
Mountain. Let us find a temple for our resting-place."

**Pien:** We are engaged in meditation. Do not disturb us further, but apply to the kitchens. [*She exits with* **Fragrant Princess.** *Master of Ceremonies knocks again.*]

**Hou:** Since they are observing the rules of their order, we should not disturb them.

**Master of Ceremonies:** There are more temples ahead, let us go on.

[*They move on. The minstrel* **Ting Chi-chih** *enters, in Taoist garb and with a basket of herbs on his arm.*]

**Ting** [*sings*]:
Straw sandals and bamboo staff
Carry me where they will through the scented hills,
To gather herbs in depths of ancient grottoes.
The setting sun etches the hoary branches,
Fresh fronds and roots of fern provide chaste fare.

**Master of Ceremonies** [*joyfully*]: Ah, a follower of the Tao. I'll ask him. [*Bows*]: Sir Taoist, we have entered these hills to celebrate a memorial service. Would you kindly direct us to a temple where we may rest awhile?

**Ting:** The gentleman there looks very like young Master Hou of Honan.

**Liu:** Who else do you think it is?

**Ting:** And you are surely Liu Ching-t'ing?

**Liu:** The very same.

**Hou:** Ha! Ting Chi-chih! How come you to be following the Tao?

**Ting:** Let me tell you, Master Hou. [*Sings*]:

Ageing and enfeebled,
I came to distrust my former minstrelsy,
And tune my voice instead to occult lay.

**Hou:** And so you have become a Taoist recluse.

**Liu:** Where have you settled among these hills?

**Ting:** Not far ahead of you is Gather Purity Temple, and that is where I cultivate the Way. If it is not too poor and lonely for you, you are welcome to stay there.

**Hou:** Excellent.

**Master of Ceremonies**: You and Liu Ching-t'ing have found an old friend and a lodging. I shall go on to White Cloud Temple to arrange for the memorial service.

**Hou**: We are grateful for your company thus far.

**Master of Ceremonies**: And I for yours. [*They take leave of each other, and he recites*]:

Here purple halls rise beside crystal springs,
And snowy breezes bear refreshing rain.

**Hou**: But the southern hills are cut off by this river before us. How shall we cross?

**Ting**: It will not be difficult. A boat is moored by the bank. We may sit in it and chat until the fisherman comes by, then he will row us across. We are only a few hundred yards from Gather Purity Temple. [*They seat themselves in the boat.*]

**Liu**: As a boy I fished in the North Bay at T'aichou for a living. I'm used to a boat like this, I'll row you across.

**Hou**: Splendid, splendid. [*Liu rows.*] Master of Ceremonies, do you realize that three years have flown since I last had the pleasure of your company, when you attended my wedding with Fragrant Princess?

**Master of Ceremonies**: True indeed. And have you received any word of Fragrant Princess since she was taken into the palace?

**Hou**: How could I? [*He brings out the fan.*] But I have always preserved this peach blossom fan. It was our betrothal pledge. [*Sings*]:

This peach blossom fan I cherish
Recalls old dreamlike days in the tower of bliss.
Though earth and Heaven grow old,
This love will endure forever.
So rudely were we parted
To fly alone, a thousand peaks between.
Within a month our happiness was ended.

**Liu**: When the Emperor fled, his consorts dispersed. Fragrant Princess must surely have left the palace then. When peace returns to Nanking, let us go back and search for her there.

**Hou**: I fear we may never find her, since so many scattered far and wide during the fighting. [*He weeps.*]

**Ting**:  There is my temple, behind that bamboo hedge. Let us land
here. [*Liu moors and they land. Ting calls*]: Boy, here are
visitors, help with their baggage. [*Boy assents from within.*]
Please enter my humble abode.

**Hou** [*sings*]:
Within the gate, the alchemist's crucible

**Ting**:
Above my lodge, the pine trees silent stand.

**Liu**:
After a thousand meanders of the stream

**Hou**:
As in a dream we enter Fairyland.

---

SCENE 40

# Entering the Way

1645, SEVENTH MONTH

[*Enter Chang Wei. He wears the broad-sleeved robe and gourd-
shaped hat of a Taoist priest, and carries a whisk.*]

**Chang** [*sings*]:
The blush of youth had faded from my cheeks
Ere half a life-span in the dusty world.
Too long I watched the puppet-play,
Wept tears, and then in turn laughed loud.
No more of folly. In these secluded haunts,
Few men have ever cherished worldly sorrows.

[*Speaks*]: Ever since I retired from the official world, I have
lived in seclusion in this White Cloud Temple under the name
of Chang the Taoist. This is my lot, to cultivate the Way and
have no more to do with the world's affairs. It was my good
fortune to be accompanied here by Ts'ai Yi-so, the bookseller, who brought five cartloads of classics and histories.
Lan Ying the painter made the same resolution, and he has
painted scrolls depicting our rustic retreat. So, since in these
bare hills I can study and let my fancy roam to my heart's

content, when the time comes for my Transformation it will be no doltish ignoramus who ascends to the clouds. The one regret that persists from my former life is my failure to repay the gracious favour of His Majesty the Emperor Ch'ung-chen. Therefore today, the fifteenth day of the seventh month, I have invited many celebrants to a major memorial service for His late Majesty. I have been fortunate enough also to secure the attendance of a former Master of Ceremonies from Nanking, who with some of the local elders will offer the prayers. Now let me call my disciple to make sure all is ready. Boy!

**Ts'ai** and **Lan** [*entering in Taoist garb, recite*]:
Farewell to dusty world;
In the clouds we gather as followers of the Way.
Greetings from Ts'ai Yi-so and Lan Ying.

**Chang**: Do you both prepare the altars and lead our brethren in the ritual. I will purify myself and change my garments so that I may offer up prayer with the utmost devotion. Truly a pure repast before the gods, an offering from the chaste hearts of men.

> [*Chang exits. Ts'ai and Lan set up a triple altar which they furnish with incense, flowers, fruits, and tea. They set up banners and tablets, and then sing.*]

**Ts'ai** and **Lan** together [*singing*]:
As the sun rises from the sea, we build our high altar.
All spirits of the sky, appear!
Lords of the stars and planets, come to audience!
Your banners float on the breeze
As prayers ascend for the seventh-month sacrifices.

**Ts'ai**: The altar is raised and furnished. All is ready.

**Lan**: And lo, here comes a throng of village elders with gifts of wine and incense.

> [*Enter Master of Ceremonies at the head of a crowd of villagers. They bear wine, incense, paper money, and embroidered banners.*]

**Villagers** [*sing*]:
Home-brewed wines we bear,
Incense purple and yellow

15. Ts'ai Yi-so: "The altar is raised and furnished. All is ready."

We've wrapped in broidered kerchiefs.
Upward we gaze, to the royal Throne
In the Jade Palace of the Purest Void,
And ask: How came our Emperor
To leave us villagers fatherless? [*They weep.*]
Now in the seventh month, deep in the folded hills,
Offerings we burn to His late Majesty.

[*They greet Ts'ai and Lan, and say*]: Reverend Sirs, we of the laity are all present and prepared for the service. Please ask His Reverence the Abbot to come forth and circumambulate the altar.

**Ts'ai** and **Lan** [*calling offstage*]: All is in readiness for Your Reverence to circumambulate the altar and perform the rites of purification.

> [*Three drumbeats. Four* **Taoist musicians** *appear.* **Ts'ai** *and* **Lan** *put on robes decorated with magic symbols, and follow behind bearing censers. Last comes* **Chang**, *in similar robe and gold mitre. He walks around the altar, carrying a vial of water and a pine branch with which he conducts the rituals of purification.*]

**All** [*singing*]:
Hands new purified
Flourish branch of pine,
Scatter healing dew
In droplets superfine.
Round the altar and around,
Thrice threefold and nine:
Banish dust, vanish lust,
From this place divine.
Incense smoke ascending,
Cloud with cloud entwine,
Airy palace towers
For his royal line.

[*Exit Chang.*]

**Ts'ai** and **Lan** [*calling to* **Chang**, *offstage*]: The ritual of purification is complete. Now let Your Reverence change your robe and offer the memorial prayer at the altar.

> [**Ts'ai** *and* **Lan** *proceed to set up the tablet of the Emperor Ch'ung-chen on the central altar. On the left are set the tablets*

*of the civil martyrs of the year 1644, and on the right the*
*tablets of the military martyrs of the same year. Soft music*
*plays. Chang enters wearing a nine-ridged hat (indicating highest*
*rank in the bureaucracy) and a crane-embroidered robe of*
*audience. His thick-soled boots also are such as are worn in*
*Imperial audience. He wears a golden girdle and carries an ivory*
*tablet.*]

Chang [*kneeling*] : Let the stars of the heavens lend brightness to
the vision of the Land of the Immortals. Let the winds and
the thunder bear word that the gates of Heaven be opened.
Here in all reverence we implore the attendance of His
Imperial Majesty Ch'ung-chen and of all noble martyrs, both
civil and military. Let the Imperial procession now appear in
all its splendour, flanked by gleaming banners and followed
by the attendant throng. Ride the white clouds to where we
humbly await Your Imperial Presence with offerings of
sacred music and hallowed wine.

> [*Music sounds. Chang makes a triple libation and prostrates*
> *himself four times. Master of Ceremonies and Villagers join in*
> *his prostrations.*]

Chang [*sings*] :
Adepts here assembled
Implore Your Majesty to descend from the azure clouds.
Leave Coal Hill, the fatal tree,[1]
Untie the silken sash,
Come relish pepper wine,
Breathe incense of the pine,
Lament no more the crimes of bandit rogues.
No earthly pomp can last a thousand years,
But in these hills your spirit lives forever.

> [*Chang exits. Ts'ai and Lan make libations at either side of the*
> *stage, then prostrate themselves. Master of Ceremonies and*
> *Villagers join in the prostrations.*]

Ts'ai and Lan together [*singing*] :
For every martyr's soul we pray
Who died on that ill-fated day.
All who found death by slow starvation,

---

1. From which, it will be recalled, the Emperor Ch'ung-chen hanged himself (see
Scene 34, n. 2).

Knife, or well, or strangulation,
Let no more rage your bosoms fill,
Join us here and feast at will.

[*They speak*]: Now pour libations and burn the spirit offerings, that the spirits may be escorted to their heavenly home.

> [*All present burn paper offerings, make libations, and
> wail.*]

**Master of Ceremonies**: Now for the first time they have been
fittingly bewailed.

**Villagers**: Having expressed our devotion, let us go to our own
pure repast. [*Exeunt.*]

**Ts'ai** and **Lan** [*calling to Chang, offstage*]: The ceremonies of
invitation are completed. Now is the time for Your Reverence to change your robes and ascend to the altar to offer
food to the wandering souls.

> [*Ts'ai and Lan set out the food offerings. To soft music, Chang
> re-enters, now wearing a turban and a cloak trimmed with crane's
> down, and carrying his whisk. After prostrating himself, he ascends
> the steps of the altar. When Ts'ai and Lan have assumed their
> positions behind him, he strikes the altar with his fist.*]

**Chang**: Though endless spread the sandy battlefields, raising our
eyes we see the mansions of Heaven; lost as we are in the
boundless ocean of sorrows, turning our heads we see the
Isles of Blessing. We commemorate the host of those who
gave their lives for their country, whether they fought hard
by the capital or in the central plains, south of the great lakes
or far in the desert northwest; whether to them came death
by water, death by fire, death by sword's edge, death by
arrow, death beneath trampling feet, or death from sickness
and starvation. Though your bones lie tangled in thorny
thickets, though your spirits flicker as will-o'-the-wisps, come
to our holy hill, our sacred altar. Come drink the cup that
agelong will quench your thirst. Come taste the grain that for
a thousand springs will be your nourishment. [*He scatters
grains of rice, sprinkles water, and burns paper offerings.
Then he sings*]:

Out on the dusty battlefield
With wild herbs overgrown,

Crimson stains of blood must yield
To slowly whitening bone.
In howl of wind, rage of rain,
Homeward gazing, they gaze in vain.
Poor ghosts who linger drear and chill:
Come eat this once, come eat your fill.

**Ts'ai** and **Lan**: Now the gifts of food have been made, it is time for Your Reverence to send forth the rays of holy light which will illumine the Three Realms[2], so that the wandering spirits may be guided each to his proper altar.

**Chang**: They have been long in Heaven, the souls of the martyrs of last year's disaster.

**Ts'ai** and **Lan**: But what of the victims of this year's struggle, Prince and ministers pitted against the north? We entreat you to seek a sign of what fates have befallen them.

**Chang**: Then attend with steadfast hearts while I offer incense and enter meditation, closing my eyes to see the more intently. [*Ts'ai and Lan stand with bowed heads, incense sticks held before them. A long pause ensues.*] No, I find no manifestation of the Emperor Hung-kuang, the two Generals Liu, T'ien Hsiung, and the rest. They must still be among the living.

**Ts'ai** and **Lan**: What of Shih K'o-fa, Tso Liang-yü, and Huang Te-kung, who died in this year's fighting?

**Chang**: Let me see.

[*He closes his eyes, whereupon there enters, to soft music, a white-bearded figure wearing court headdress and crimson robe. His face is covered with a yellow silk cloth, and he has a retinue of attendants carrying streamers of silk such as decorate shrines.*]

**First Apparition**: I, Shih K'o-fa, former Field Marshal and President of the Board of War, am newly appointed Original of the Purple Void, in the Palace of Great Purity. To this post I now ride.

[*He mimes the act of riding, and exits. A second figure, in gold armour and with a red silk cloth over his face, enters to drums and pipes. His retinue carry banners.*]

---

2. The Three (Buddhist) Realms of Desire, Form, and Formlessness.

**Second Apparition**: I, Tso Liang-yü, former Earl of Southern Peace, am newly appointed Heaven-soaring Envoy. To this post I now ride.

[*He exits. A third figure enters with banners, drums, and pipes. His armour is silver, and the cloth over his face is black.*]

**Third Apparition**: I, Huang Te-kung, former Earl of Southern Tranquillity, am newly appointed Heaven-roaming Envoy. To this post I now ride. [*Exit.*]

**Chang** [*opens his eyes*]: Wonderful! I have just had visions of Their Excellencies Shih K'o-fa, Tso Liang-yü, and Huang Te-kung, each riding to assume a glorious new appointment in Heaven. [*Sings*]:

Celestial steeds astride the clouds,
In heroes' pride they go.
Heavenly music sounds on every side,
Banners and parasols wave,
Swords, robes, and insignia befit
The majesty of other-worldly office.
High Heaven recognized their worth,
And now they ride in glory.

**Ts'ai** and **Lan** [*bowing with folded hands*]: Homage to Heaven's Lord! Thus virtue reaps reward, and the justice of Heaven is displayed for all to see. [*Turning to Chang*]: But what retribution has befallen the traitors Ma Shih-ying and Juan Ta-ch'eng?

**Chang**: Let me see.

[*Enter, running, a fourth figure, with dishevelled hair and clothes.*]

**Fourth Apparition**: After a lifetime of misdeeds, I, Ma Shih-ying, met my end in the T'aichou Mountains. [*Following him comes the **Spirit of the Thunderclap**, who chases him around the stage. The **Apparition** kneels, clutching his head.*] Have mercy! Have mercy!

[*The **Spirit** strikes him dead, strips his body, and departs. Enter a fifth figure in court robes and girdle.*]

**Fifth Apparition**: Done it! A superb achievement for Juan Ta-ch'eng, to cross this Ridge of the Immortals!

[*He climbs a peak, whereupon the **Mountain Spirit** and attendant*
**Yakshas**[3] *enter and push him off. He falls to his death.*]

**Chang** [*opens his eyes*]: Horror, horror! A vision of Ma Shih-ying
struck dead by a thunderbolt in the T'aichou Mountains, and
Juan Ta-ch'eng fallen to his death from the Ridge of the
Immortals. Each with his skull cracked open, terrible to
behold. [*Sings*]:

Bright is the image in the karmic mirror,
Close is the mesh of Heaven's all-compassing net.
Flee where you may over a thousand hills,
Thunder Spirit and Yakshas will hunt you down.
Those who have scooped the brains from so many skulls,
Will scarcely feed a dog with their remains.

**Ts'ai** and **Lan** [*hands folded*]: Homage to Heaven's Lord! Thus
evil meets retribution, and the justice of Heaven is displayed
for all to see. [*Turning to **Chang***]: Your attendants still lack
the fullest understanding. We beseech Your Reverence to fill
our ears with truth.

[*While **Chang** raises his whisk and sings at the top of his voice,*
**Master of Ceremonies** *and* **Villagers** *re-enter to listen respectfully,*
*incense sticks held before them.*]

**Chang** [*sings*]:
Every mortal creature's
Misdeeds, however small,
However closely hidden,
To his account must fall.
And yet the karmic circle
Each merit will recall,
Reward and retribution
Made visible to all.
North succeeds to South,
State gives way to state,
Each dynastic cycle
Predeterminate.
Just men and the ungodly
Meet their appointed fate,
Sure of resolution,
Whether soon or late.

---

3. Demon Messengers from Hades, in popular Buddhist belief.

[*Master of Ceremonies* and *Villagers* kowtow and exit. Enter
*Fragrant Princess* with *Pien Yü-ching*.]

**Pien**: Happiest in all this world are those who devote themselves
to acts of piety. In the company of Taoist priestesses we have
set up banners before the altar to the Empress Chou, and
now we come to hear the Abbot in his sermon hall.

**Fragrant Princess**: Am I permitted to accompany you?

**Pien**: See, here is a throng of Taoist priests and laymen, there can
be no harm in our presence as observers.

[*Pien* prostrates herself before the altar, then takes up a position
at one side, with *Fragrant Princess*. Enter the minstrel *Ting
Chi-chih*.]

**Ting**: Hard to ensure return in mortal form; mysterious and secret
is the Way. [*He prostrates himself before the altar, then rises
and calls offstage*]: Master Hou, come see the sermon hall.

[*Hou Fang-yü* hastens onstage.]

**Hou**: At last! Long have I suffered in the dusty world. Now to
seek bliss beyond its narrow confines. [*He follows* **Ting** *to a
position at the other side of the stage from* **Fragrant
Princess**.]

**Chang** [*pounds his lectern*]; You, my hearers, hearts turned to
piety: know that only the total voidance of your dusty
desires can free you to rise towards purity. One single speck
of lingering mortal passion, and you are condemned to a
thousand further revolutions of the wheel of karma.

[*Concealing his face with his fan,* **Hou** *peers at* **Fragrant
Princess***, and starts in astonishment.*]

**Hou**: That is my Fragrant Princess! How can it be that I find her
standing here? [*He hurries over to* **Fragrant Princess** *and tugs
at her hand. She is equally startled to see him.*]

**Fragrant Princess**: It is Master Hou! Oh, the longing for you has
almost caused my death! [*Sings*]:

Ah, when I recall
The abruptness of our parting!
No bridge was ours, to cross the Milky Way;

Higher than Heaven seemed the walls between us.
No letters could we exchange,
Dreams were a vain recourse,
Longing was endless;
And when I left the palace,
Ever more distant wanderings seemed to face me.

**Hou** [*points to the fan*]: Gazing on the peach blossoms of this fan, I have asked myself how I could ever requite you. [*Sings*]:

The blossoms on this fan:
Were they really formed from bloodstains?
Or are they the petals that rained down
When the holy Abbot preached?[4]

> [**Hou** and **Fragrant Princess** *look at the fan together. Then they are dragged apart by* **Ting** *and* **Pien**.]

**Ting**: You should not discuss private matters while the Abbot is in the middle of his sermon.

> [**Hou** and **Fragrant Princess** *take no notice, and* **Chang** *pounds his lectern again.*]

**Chang**: Tchah! What kind of fractious children are these who babble of love before this sacred altar? [*He hastens down, tears the fan from the hands of* **Hou** *and* **Fragrant Princess**, *and flings it to the ground.*] This a place of sanctity, not to be defiled by wanton youths.

**Ts'ai**: Ai-ya! But Your Reverence knows this man. It is Hou Fang-yü of Honan.

**Chang**: And the girl?

**Lan**: I know her. She is Fragrant Princess, who became Master Hou's bride.

**Chang**: And what has brought them here?

**Ting**: Master Hou is residing at my Gather Purity Temple.

**Pien**: And Fragrant Princess at my Foster Purity Temple.

---

4. According to Buddhist legend, when the Abbot Kuang-ch'ang reached the climax of his exposition of the sutras, a shower of flower petals fell from the sky.

**Hou** [*bowing to Chang*]: And you, sir, are Chang Wei, from whom in former days I received much favour.

**Chang**: Master Hou, I am delighted to see you released from prison. Did you know it was because of you that I left the world to follow the Way?

**Hou**: No, I had no means of knowing that.

**Ts'ai**: I also left the world on your account. I shall tell you the story all in good time.

**Lan**: And I came here as escort to Fragrant Princess in her search for you. I little dreamed that we should find you at last.

**Hou**: How shall Fragrant Princess and I ever repay the debts we owe to you, Ting Chi-chih and Pien Yü-ching, who gave us refuge, or to you, Ts'ai Yi-so and Lan Ying, who aided our search for each other?

**Fragrant Princess**: And Su K'un-sheng also accompanied me here.

**Hou**: And Liu Ching-t'ing came in my company.

**Fragrant Princess**: We owe so much to Su and Liu, who stayed loyally beside us in defiance of all hardships.

**Hou**: When we are home once more as man and wife, we shall endeavour to repay their kindness.

**Chang**: What is all this meaningless chatter? How laughable to cling to your amorous desires when the world has been turned upside down!

**Hou**: Sir, you are mistaken. The marriage of man with maid is the source of human relationship. Sorrows of separation, joys of reunion, all these are the fruits of love. Why should you object to our discussion of them?

**Chang** [*angrily*]: Pshaw! Two piteous passion-clinging bugs! Where now is the nation, where the home, where the prince, where the father? Can't you get rid of this miserable infatuation? [*Sings*]:

Alas for silly youths,
Ignorant of the changing of their world.
A stream of lascivious chatter,
Hand in hand they plan their marital bliss,
Here, in the very presence of the spirits!
Can't you divine love's final dissolution,

Hear the flapping of wings
As the mandarin ducks fly apart,
See the shattered fragments
Of the jewelled mirror of union?
Are you not ashamed to hear
The laughter your performance brings?
Are you not ready to follow
The broad highway of Escape?

Hou [*bows*]: I hear your words and wake from my dream,
drenched in a chilling sweat.

Chang: Do you understand them?

Hou: I understand.

Chang: Then if you do, salute Ting Chi-chih as your tutor. [*Hou
does so.*]

Fragrant Princess: I also understand.

Chang: If you also understand, salute Pien Yü-ching as your tutor.
[*She does so.*]

Chang [*to **Ting** and **Pien***]: Help them change into Taoist robes.
[*They do so.*]

Ting and Pien: Ascend to your seat, Your Reverence, so that we
may present our disciples.

[***Chang** takes his seat, and **Ting** and **Pien** lead **Hou** and **Fragrant
Princess** to prostrate themselves before him.*]

Ting and Pien together [*singing*]:
Crop the sprouts of love
And see them wither, the sprigs of gold and jade.
Root out passion
From these descendants of the dragon and phoenix.
Life is brief as bubble of foam,
Short as spark, struck from stone.
Let them spend their remnant years
Following our doctrine.

Chang: For the male, let the south be his direction. Let Hou
Fang--yü depart for the southernmost hills, there to cultivate
the Way.

Hou: I go. Understanding the Way, I perceive the depths of my
folly. [***Ting** leads **Hou** offstage.*]

**Chang**: For the female, let her direction be the north. Let Fragrant Princess depart for the northernmost hills, there to cultivate the Way.

**Fragrant Princess**: I go. All is illusion; I know not that man before me.

> [*Pien leads* **Fragrant Princess** *offstage, the opposite side from Hou's exit.* **Chang** *descends from his seat and utters three great shouts of laughter.*]

**Chang** [*sings*]:
See them take their leave
With never a backward glance.
My task it was to shred the peach blossom fan,
That never more the strands of folly
Shall bind the heart of man and maid.

White bones are laid in the dust,
The southern realm concludes its span.
Dreams of revival fall to earth
In shreds with the peach blossom fan.

---

# Epilogue

## 1648, NINTH MONTH

> [*Enter* **Su K'un-sheng** *in the guise of a woodcutter, a bundle of faggots on his back.*]

**Su** [*recites*]:
At the limits of my vision
Hoary cliffs line the sky,
A thousand reddening branches
Touch my head as I go by.

[*Speaks*]: Wild tigers share this cloudy fastness, dodging as I do the arrows of the world. On Nanking's wall the ghosts moan nightly, Yangchow's wells are stuffed with corpses, and though my own life dangles from a thread, I am rich in stories of the fall of the South. [*Pause.*] Three years have passed since I accompanied Fragrant Princess into these hills. Rather than return home, I have lingered here on Bull's Head Mountain, sleeping in the wilds and earning my keep by gathering wood. Liu Ching-t'ing made a similar resolution; he bought a little boat and works as a fisherman. We rejoice in these ancient forests deep in the hills, cut off from men by the broad river. Here at our daily meetings I beat out a rhythm with my axe-head on his prow, and we sing loud and free for our own pleasure. I have finished work early today, since I am expecting him to visit for a good chat. It is time he was here.

[*Su sets down his load and naps for a while. Enter Liu Ching-t'ing as a fisherman rowing his boat.*]

**Liu** [*recites*]:

Silver-haired old fisherman,
My tale already told,
But more content with this retreat
Than any hermit of old.

[*Speaks*]: It is three years since I escorted Master Hou Fang-yü into Taoist seclusion. I have stayed on to work as a fisherman while I spin the events of dynastic collapse into romantic tales. A day like this, with the sky clearing after autumn showers and the river shining like silk, is just right for a drink of wine and a heart-to-heart chat with Su K'un-sheng. [*He points*]: And look, there he lies wine-fuddled on the bank. I'll wake him. [*He mimes the act of mooring and stepping ashore, and rouses Su.*]

**Su**: Good, you're here.

**Liu** [*folding his hands in salutation*]: I see you've been drinking behind my back!

**Su**: Now where would I obtain wine, when I haven't sold my firewood yet?

**Liu**: Nor have I sold any fish. Not a copper between us —what's to be done?

**Su**: Here's what we'll do; you bring water and I'll contribute firewood, and we'll brew tea and have some "pure talk"!

[*Enter the old **Master of Ceremonies** bearing lute and wine-jar.*]

**Master of ceremonies** [*recites*]:
> Busy or idle,
> By hill or stream,
> Win or lose,
> All's a dream.

[*Speaks*]: So! Here are my old friends Su and Liu!

**Su** and **Liu** [*greeting him with folded hands*]: What brings you here, sir?

**Master of Ceremonies**: I have been residing by the Swallow Pier. Today being the seventeenth day of the ninth month, the birthday of the God of Wealth, I have visited his shrine with some friends in these hills. I am just on my way back.

**Su**: But why the lute and the jar?

**Master of Ceremonies**: Don't laugh at me, but I have composed a "spirits' song" which I have entitled "Questions to Heaven." I played and sang it today, and when our little gathering broke up I was awarded this jar of wine. It is my good fortune to have chanced on you gentlemen. Please help me to drink a few cups.

**Liu**: Oh, we couldn't do that.

**Master of Ceremonies**: This is what is known as "sharing each other's good fortune."

**Su** and **Liu**: Excellent, excellent! [*They seat themselves and drink.*]

**Su**: Could we please hear your "spirits' song"?

**Master of Ceremonies**: Indeed yes. I should very much welcome your advice. [*Su and Liu clap in rhythm as he strums his lute and sings*]:

> Fifth year of the new reign,
> The era of Shun-chih,[1]
> In autumn, the ninth month,
> Day the seventeenth —
> Fit time for celebration!
> We beat the sacred drum,
> Unfurl the spirit banners,

---

1. Shun-chih, reign-title of the first Manchu Emperor, 1644-1662. The fifth year is 1648.

Neighbours here assembled.
Among them is this singer,
Ageing refugee,
White locks properly shorn.
Ancient shrine
Dating from Tsin and T'ang,
Beam and lintel
Of fragrant cassia,
Vessels of gold and jade,
Pillars of crimson lacquer,
Walls gleaming white,
Murals finely crafted.
Brilliant, awesome,
The tablet of the god,
Jewels of mine and ocean
In comprehensive display.
Where is the ancestral temple,
The shrine to prince or tutor,
That can boast such throngs of celebrants?
Friend vies with neighbour
To burn the most fragrant incense,
Offer the finest wine.
Under this bamboo rain-hat,
Here I stand,
Tug my beard and sigh:
Is it the Creator's will
That the poor stay poor,
The rich continue rich?
Like you I was born
In this month
On this day,
But my purse is empty.
My stove is cold,
I live a mere beggar;
Already my span has filled
A cycle of sixty years,
And twilight swiftly nears.
"Rather a dog in days of peace
Than a man in troublous times,"
But no peace have I known.
This jade cup I offer.
Come sit on your jewelled mat,

I will attend your feasting.
Let it be clear determined
If I have spirit power
Or mortal ineptitude.
Knocking my head on the ground
I call on your palace attendants,
With open eyes and ears,
To re-examine my file,
Set the record straight,
Dispel discrimination.
Though distant your halls of gold,
Remote your purple portals,
In high Heaven, far as a dream,
We shall welcome your coming,
We shall escort your return
With coursers swift as the wind.
Dance and song will end,
Meat and fowl be cleared away,
Our company disperse.
Then I shall lean at sunset
Against an ancient trunk
In solitary thought.
Perhaps a true division
Gives riches to the turbid
And to the pure a fair name;
The balance must require
The man of inward wealth
To lack external goods.
Genial as fire
Is the God of Wealth,
Father and mother to common men;
Cold as ice
Is the God of Letters,
Patron and guide of the learned.
Even the spirits have their faults,
The sages their shortcomings,
And who fulfills his desires?
Earth has its hollows,
Heaven its cracks,[2]

---

2. Heaven was cracked when the legendary rebel Kung-kung, raging in defeat, crashed against one of the pillars which support the sky. See Scene 8, n. 3 for Nü Kua's repairing of the sky.

This is the law of creation.
Having released
The troubles of my bosom,
I can smile again.
The river flows,
Clouds roll on;
Why should I doubt?

[*He puts down his lute and says*]:   A very poor effort, I'm afraid.

**Su**: Brilliant! It vies with the songs of the great Ch'ü Yüan himself.[3]

**Liu**: We have failed to treat you with proper respect. We didn't realize you were a reincarnation of the God of Wealth in person!

**Master of Ceremonies**: Please finish off this wine now.

**Su** [*running his tongue round his lips*]: It's hard when there's nothing to go with the wine.

**Liu**: I have a little something here.

**Su**: What do you have?

**Liu**: You must guess.

**Su**: If it's yours, it has to be fish or shellfish of some kind.

**Liu**: Wrong.

**Su**: What else could it be?

**Liu**: My tongue.

**Su**: Well, of course, your tongue can go with the wine. But only for yourself. How can you offer it to others?

**Liu**: Don't you know the old story about "reading the *Han History* as you drink?"[4] This tongue of mine can narrate the tales of the Han History, so it's something to go with the wine.

**Su**: Then I'll pour for you, and you can narrate the *Han History* for us.

---

3. See Scene 8, n. 1.
4. *Han History:* the great history of the former Han dynasty, 206 B.C. — A.D. 25, by the Pan family in the later Han period (A.D. 25-221). The story of "reading the *Han History* as you drink" refers to the Sung poet Su Shun-ch'in, 1008-1048, who became so engrossed in the book, reading as he drank, that he emptied cup after cup.

**Master of Ceremonies**: Splendid! I'm only afraid it's too long a
    story for the wine we have left.

**Liu**: If the *Han History* is too long, I've got a new ballad which I
    call "Nanking Autumn." I can sing that instead.

**Master of Ceremonies**: It is about the events of recent years?

**Liu**: It is.

**Su**: These are all matters we ourselves have seen and heard. If you
    make a mistake, we shall demand a forfeit.

**Liu**: There will be no mistake, I can guarantee. [*He strums and
    recites*]:

A few plucks of the string
Convey six reigns' vicissitudes,
The protests of a thousand ages.
A lifetime by lake and seashore
Makes the myriad hills resound.

[*He sings to his lute in the manner of a blind girl ballad
monger*]:

A moonlit haze of grief recalls
When the house of Sui destroyed the Ch'en[5]
How powdered court ladies hid in the well
And the very earth was perfumed;
Willow floss clung to gleaming coiffures
And parrots squawked in doleful warning.
The glory of Ming moved south for a space,
And the heirs of disaster flourished like flame.
In courts of idleness patterned on Ch'en's last ruler,
Little did they heed the threatening northern bows.
Beauties with eyebrows like moth antennae
Were chosen to sing *The Swallow Letter*,
Leading musicians and dancing-masters
Plied their skills for the royal delectation.
Verses in voluptuous late-T'ang styles,
Robes and coronets of the early southern courts.
In a hundred boudoirs, jewelled mirrors
Reflected the fondness of regal amours.
Warning beacons beyond the walls
Burned unseen by the revellers

---

5. See Scene 18, n. 1.

16. Su K'un-sheng: "It's hard when there's
nothing to go with the wine."

On gilded barges off the Isle of Egrets.
Honest men feared the minister's wrath,[6]
Saw through his lies, but fled to the hills.
Careless of past faults, Juan Ta-ch'eng
Fawned on the might of Ma Shih-ying,
Tricked and betrayed all who opposed him,
Slaughtered his foes with borrowed blade.
Marshal Shih wept on Plum Blossom Ridge,
General Tso bravely drove on Wuchang,
But unguarded crossings welcomed the foe,
Treacherous moves blocked the loyal defence.
Yangchow's carved pillars crashed to the ground,
The singing stopped and the halls grew chill.
Friendless the dragon roamed through the seas;
Helpless the phoenix flapped in the dust,
Our Emperor was delivered up, a captive bound,
And Huang Te-kung's blood by his own hand shed.
Weeds choked the springs of the royal pools,
Dusk hid the road to the Imperial Tombs,
To city after city the gates swung open,
Gallant defenders were foiled at every turn.
More than one lord of the Ming met disaster:
Chien-wen a wandering monk, Ch'ung-chen self-destroyed,
Cheng-t'ung a war captive, Cheng-te a degenerate.[7]
To these add Prince Fu, a twelve-month sovereign,
His memorial a line or two of bitter tears.

**Su**: Wonderful! Everything absolutely true!

**Master of Ceremonies**: Though it is no more than a ballad in
form, it has the quality of a song by our distinguished
contemporary Wu Wei-yeh.[8]

---

6. This ballad by Liu Ching-t'ing is in strictly classical language, replete with
allusions. Several of his comments on his contemporaries are couched in terms of
historical figures. Here, for example, the minister intended is Ma Shih-ying, but the
allusion in the original line is to Chao Kao, chief eunuch of the First Emperor of the
Ch'in dynasty. Chao Kao brought a deer into court and forced the officers to prove their
loyalty to himself by swearing that he was correct in proclaiming the animal to be a
horse (much as Hamlet tested Polonius). In complete contrast with this heavily allusive
language is the plain "Northern" style of Su K'un-sheng's song-set which follows.

7. The Ming emperors who met these unhappy fates reigned at the following times:
Chien-wen, 1399-1403; Cheng-t'ung, 1436-1450; Cheng-te, 1506-1522; Ch'ung-chen,
1628-1644. Prince Fu, of course, is the Hung-kuang of our play (1644-1645).

8. The scholar-poet Wu Wei-yeh, 1609-1672, was one of the most gifted of the men
who opposed Ma Shih-ying and his faction.

**Su**: Another cup of wine, to salute the progress of your art. [*He pours.*]

**Liu**: But I still have nothing to go with the wine.

**Su**: Well then, I have a little something to help it down.

**Liu**: If you're to provide it, it's bound to be coarse mountain fare of some sort.

**Su**: Not at all. I brought it back specially from Nanking yesterday, after selling my firewood.

**Liu**: Then let us enjoy it together.

**Su** [*points to his own mouth*]: It's *my* tongue this time.

**Master of Ceremonies**: What do you mean?

**Su**: I'll tell you: it was three years since I had been in Nanking, and I took a sudden notion to go there to sell my firewood. The road led past the tomb of the Founder of the Ming,⁹ and I saw that sheep were grazing in the sacrificial halls.

**Liu**: Ai-ya! And what of the Imperial palace?

**Su**: Crumbling walls, ruined chambers, weeds and brambles everywhere.

**Master of Ceremonies** [*brushes away tears*]: Who could have forseen such a state!

**Su**: I went on to the Ch'in-huai pleasure-quarter, where I stood for hours without seeing a living soul.

**Liu**: You should have taken a look at the Longbridge district, where you and I spent so much of our leisure time.

**Su**: Don't imagine I didn't. Not a plank of the bridge left whole, and the old pleasure-houses just a heap of bricks and tiles.

**Liu** [*beats his breast*]: Ay, what dreadful news!

**Su**: As I hurried away, my heart was filled with grief, and I composed a song-set in Northern style which I have entitled "Lament for the South." Let me sing it for you. [*He beats a tempo for himself on a block.*] Listen to this woodcutter. [*Sings, in the Yi-yang style*]:

From pine-clad hills and flowering meadows,
Back to Nanking, head raised in expectation.
Survivors camped in decaying forts,

---

9. Chu Yuan-chang, whose reign-title was Hung-wu (1368-1399).

Starved horses sprawled in deserted trenches;
And over the wasted suburbs,
The city wall reflected the setting sun.
Sporadic fires had blackened
Catalpas guarding the Founder's Tomb;
Long fled were the eunuch attendants,
Their place assumed by shifting flocks of sheep.
Refuse of bird and bat littered the hall,
Dead leaves and dried twigs carpeted the steps.
Where acolytes should be sweeping,
Herdboys had made a mark of the dragon tablet.
Next, the royal palace:
White marble pillars in a heap of ruins,
Red-plastered walls a crumbling sea of dust,
Shattered tiles in profusion,
Hardly a glazed square left in any window.
None but the swallow posturing
Before the Screen of Audience,
Only the tall weeds marching
Down the central avenue;
And resident in the palace,
No one but beggars and men dead of starvation.
The Ch'in-huai pleasure-quarter, where we spent our days:
Torn window-papers rustled in the breeze,
The river lapped across broken sills,
No sight but filled the eye with sorrow.
Where now do flutes play soft
For the powdered beauties we knew?
At the Midsummer Feast the lantern boats are dark,
At Midautumn the wineshop flags stay furled.
White birds hover,
Green waves roll,
Butterflies woo the yellow blossoms,
Leaves turn red with none to notice.
Remember the bridge that crossed Green Creek?
Not one of its scarlet planks is left.
The stream flows on, but few men cross;
And in the cold sunset
Only a single willow dances slow.
I came to the old pleasure-house :
No need to knock,
No fear the dog would bark.
A dried-up well, an abandoned nest,

Moss-covered tiles, the steps sprouting weeds.
The trees we planted, you and I,
Had been stripped at random for fuel —
And whose were the ashes of this cooking-fire?
I, who have heard the orioles greet the dawn
In the jade halls of Nanking's elegance,
Who have watched spring bloom on the Ch'in-huai river
    walks —
How could I dream that all would vanish
Like the melting of ice?
I saw the crimson balconies rise,
I saw the feasting of the guests;
I have seen all lie in ruins.
Where moss creeps over the rubble,
In times long gone I dreamed of love and glory.
Now I have seen it all, the rise and decay
Of half a hundred years.
They passed from here, the owners of those mansions:
Grieve not that lakeside demons weep by night
And the owl perches on the phoenix terrace.
It was so real, the dream of Ming revival,
It is so hard to give up the land we knew,
So hard to believe the map has been re-drawn.
Here is a song-set in lament for the South:
Let me wail unchecked as old age hastens nigh.

**Master of Ceremonies** [*brushing away tears*]: That was truly
magnificent, but it brought so many tears.

**Liu**:  For myself, I don't think I can bear to drink any more. Let's
just chat for a while.

> [*Enter **Hsu Ch'ing-chün** wearing the black uniform of a magis-
> trate's runner of the Manchu regime.*]

**Hsu** [*unseen by the others, recites*]:
    I, who once escorted His Majesty,
    Now stand guard to a district judge.
    What hope for advancement have I,
    A nameless runner for a local court?

[*Speaks*]:  I am Hsu Ch'ing-chün, descendant of the Duke of
Wei. Born to wealth and eminence, I lived a life of luxurious
ease. But with the overthrow of the Ming dynasty, my family
collapsed and I found myself alone in the world. The only

way I could earn my living was as a magistrate's runner here in Shang-yuan County. I hold an official warrant to track down loyalists who have gone into seclusion in these hills, and that is what I am engaged in now. [*He looks about*]: Ha, there on the river bank is a group of old men sitting at their ease. To strike up a conversation, I'll ask one of them for a light. Truly, compared to my distinguished forebear I am the tail of the dog; and these refugees from the new regime draw in their necks like turtles. [*He greets the others*]: Can any of you gentlemen provide me with a light?

**Liu**: Please join us. [*Hsu sits down.*]

**Master of Ceremonies**: You wear the dress of an officer of the magistrate's court.

**Hsu**: That's who I am.

**Su**: If it's a light for your pipe that you want, I have some fine tobacco here. Please take a fill. [*He fills and lights Hsu's pipe.*]

**Hsu** [*smoking*]: Very fine tobacco. [*He pretends to be dizzy and slumps to the ground. Su helps him sit up.*] No, don't tug at me, just let me have a little rest and I'll be all right. [*He feigns sleep.*]

**Liu** [*to Master of Ceremonies*]: I recall that three years ago you were intending to bury the robes of Marshal Shih K'o-fa below Plum Blossom Ridge. What ever happened to that plan?

**Master of Ceremonies**: I joined forces with a goodly number of loyal friends, and we gathered at Plum Blossom Ridge to summon the soul of Marshal Shih and to bury his relics. It was a fine commemoration, except that we did not set up any tablet to him.

**Su**: A deed well done. But what a pity there was no one to bury General Huang when he loyally sacrificed his life by the roadside.

**Master of Ceremonies**: That has been taken care of. I gathered together some of the village elders and we buried him and set up a tomb, quite an imposing one.

**Liu**: These are two major acts of merit you performed.

**Su**: I don't think I ever told you gentlemen that when General

Tso died in battle and all his comrades were scattered, it was I who placed him in his coffin.

**Master of Ceremonies**: Well done, well done. And now I hear that his son, Tso Meng-keng, has inherited the title and has taken the coffin back to the ancestral burial-ground.

**Liu** [*wiping his eyes*]: General Tso was a personal friend. I had Lan Ying paint a posthumous likeness of him, and asked Ch'ien Mu-chai to inscribe it for me. Now I am able to commemorate my friendship with General Tso by sacrificing to his portrait at the appropriate seasons.

**Hsu** [*opens his eyes and says to himself*]: From what they say, these are all loyalist recluses. [*He rises to his feet*]: Are all you gentlemen recluses here?

**Su**, **Liu**, and **Master of Ceremonies** [*rising and bowing*]: You flatter us, sir. Why do you ask this?

**Hsu**: Surely you must have heard. The Board of Rites submitted a memorial requesting that loyalist recluses be sought out wherever they may be. The Pacification Commissioner posted notices everywhere, and it is weeks since we received the directive from the Provincial Governor, but not one man has come forward in response. The prefectural and county authorities are very concerned, and are sending us runners out to search. If you three gentlemen truly are such persons, please come along with me at once.

**Master of Ceremonies**: You are mistaken, friend. These recluses you speak of are famous scholar-officials who refuse to leave their retreat in the mountains. I was merely a Master of Ceremonies, with no real claim to learning, and I could not think of accompanying you.

**Su** and **Liu**: We are just a couple of entertainers, a story-teller and a ballad-monger who now make a living as fisherman and woodcutter. We are even less qualified to go with you.

**Hsu**: You don't understand. The famous scholar-officials, the great men of affairs, all these left their retreats three years ago. It's exactly your kind that we are looking for now.

**Master of Ceremonies**: Bah! For the court to seek out hermits and invite them to come forth is a serious undertaking. Local officials should issue invitations with due ceremony. There

should be none of this tracking down. You runners are up to
no good, I'm certain of that.

**Hsu**: It's nothing to do with me, I'm simply carrying out the
warrant issued by the magistrate. Here it is — look! [*He
makes ready to arrest them*]

**Su**: What a thing to happen!

**Liu**: Hadn't we better be off?

**Master of Ceremonies**: You're right. This is our last chance. We
didn't hide ourselves thoroughly enough.

> [*They hurry off in different directions, too fast for Hsu to
> catch up.*]

**Hsu**: See them scramble up cliffs and over gullies! All gone
beyond trace! [*Sings*]:

Through the marshes, through the hills,
Everywhere we hunt them
On order of the Court.
The green warrant bears their names,
A crimson circle by each,
But in their white robes off they scurry.

[*He stops to listen, and says*]: Somebody far away is reciting
a poem, by a brook or under the trees. I'll go wherever it may
lead and see if I can't find them. [*He hastens off.*]

**Voices** [*off stage singing*]:
Fisherman and woodcutter
Chatting of the past,
Each to each recalling
Dreams that did not last:
Scorn for the swallow letter,
Praise for the painted fan,
Sighs for old companions
Ere grief befell Chiangnan.[10]
Parting words of sorrow
To sky's rim will resound,
As in the turning of the years
The Feast of the Dead comes round.

---

10. Chiangnan, "south of the (Yangtze) River," old term for the lush region of
which Nanking is the center.

fan

**DATE DUE**

| OCT 20 1976 | | | |
|---|---|---|---|
| | | | |
| | | | |
| | | | |
| | | | |
| | | | |
| | | | |
| | | | |
| | | | |